Ouida

Idalia

A Romance

Ouida

Idalia
A Romance

ISBN/EAN: 9783742826558

Manufactured in Europe, USA, Canada, Australia, Japa

Cover: Foto ©Andreas Hilbeck / pixelio.de

Manufactured and distributed by brebook publishing software
(www.brebook.com)

Ouida

Idalia

COLLECTION

OF

BRITISH AUTHORS.

VOL. 906.

IDALIA BY OUIDA.

IN TWO VOLUMES.

VOL. II.

IDALIA.

A ROMANCE.

BY

OUIDA.

IN TWO VOLUMES.

VOL. II.

COPYRIGHT EDITION.

LEIPZIG

BERNHARD TAUCHNITZ

1867.

CONTENTS

OF VOLUME II.

IDALIA.

CHAPTER I.

"The Devil tempted me, and I did eat."

In the Neapolitan palazzetto, which was the residence of Victor Vane, the light of the summer morning made its way through half-closed blinds, the odours of orange and myrtle were heavy to oppression on the air, the waters beat a lulling measure below, at the foot of the little pier; it was still, soft, indolently charming, slumberously restful in the noontide hush; yet he himself—commonly so calm, so languid, so supreme an artist in the science of lazy pleasures—had no repose in it or in his own life. He was pacing up and down the chamber that opened on the terrace with a restless impatience, a feverish irritation with all things that were about him. He drank down some claret fresh from the ice; it seemed to have no coolness in it; he twisted some grapes asunder, and they seemed to parch his mouth; he smoked an opium-filled narghilé, and flung the tube away with a curse—the nicotine had lost its charm, and irritated where it was wont to soothe then he flung himself down on a couch, with his head dropped on his hands, and sat there immovable many moments, with a quick shudder running through his limbs, and the silence about him like a dead intolerable weight. For now that his work was done he loathed it; now that he had betrayed her, he could have killed himself; now that he had given her over to captivity and torture, he was haunted, and wrung, and maddened with the thoughts that for ever pursued him. Yet—he would not have undone it if he could; he would not have foregone his revenge had it been in his power; since she was denied to him, he loved to know that she suffered, that she had pain, and fetters, and shame, that she would live to wish she had listened to his love, and to feel the cost of having mocked him and repulsed him.

She had refused him all the sweetness of passion; he would not have loosened his hand on its vengeance. Since she could never be his, let her lose all likeness of herself, and perish as she might! There was fierceness enough in him to feel that ruthlessly; there was sufficient savageness in him beneath the polish of the world and the serenity of his egotism to be eager— thirstily and brutally eager—to know that what was beyond his reach, what he sought vainly, what he desired unavailingly, would be scourged, and defaced, and insulted, and shut out from all place on the earth. And yet, though he had given her up to her suffering, and would not, had he owned the power now, have released her from one pang of it, he suffered himself— suffered a torture not less than that to which he had delivered her. He knew the doom that would be hers under the revenge of a Church and a State so bitterly incensed against her; he knew that the net which had enclosed her would never unloose to let her issue with her life; he knew that if she ever came forth from the captivity into which he had betrayed her, it would

only be when bondage, and stripes, and the companionship of infamy, and the approach of age, would leave
no trace on her of all which she once had been; he
knew—for against them all his hatred had been borne
and his skill arrayed—the full meaning of the tyrannies of Bourbon and of Rome: and there were times
when his passion endured agonies at the memory of
the scourge that would cut the fairness of her skin, of
the rough hands that would unveil her beauty, of the
gaol-ruffians who would strip the delicate raiment off
her limbs, of the villanous glances that would gloat
unchecked on her fallen loveliness.   Mercy he had
none; such love as he had borne her was of the
character to change into a relentless and envenomed
hate; but it was passion still, and there were times
when the thought of her yielded up to her adversary's
will, and buried for ever beneath the stones of a
dungeon-vault, drove his own revenge back into his
heart, and tortured him not less than that revenge
could her.   Moreover, he had betrayed her; he had
sold her into the hands of her foes, and though the
subtle art of silken treachery had long been a science
in whose proficiency he took his highest pride, there
was manhood and there was dignity enough in him to
make his forehead burn with a red flush of shame
when there rose in remembrance before him the
challenge of her eyes, and to make him long to
know her dead in her youth, so that those eyes
should never be turned on him in accusation and
rebuke.

"Great heaven!" he muttered in his teeth, where
he lay with his head sunk on his arms, "if she would
only have *believed* I loved her!"

That was the one misery which had goaded him on to his crime. For once in his life he had been in earnest; for the sole time, from his boyhood up, an emotion genuine, however alloyed, had risen in him. In what he had felt for Idalia he had been true, with a truth he had never known before; for her he would have become anything that she had bidden him; to win her he would have endured and achieved all tasks she could have pointed out; and in the single hour in which this sincerity and this reality had possessed him, his own sceptical mockery had recoiled on him in hers; he had been powerless to induce her to hear one beat save that of egotism in his heart; he had been powerless to make her credit one throb of love or loyalty in him. That she should have rejected him he would have pardoned her; that she *disbelieved* him was the iron which went so far down into his soul, and changed every desire in him into one cruel thirst—the thirst for his vengeance and for her destruction. She had contemptuously doubted the force of his love. Well! he had said in his teeth that she should feel that force—feel it in the weight of fetters, in the burden of ignominy, in the oppression of dungeon solitude—feel it till she cursed the day that ever she braved it and mocked at it.

Awhile ago, and he would have laughed in the beard of any man who should have told him that such barbaric folly, such desert passions as these, could ever blind and rule him. Now he never resisted their sway, but let them burn out his strength and consume his intellect as they would. There were times when he shook opiates into his wines with a hand that recked little whether it shook too little or too much, and would have poured out a death-dose without a tremor; times when ambition seemed worthless as autumn leaves, and he loathed life because life could never yield to him the beauty of one woman. All who once loved Idalia drank of a mandragora that left them little of their natures, nothing of their wisdom. Even he had no antidote against it, but let it steal away his brain and pour its fire through his limbs till the soft courtier grew a brute, till the subtle politician became a fool, till the gentleman turned a traitor.

A sound in one of the many chambers leading off from the terrace-room in which he was, roused him. He was still too much governed by long habit and discipline not to recover himself instantly. Whatever he felt was only given way to in loneliness; no looker-on could see any change in his delicate, immutable face, in his soft calm smile, in his easy velvet indolence; he would have profited little by his long study of the world if he could not have held his own in finesse to the last.

Into the apartment, with little ceremony and no apology, Conrad Phaulcon came. His disguise was perfect. He was used to assume one at any hour and for any need; and in the dress of a melon-seller, with his fair skin stained and his auburn beard dyed black, his closest friend might have passed him by, his sworn foe failed to challenge him. He neither paused to watch nor ask if his host penetrated the mask as he swept up towards Vane, his mobile mouth working, and his large brown eyes aflame.

"Is this true?"

Victor had known him before he had heard his voice, and was on his guard. He shrugged his shoulders where he leaned against the side of the vine-shadowed window.

"You incarnate volcano! you will destroy us all some day! An ostensible melon-seller forcing his way in to me in this fashion! Have you ever stopped to remember what the household can think?"

"Felix admitted me, and I gave him the password. But, answer me, for God's sake, what of Idalia?——"

"What of her? Why, this of her, *caro*, that she is the subject for a tragic study by that eminent artist Monsignore Giulio Villaflor, to which you will form a companion picture if you trust to a basket of melons to pass you unnoticed through Naples."

The words were quite cool, quite unstudied, with just enough of regret in their half-languid banter to keep them from being mockery. Phaulcon's fine frame shook passionately as he heard; under the olive dye his cheek grew ashen; he threw himself down and sobbed like a child, wept as if his heart would break, in uncontrolled emotion.

His friend stood looking at him some moments in silence with a certain impatient disdain. This Greek, handsome as an Apollo, cruel at times as a Nero, and stained deep with many a crime, was yet as a child in the sight of the more controlled and astute Englishman; a child in cowardice, in impulsiveness, in caprice, in tyranny, in emotion, with all a child's unguardedness, recklessness, mobility, and love of torture.

"Naturally, you regret!" he said, at last, very softly. "You have not even killed your goose with the golden eggs yourself, my poor Conrad, but see bird and gold both stolen at a blow! Very naturally, you regret!"

The silken irony, the mockery of pity, stung Phaulcon like a shot. He started up, dashing the waves of his hair out of his eyes, while great drops of dew stobd on his forehead.

"Can you credit me nothing better than that?"

"*Caro mio*, how can I credit you with anything better than caring for money? It is the one prudential virtue which the world *does* crown!"

The Greek's teeth crushed his silken beard, while his features quivered with the vivid, uncontrolled emotion of his changing temperament.

"I am not thinking of her wealth; I think of *her* —of my own sins to her, of her beauty, of her genius, of her life."

His voice sank in a deep sob; he spoke but the truth for the moment; he thought for the instant not of himself, but of Idalia; not of his own danger, not of his own loss, but of her torture. He loved her in his wayward, tyrannous way; and for awhile the love alone remained with him.

"She is in the power of Villaflor!" he said, fiercely. Remorse was in him, and remorse made him long to wreak some savage vengeance somewhere; he would have little cared how or on whom.

"They say so. You know as much as I do. It has been a terrible blow to us; to keep quiet, and cover as much as we can, is all we shall be able to do. There was great carnage at Antina, and the arrests swept off all the musketry spared—among them your Countess. Indeed, she was doubtless the chief object of all."

"Where have they taken her?"

He spoke in his throat. At that moment he would have rather had a hundred balls fired into his own breast than have heard this of the woman he had so pitilessly chained and tormented.

"*Poverino!* how can we tell? It is not the fashion of the court to disclose its secrets, nor of Monsignore to let profane eyes see where his nets are spread."

His voice was unmoved, and almost careless, though it wore a natural gravity of regret, but in his heart he endured an agony greater than that of the man before him; the thought crossed him, to what fate would the Prince-Bishop devote a captive of the sex and the years and the charms of the prisoner he had betrayed to him?

Phaulcon's hand clenched; the muscles of his throat and chest, where the loose shirt of the *contadino* left them to view, swelled to bursting. Idalia was his treasury, his sovereignty, his world, his sceptre; without her he was nothing; of her he had made with a twisted mixture in him of fear and homage, of tyranny and weakness, of hate and love, an empress who to him alone out of all the earth was a slave, an enchanted wand with which he summoned what he would, an idol that he treated as hunters treated their statue of Pan when they reviled him because they needed more wealth than he gave, and yet feared him with a strange mingling of dread, of reverence, and of jealous love.

"Villaflor?" he repeated hoarsely. "That Satan of the Church? Better she had gone at once to her death. Are you sure? How can you know?"

Vane had let slip in a momentary incaution the

name of his great priestly confederate; he veiled the indiscretion with his finest tact.

"How can I doubt?" he said, with an acrid impatience that passed well enough for aversion to a mutual and omnipotent foe. "Was Giulio Villaflor ever absent from such errands as those? Did his brain ever fail to hatch such plots as those by which the maskers of Antina were entrapped, however little his hand might be seen, or his will be guessed in them? His special hatred always bore down on the Countess Vassalis; there is no more doubt that he works beneath this, if he do not wholly originate and govern it, than there is doubt that the sun is shining out yonder."

Phaulcon swore a mighty oath in his teeth as his lips shook, and his face flushed purple.

"If he harm her, I will find my way into his palace and drive a dagger down his throat, though he stand at the altar itself!"

"*Carissimo!* what would that avail, except to have you hanged, or disposed of in a still less humane fashion? Be reasonable. Tragedy will avail nothing. If you killed Villaflor, there would remain a score of monsignori to take his place and play his cards. The arrest of Madame de Vassalis is a terrible stroke for us —we could better have afforded to lose fifty men than to lose your irresistible Idalia; at the same time we shall not better her, and we shall surely imperil ourselves and all our projects, if we go like men in a melodrama, slaying priests and calling on the gods for vengeance."

"What! You would have us stand calmly by in inaction while she may be—may be——" The words

choked him; he knew what the power of Giulio
Villaflor meant to all, meant above all to a woman.

"Inaction! What action can you suggest?"

The Greek was silent; his swift thoughts swept, far
over a thousand schemes that rose only to bear with
them the sentence of impossibility.

"I—as eagerly as yourself—would be the first
to try all things, and to risk much in the service of
the Countess Vassalis," pursued Vane, with the soft,
even, almost unnatural calm which he had held throughout his interview with the Roman prelate. "But,
frankly, I see nothing that is to be done with any sort
of benefit. To penetrate the secrets of the government
will take time, and, what we have very little of, money;
to avow ourselves her partisans will be only at once to
share her imprisonment and be lodged in the casemates
yonder; to attempt a rescue requires the one thing we
do not possess—knowledge of where she has been
taken. What remains? We are as helpless, so far as
I can see, as if their chains were already about our
limbs. There is nothing for it—yet at least—except to wait and watch."

Phaulcon sank down again, with his head drooped
and his hands locked savagely one in another.

"You are right, I dare say," he said, bitterly; "and
very cautious! But—you never loved her."

There was not even the flicker of an emotion, not
the faintest flush on his companion's face; but a smile
passed for a second over his listener's lips; he had not
loved her!—he whose thwarted love had betrayed her
to her fate! The Greek's utter ignorance was almost
ludicrous to him.

"Your heart and your conscience have come into

sudden play, Conrad mio," he said, indolently. "I never knew before that you kept such old-world weaknesses; no one would have accused you of them!"

"Well! I have been guilty enough to her!" he answered, sullenly, with a dark red flushing his cheek; he was ashamed of his better emotion, as the man he was with now had always made him ashamed of any purer or higher touch that lingered in him.

"It is rather late in the day to think of that!"

"Too late!—my God!"

A terrible remorse was on him, passing, fitful, evanescent, but very ardent, very contrite, whilst it was in its first poignancy, whilst he thought of the ghastly doom in which had closed the splendid life that he had made and marred, the career to which he had wooed and to which he had enchained the youth and the power and the genius of Idalia—a remorse in which he suffered acutely; in which the uncertainty and the peril of her unknown fate were tortures to him; in which he seemed very vile, very accursed in his own sight.

His friend looked on impatiently; it incensed him to see this callous, thoughtless, tyrannous, unscrupulous Greek moved by her danger thus; it made his own traitor-shame weigh heavier on his heart. He did not lose his self-command; but he spoke almost insolently, on the spur of the misery that he choked down out of sight.

"Your beautiful Countess is too fair for the scourge and the cell, there is no doubt of that. I dare say she will never be condemned to them. Giulio Villaflor has too good a taste for such dainty paintings to shut them in solitude; he will not be likely to let so rare a

flower wither in a prison-court. Miladi Idalia has
better coin to buy indulgence with than all the gold of
Europe!"

In his own wretchedness it was a cruel relief to
him to fling dishonour at the woman he had betrayed,
and to torment the man whose self-accusing contrition
made him feel more sharply his own baseness.

Conrad Phaulcon started up impetuously, with
deadly blasphemies muttered under his breath, as he
paced the chamber like a leopard lashed to fury.

"You do not know Idalia," he said, savagely. "She
would die sooner—"

Vane laughed a flippant, nonchalant, silvery laugh.

"Oh, believe me, fair women are not so enamoured
of the ugliness of death; and—as for the rest—she
has gone very far for the sake of public liberty; she
will scarce grudge a good price for personal freedom.
Not know Idalia? *Altro!* I don't think, with all
your title to her confidence, that you know her very
thoroughly yourself. Perhaps she will treat with Villaflor *de couronne à couronne.* We are playing a losing
game; she will have the tact of her sex and go over
to the stronger side. She is far more fit for courts
than conspiracies. She could make good terms, I have
little doubt, and I would back her to match the bishop
in subtlety,—I could scarcely give as much praise to
any one else in Europe."

"You mean that—"

"That she will forsake us and coalesce with the
royalties. All women are rakes at heart, as Pope
says, and he should have given an alliterative line to
it,—all women are royalists. They may talk liberalism,
but they are Optimates to the core, and adore a despot,

public or private. Madame de Vassalis will see herself in imminent danger; she will barter herself and her knowledge and her power to buy her emancipation. Not a doubt of it. She is a republican; she is of the advanced school; she is '*of us*'—oh yes! but she is a woman of the world, a wonderfully clever one too, and she will do what is expedient, and never die for a chimera."

He more than half believed what he said; he saw far into Idalia's character, but not far enough to fully gauge its depth. He had, moreover, a natural disbelief in the existence of any nature proof against a bribe, or capable of preferring a creed to a sovereignty. The Greek looked at him with fiery scorn.

"You think that? I tell you that, rather than play for one hour into the hands of King or Church, Idalia would suffer a hundred deaths. Her word is her bond, and treachery has no place with her; she will never buy liberty by a renegade's cowardice—"

"Sublimely virtuous, but—scarcely true, I fancy. Miladi is too world-wise to be an idealist."

He spoke carelessly: but such conscience as was in him, and all manliness that had not been polished away by the plane of sophism and of expediency, were pierced to the quick by the words that unwittingly stung him so closely.

"By the way," he went on carelessly, "I dare say that the Court, having snared her, would be willing to treat with you. What do you say, amico mio? You have not made a very good thing of Liberalism; would you try Absolutism for a time, and change the Phrygian bonnet for a Neapolitan coronet?"

"*I!*"

"Well—you. If they do not take you prisoner too, you may conclude very good terms just now, in all probability. Our party is bruised, but not killed. We have danger enough in us to render us worth bribing, though not strength enough to give us a straw's weight of success. Under the circumstances, you might make a very lucrative bargain. There is no reason on earth why a democratic *condottiere* like you, my good Conrad, should not be metamorphosed into a courtier and a son of the Church. What do you think of it?"

Phaulcon's eyes had fastened on him throughout his speech with a glistening light that he—he who had told the Prince-Bishop that he could buy this man at a moment's notice—had construed as the eagerness for change, for security, and for a costly bribe, of an avaricious and reckless adventurer. As he ceased, the Greek's rich voice broke across his final words like thunder.

"By Heaven, if I thought you spoke in earnest I would kill you where you sit! If I did such villany as you hint at, I should deserve the shot or the steel that would find its way to me as surely as night follows day. *You* tempt me to such shame—you!"

Victor raised his hand with a slight warning gesture; the gesture that controlled his companion's tumultuous passions like a spell.

"Why not?—*to try you?* Frankly, I scarce gave you credit for such sublimated idealogy and self-devotion. Do you mean to say that you would rather swing or be shot by the Bourbons to-morrow than get a court place and an Italian title?"

He spoke with a contemptuous, incredulous insolence; he would as soon have expected Vesuvius to vomit gold and diamonds as to find anything like loyalty and probity in the man he dealt with—a man who checked at no crime, and knew no contrition.

The Greek flushed restlessly and painfully under the brown dye of his skin.

"Sneer as you will," he said, sullenly, "I have so much conscience in me, whether you believe it or not. I am vile enough, I dare say, but I am not so vile as *that*. There are few sins I have not plunged into, there is not one that I fear; but a renegade I never was yet, and never will be. By Heavens! if I felt myself turning traitor, if I thought that my strength would fail me to keep true, I would set the mouth of a pistol against my own head before my lips had time to dishonour me!"

In the moment he was true; in the moment the one higher thing in his nature asserted its domination; with all his falsity, his guilt, his ruthlessness, his baseness —and these were very black—he was loyal to an idea, he was faithful to a bond. He would betray others without a scruple, but he would not turn a traitor to his cause; he had so much still left of affinity with the codes and the freedom that he ostensibly served. It went far to redeem him, all warped and erring though it was—went far to raise him above the higher intelligence and the finer subtlety of the man who tempted him.

Vane heard him with an acrid wrath; this madman, this tool, this wax in his hands, this guilt-stained adventurer, whom he thought no more of than he thought of any pistol that he could use as he would, full of danger to others but to him a mere toy of wood and of steel, shamed him, stung him, escaped from him.

What Conrad Phaulcon shrank from as too foul to stoop
to must be foul indeed!

"I congratulate you on your new nobility, mon
cher," he said, indolently, with that covert sneer which
the Greek had learned to dread as a hound dreads the
lash. "I did not know there was anything you *had*
scruples about, but I am glad there should be;—it is
a new experience! I take your assurances, however,
cum grano salis;—you are quite wise to make them
so fervently, seeing that, as you observed, a shot or a
stab would follow your desertion as surely as night
follows day. And now, you will allow me to remark
that you are very imperfectly disguised, that you will
involve me very disagreeably if you are discovered
here, and that I shall thank you to remove yourself
from Naples at once."

"But Idalia?"

"You can serve Idalia in nothing by putting yourself and every one else in jeopardy. The Church has
her; the Church does not lightly let go its prey. All
that can be done, you are sure, will be done——"

"But——"

Victor lifted his hand again; a very slight gentle
movement, but before it the fiery impetuosity, the
mutinous impatience, of the Greek fell into a soldier's
submissiveness, a spaniel's docility. In their armies
there were many ranks, but there was only one discipline—implicit obedience and silence unto death.
If his chief had bidden him throw himself from the
heights of Tiberio, Phaulcon would have cast himself
headlong down without a question, when once they
stood on the ground which that slight gesture warned

him they were on now—the ground of authority on one side, of obedience on the other.

"Leave all to me. And for the present quit Naples while you can—if you can. Go to the old quarters at Paris immediately, and there await instructions. Adieu!"

Phaulcon's eyes looked at him with a piteous entreaty; he did not speak, but the great muscles of his throat swelled and throbbed, and his nervous hands clenched; the mute appeal spoke better than any words his prayer against that merciless dismissal.

"Go, *caro*," said his tyrant, gently; but the gentleness was immutable and cold. "If you feel such tenderness for your fair Countess, you should not have drawn her into such dangerous paths. Make yourself easy; she can take care of herself; there are few men —and I doubt if Giulio Villaflor be one of the few— who can match the wit and the science of La Vassalis. Now, go; your presence is embarrassing, and your melons are a blunder; but you always would be so impetuous! *Bon voyage;* and if the Bourbonists should stop you on the way, remember—and die mute. An unpleasant and discourteous allusion, I confess; but one must face possible contingencies."

Conrad Phaulcon looked at him one moment with a fierce glare under his curling lashes; but for the bond that bound and the authority that fettered him, he would have tossed up the Northerner's slender frame in his strong lithe arms, and dashed on the marble without those subtle astute brains that baffled and that ruled him. Then he dropped his head as a chidden hound drops his—and went.

Alone, his chief sat motionless, his eyes fixed, his

arms resting on the table before him, his face white
and rigid as though its profile were the profile of a
marble bust. He had been bitterly stung, though he
had never shown it; he had been deeply moved, though
he had given no sign of it. This lawless tiger, this
velvet-skinned wild brute, this worthless adventurer,
this mountain-thief, who shot men as willingly as he
shot sea-birds, had flung off treachery as a villany too
black for him; and he—a scholar, a gentleman, a
wit, a man who ridiculed the barbaric errors of crime,
and who knew that he had in him intellect to compass
the statecraft of half a world—had found no issue for
his ambitions, no crown to his career, no end for his
attainments, except a traitor's shame! No rebuke from
pure or lofty lives would have made him feel his own
degradation so deeply as the revolt of the man whose
hardened guilt he had known so long, and whose
scruples he had never before found check at any baseness that was offered him; the man in whom he had
himself killed all remnant of better instincts, and whom
he had looked on as a mercenary, to be hired at will
for any infamy, by whichever side could bid the highest.
No scorn from those of stainless honour or of blameless
deeds could have cut him so unendurably as the contempt for his own sin of renegade betrayal which had
flashed from the glance and lashed him in the words of
the Greek, whom he had known steeled to all remorse
and careless of all disgrace.

"Faugh!" he thought, with a disdainful bitterness
that availed little to reconcile him to himself; "his is
just such bastard honour, such childish folly, as we see
a thousand times over in the most shameless scoundrels
of Europe. The brigand murders at his fancy, and

reverences a leaden saint in his hat; the brutes of the Abruzzi flay their prisoners, and pray to the Madonna; the soldiers of the Pope kill women and children as they would cut the throats of pigs, and tremble when their master blesses them on Easter-day;—it is all over the world, that trash of superstition, that fit of spurious repentance, that ague-attack of poltroonery which men, because they are ashamed of it, dignify into conscience or creed! He would sell his soul to the devil if there were such a thing as a devil, and yet he prides himself on clinging to an idea which he has never followed except for the sake of adventure and self-interest, and to a cause which he has never embraced except as a vent for his own listlessness and discontent! And men call that king of straw, that random folly, that weakness cloaked in borrowed purples, *honour!*"

But the ironies that he wove to himself, the contempt in which he strove to steep and still the pangs of shame that Conrad Phaulcon's single virtue had awakened, had little potency. He was a gentleman, and the disgrace of his sin was as gall to him. Something of that humiliation and unendurable hatred for his own act which made Iscariot slay himself, finding no value in the silver pieces for whose glitter he had wrecked his peace and sold the guiltless, smote even through the ice-mail of his graceful callousness, the steel cuirass of his worldly policies.

And—though cowardice had no place in him, as it had in the fiery but mobile temper of Phaulcon—a shiver ran through him as he thought of those words—"the shot or the steel that follows the renegade, as the night follows the day." He knew that they were no hyperbole, no metaphor; he knew that men who were false to the political Order of which they were sworn, died so by that Order's vengeance, almost as surely as darkness falls on the sun's setting—died with a daggor-stroke in the winter nights of Rome, a pistol-shot in the gay chambers of Paris, a blow from behind in the riotous carnival times of Venice; died wherever they were, struck by unerring hands, and knowing that it was but wild justice for their own Judas sin, though the world saw in their fall but some common street scuffle, some murder of continental lawlessness, some thief's assassination for a few gold coins.

He knew it, and a chill tremor passed over him as he mused. But a few months before, a sculptor had been found at the door of his studio in Rome with a great wound slashed across his breast, and the blood choking his voice, so that he died speechless. The talk of the day had drafted that death in amongst the deeds of violence that Roman thieves will deal in, and babbled of the insecurity of life under the Papal tenure, and of the sad fate of the young genius struck down for a few bajocchi on his own threshold. Victor Vane had been aware, as many like him also, that no Roman thief had been the dealer of that stroke home to the lungs as the sculptor felt his way up the dark winding staircase, whose blackness the oil flicker of a single lamp only rendered deeper gloom; but that it had been a pitiless vengeance for an oath taken in boyhood, and in manhood broken.

He knew it; wherever he went, whatever he did, howsoever high he rose in eminence, whatsoever fruitage he gathered from the seed of treachery, the possibility of that doom would pursue him, the dread of it would haunt him—a worse fate than the stroke itself, sharply and swiftly dealt. The sword would ever hang above his head wherever his banquet should be spread, whatever nobles and princes should be summoned to it. Let him dupe his early comrades, or reign in his new sovereignties as he would, he could never dismiss this from him —this chance, that soon or late the vengeance for his desertion would search him out, and strike him in the hour of his surest security, of his proudest triumph.

Yet the step was taken; there was no receding now, and he knew that he had in him to rule empires if once he could grasp but the hem of power. He ground his teeth where he gazed down on the mosaic on which his arms rested, with the sharply-defined delicacy of his features, death-white in the golden sun-glow that fell through the broad leaves of vine.

"I was wrong to say there is no devil," he thought; "there is one that cripples the strongest and tempts the wisest, and sets the fool above the sage, and kicks genius into a hovel to die, and gives diadems to idiots, and makes great lives plod wearily for daily bread round the ass's mill, and in the ass's shafts; there is a devil that runs riot in the world, flinging all the prizes to the dullards who let them rust, and tossing all the blanks to the men who only want a chance to prove their mettle; there is a devil that leaves thrones to brainless dullards, and scratches out the winning blood from every race because it has no pedigree, that fills swine's troughs with pearls, and seals lips that drop eloquence; there is a devil that flings the wheat to the flames, and calls the chaff blessed bread, that lames the boldest ere they can start, and curses the new-born child in his cradle; there *is* a devil—the devil of Caste!"

When the failings of Democracy are hooted against her, one fair thing in her should be remembered—that in her sovereignties this one deadly bitterness, this passionate, poignant regret for all he *might have been*, had not Position warped, and cramped, and proscribed, and starved him, can come unto no man.

And there is no evil worse than this; for by it the man casts back on accident (and often with a terrible justice) all the errors, the failures, the sins, and the disgraces of his life. "I never had a fair field!"—it may be sometimes a coward's apology; but it is many a time the epitome of a great, cramped, tortured, wasted life, which strove like a caged eagle to get free, and never could beat down the bars of the den that circumstances and prejudice had forged. The world sees the few who do reach freedom, and, watching their bold upward flight, says rashly, "will can work all things." But they who perish by the thousand, the fettered eagles who never see the sun; who pant in darkness, and wear their breasts bare beating on the iron that will never yield; who know their strength, yet cannot break their prison; who feel their wings, yet never can soar up to meet the sweet wild western winds of liberty; who lie at last beaten, and hopeless, and blind, with only strength enough to long for death to come and quench all sense and thought in its annihilation,—who thinks of them—who counts them?

Where he sat, with his teeth clenched and the nerve of his lips twitching, the finished tactician cursed his fate as passionately as any Gilbert on his death-bed,

any Mirabeau in his dungeon. A consuming passion
was upon him; and under it his philosophies mocked
and his worldly wisdom forsook him. It had made him
a traitor; it made him now weak as any woman. While
he had lightly laughed with a scoff to the Greek of her
sorcery over the Italian Prelate, his heart had been sick
with jealousy and dread. He had remembered too late
what manner of man Giulio Villaflor was; what manner
of ransom the voluptuous Churchman was likely to
exact from such a captive as he possessed now. He
had thought too late that, in yielding her up to her foe,
he was delivering the woman he loved to one who
would feel the spell of her beauty as utterly as he, and
would be armed with the power to do with that beauty
howsoever he would. So that he were revenged on her,
he had never heeded how that vengeance might recoil.
It smote him keenly now, as he mused on the amorous,
ruthless, unscrupulous priest to whom he had surrendered her.

In the power of Giulio Villaflor!—he turned hot
and cold as the memory passed over him. He had
delivered her into bondage, that she might be shut away
from all eyes—that her smile might be seen of none
—that what could not be his should be no other's—
that the empire of her sorcery should end for ever in a
life of ignominy, of suffering, and of slavery. But now
he shuddered where he sat immovable, with the yellow
light streaming down through the vine; he had given
her over to one who never spared, to one who would
look on her loveliness at once with the admiration of a
voluptuary and the sway of a tyrant; to one who could
offer her release from lifelong misery as the purchase
coin of her love, or could take it, if denied, with the

mailed grasp of an irresistible and irresponsible dominion.

It fascinated him with its very horror, it enchained him with its very torture, this thought which he had flung at the name of Idalia, to insult her and to taunt his companion, and which grew into a phantom that he could not exorcise, a vision that he could not drive away. Every second was horrible to him; he saw the sovereign grace, the proud glance of the woman he had betrayed; he saw the full lustrous eyes of the arrogant priest as they would be bent upon her; and he writhed as under some bodily agony—he had dealt himself a sharper torment than any he had condemned her to endure. He had given her to bondage—yes, but he had given her also to Giulio Villaflor!

There are women who rouse a passion far more intense than can be held in the word love, which makes the man who feels it lose all semblance of himself, which sweeps away his memory, his honour, his reason, his ambitions, his very nature, and leaves him no sense of anything save itself. This was the passion which made her traitor now—cold, and keen, and subtle, and world-worn, and sceptical as he had been—choke down the great sobs in his throat, as he thought:

"Only to know her dead, so that no other can ever look on her; only to know that! Dead, dead, dead! she would seem mine then. And yet—I should rifle her grave like the madman in legends, for one sight of her face, for one touch of her lips!"

CHAPTER II.

The Captive of the Church.

In the interior stood a small castellated building flanked with towers of a singular solidity and strength, and casements built deep into the solid masonry, the narrow slits and dwarfed arches of the early centuries. The country round was dreary;—marsh and osier bed, with the rushes turning from spring green to autumn hues as the season varied, and to the left, interminable olive-fields, bounded in the distance with a sombre line of cypress, had little beauty, even when the southern sunset gave them its glow; and the place where the building stood, a black and broken pile of irregular rock, with a lake below, hemmed in by dark and stunted trees, lent only a deeper gloom and loneliness to the landscape. In the middle ages the towers had been a robber's stronghold, called the Vulture's Nest, and sorely feared by travellers; now, it was Church property, a few Cistercians held it as their convent, and, if it were ever used for other purposes, the slow swinging of the matins' bell, which dully droned over the désolate lands around, stilled all rumour of the fact.

A tempestuous sun was setting in the west;—intense fire lighted for the moment all the rugged and monotonous expanse, flamed in the salt and sluggish waters of the tarn, and reddened all the arid desert of the parching turf. Through a lancet window it shone into a darkened barren room; the grey stone floor uncovered, the pine-wood walls as bare, and the meagre furniture of a convent cell the only things that garnished it. To and fro in the narrow limits paced, as a lioness

may pace her den, Idalia. She was a prisoner of a
King and of a Church—two gaolers that never in any
age have loosed their prey.

The hour had come that she had long foreseen must
sooner or later be her fate; she was in the hands of
foes whom but a tithe of all that she had done would
have sufficed to hound to their worst fury. Fear was
not in her now; the blood of Artemisia and of Manual
was in her veins, and the fire of the Sea Queen and of
the Imperial Soldier flamed too hotly and too proudly
there to let dread enter. But a terrible chafing sense
of utter impotence, a longing to dare, to defy, to
vanquish, while she was here a captive, a fearful knowledge, a passionate regret for all that she had lost, for
all she might have been, made the slow moments' tor-
turing passage unendurable—made her hands clench,
her eyes flash, her whole frame quiver and rebel in
mighty longing, in fearful bitterness.

She knew that she had in her what would have
found power to rule an empire—and she was here the
prisoner of a Priesthood!

But a more intense and a more poignant pang than
that of her own adversity, of her own peril, was in her
for other lives lost through her—for the manhood that
had reeled and fallen at her feet, for the sightless eyes
that had looked up to hers, for the dead, slaughtered
through a too true adherence to her will, a too obedient
rendering of her word. True, the liberty for which
they had conspired was the just heritage of man, and
the noblest cause for which human life can ever be laid
down; true, it was for their country, and that country's
welfare and freedom, that they had fallen; but this was
no opiate to still the remorse that pierced and pursued

her. She knew that the cause had been far less to those who had died before her than the smile of her own eyes; she knew that with her beauty, and her power, and her sorcery, she had wooed them to passion only to drive them there, by their fealty to her, to perish like netted stags. She knew that it had been through the beguilement of her own unsparing temptation, her own ruthless witchery of fascination, that those who had been murdered in the night just gone had entered on a career which, without her, they might never have embraced.

The very masked banquet at which they had been trapped and slain had been given through her, given for her, and turned by her to that end for which the soldiers of the King had shot them down as rebels. She knew that but for her they would be living now in the fulness of their freedom and their manhood; and the remorse of an assassin seemed to weigh on her and haunt her, with the blood-red glow of that dying sun, in which the uplifted eyes of Viana, as they had sought hers through the mists of his last agony, seemed ever to gaze on her.

She was proud, she was daring, she was unscrupulous, she was self-controlled to a marvel, she was, as men counted, cruelly heartless; but in that moment Idalia could have doomed herself to the curse of any eternal travail of expiation—in that moment she could have rent out her living heart where it beat, and have flung it to the kites that hovered in the dusky glow of twilight as the vilest, darkest, most accursed thing that ever beat with life. She had the coldness of the world, and the pitiless serenity of one long used to study strong emotions only as tools to power; but beneath her acquired calm and cynic indifference the fervency of southern nations still slept in her, and she loathed herself with the fierce unsparing hatred with which men hate their direst foe.

She did herself injustice in much, and loaded herself with heavier reproach than that which had a right to rest on her; but it is ever thus with natures strong, bold, imperial, and used to command, when from the exercise of unmerciful dominion they change to the lash of self-rebuke and self-detestation; as kings in monastic days laid down the sceptre and took up the scourge.

Of her own fate she scarce took a thought; she knew well enough that little mercy would mingle with it; but all her heart, all her mind, all her longing, were with those dead men who had perished for her, those noble and dauntless lives which had been struck down around her as though they had been murrained sheep. In her youth, in her beauty, in her wealth, in her supremacy, she was flung into captivity, and knew that endless imprisonment, if not the shame and labour of some still more humiliating torture, would be her doom, but no throb of pity was in her for herself; the only thought upon her was the thought of those whom she told herself that she had murdered.

The bolts of the cell were undrawn with a slow grating sound; she turned and faced the door; it opened, and Giulio Villaflor entered the chamber. The ruddy flame-like light just fading in the west was shed full upon her; the masque dress she had worn had not been changed, and the diamonds on it flashed amidst its scarlet, its black, and its gold; in her weary musings she had thrust back from her temples the masses of her diamond-crowned hair, and, though her face was very colourless and her eyes heavily circled, she had never looked more magnificent than she looked now, as she turned with an empress's challenge.

Villaflor, entering with the courtly step of his habitual grace, started and paused, with a soft oath murmured involuntarily in his surprise and his admiration. He had seen her in Paris, in Spain, in Vienna; but in that instant her loveliness literally struck him blind; he came to arraign a captive, and a queen faced him in haughty and silent disdain. Fluent, facile, a statesman and a churchman, a libertine and a courtier, he had for the moment no words; he was held in check by his own rebel prisoner.

She looked at him, and a slight smile of contempt passed over her face.

"Ah! I thought so," she said, calmly. "So *your* lambs were the wolves, holy father?"

The Prince-Bishop changed colour ever so faintly, the sarcasm of the accent rather than of the words pierced his armour of omnipotence and self-love; he understood why men had dreaded the lash and the steel less than they had dreaded the lightest touch of this woman's scorn. But he was a powerful and accomplished personage, to whom defeat or opposition were heresies unknown; he recovered his momentary discomfiture, and came nearer to her, the warm afterglow on his stately stature and his handsome majestic form, while his lustrous eyes smiled gently.

"My daughter, it has grieved us sorely that you should have been so long in rebellion against the Anointed of God; and believe me, the harshness of coercion has only been resorted to in the last extremity, and with the deepest reluctance and regret."

Idalia where she stood turned her head, and let her eyes rest full on his, with a meaning more than any words could ever have expressed.

"Monsignore, it will be as well for us to lay aside these euphuisms. Neither of us believes them, and they weary both. Let us suppose them already uttered, and speak more truly—if a priest can speak so. I am your captive; it has long been one of the supreme ambitions of your life, and one of the most relentless efforts of your Church. I have baffled you long; you have trapped me at last. There is no more to be said."

Monsignore, the silken and astute diplomatist who wove the finest meshes of Court and Vatican intrigue, and was to be embarrassed by no living antagonist's skill, felt the blood burn under his olive skin, and felt the weakness of a bitter anger rise in him beneath the brief, tranquil, ironic words of his captive. Monsignore was never angered, the dulcet sweetness of his bland repose was never stirred by so provincial and unwise a passion; and he knew her power by that pulse of wrath she could stir in him. Yet he restrained it perfectly; he bowed with the grace for which he was renowned at St. Cloud and Compiègne.

"Pardon me, *figliuola mia*—"

"Pardon *me*, Monsignore! I am not of your communion; call me simply Madame de Vassalis."

The Prince-Bishop made a gentle deprecatory gesture with his white and elegant hands.

"Even those who have strayed from us we still hope to reclaim; and I speak as beseems me in the ·

name of the Church. You have thought 'there is no more to be said,' since by force you have been brought within our authority. You err greatly; there are many things."

Her old superb, disdainful smile came on Idalia's face; the entrance of the churchman had roused in her all her native pride, all her worldly brilliance, all her royal defiance; she knew well enough with whom she had to deal, and the assumption of authority awoke in her all her dignity and dauntlessness.

"Many things?" she repeated, tranquilly. "Possibly! You would wish to know from me—your captive —the secrets of my party, the names of my associates, the securities of my wealth, many other matters that you consider have become yours by right through my conquest?"

Giulio Villaflor looked at her curiously, a little bewildered.

"It is so, my daughter," he said, blandly. "We would rather, you will be sure, receive · these—our rights, as you justly say—voluntarily from you than be compelled to extract them by harsher means."

She laughed a little; a soft, mocking, ironic laugh.

"I imagined so. Well—it is as I said; there is nothing to be discussed between us; for all the weight of your Church, all the steel of your Swiss, will not force one word from *me*."

Monsignore started, and the purple blood flushed under the olive of his cheek and brow; his lips quivered, his teeth clenched on the full scarlet under lip. It was so utterly new to Giulio Villaflor to be mocked and bearded—and by a woman too!

His dulcet courtliness gave way, his mellow and

honeyed sweetness curdled, the fire flashed into his eyes that had used to burn in the darkling glance of the men of his great hierarchy when Savonarola braved them or Kings defied their legate.

"'Will not' is never said to Rome!" he answered, with the haughty grandeur of the mighty days of the Papacy.

She faced him with a sovereignty not less disdainful and supreme.

"Indeed! I think many who have said it have been slain by Rome, silent unto death!"

His face darkened more and more; "contumacy" was the deadliest sin in his eyes; he would have stricken it out with the iron heel of Torquemada or Ximenes.

"Some crave death, and are forbidden it; they must *live* to do our bidding."

The words were uttered low, and the menace, though vague, was pregnant. For the moment there was intense silence, but her eyes never shrank, only in them deeper and deeper gathered the mute and fiery scorn.

"You threaten me," she said, with cool, contemptuous carelessness, reckless how she provoked, so that she stabbed him. "It is scarcely worth while to so stain your manhood and your calling, Monsignore. I am in your power. There is little dignity in menace to a prisoner."

The kingly potentate, the silken churchman, the absolute tyrant, the tortuous courtier, shook in all his limbs with rage. She took his weapons from him, she rent his panoply, she silenced his eloquence, she pierced his nets, and an insidious passion crept in on him. She looked so beautiful there, in the fading russet light, with her Greek grace and her ironic pride, and her fettered, untamed, deathless royalty!

"She is a Semiramis! She is a sorceress!" he muttered in his throat, as he turned and paced the cell a moment, to still the feverish, angered, impatient bitterness rising in him and unnerving him. He felt to her as in the days of the Middle Age men felt to those women whom they sent to the stake for the dangerous sorcery, the white magic, of their too great charms.

She waited there, serene, unmoved, her eyes looking outward at the desolate and barren marshes, her hair slightly pushed back from her brows, the richness and the glitter of her masque dress the sole point of colour in the grey gloom of the cell. She looked like a picture burnt in on the darkness of the naked prison wall.

His glance, licentious and ruthless under the velvet gentleness of his long-studied regard, devoured her loveliness with thirsty, astonished admiration. He had said of her that she had the daring of the Cæsars, but he thought now that she had the intoxication of a Cleopatra. He had heard of her power, he had heard of her witchery, he had heard of the insanity of men who loved her and thought a world well lost for her; he felt and understood the meaning of those stories now. And a proud, eager, cruel light dawned on his face. "*Altro!*" he murmured to himself, with the mocking smile of his full lips. What mattered it—her defiance, her beauty? She was his captive! Nominally the king's captive, virtually his. What mattered resistance?

He paused before her, subduing the glow of his thoughts beneath the fall of his silken lashes, long and soft as the lashes of women; and his voice had its sweetest melody.

"Madame de Vassalis, hear me. You have said justly you are a prisoner; in the power of a sovereign you have conspired against, of a government you have sought to undermine. To underrate your sway for rebellion and for evil would be absurd; it has been vast, and wrought by the surest spells that subjugate the heart and the soul of man——"

Her delicate, merciless smile arrested the words on his lips.

"What do *you* know of those spells, holy father?"

Though her life was in this man's power, to use as he would, she could not restrain the irony that gave her, the captive, so keen a weapon against her tyrant. A smile for which she could have killed him gleamed under his drooped lids.

"Had I never known them until now, this moment had sufficed to teach them!"

A haughty impatience swept over Idalia's face.

"Sir! I have had my surfeit of such compliments. From a priest I may surely look for immunity from their weariness."

The tiger-glitter glistened more darkly in his soft brown veiled eyes. How could he deal with this woman? Menace had no terror for her, homage no charm! Unconsciously his voice hardened and grew more imperious; she was the first who had ever braved or baffled him.

"Madame," he pursued, disregarding her words,

"you know that you are liable to the full rigour of the law?"

"I know that I am in the power of those who never failed to use that rigour with or without right!"

"The church cannot err," he said, with the certain fiery majesty which, tyrannous and blind in its own belief of infallibility as it was, was yet the truest and greatest thing in him. "You fall within the pale of its most severe justice; yet the church, as you know well, will not deal with you; your sins will be left to the Secular Arm. Your wealth will be confiscated, your power crushed, your life passed in a felon's cell. You must know this."

"My wealth cannot be confiscated," she answered, negligently, "for there is none of it lodged in Italy; you could scarcely imagine me so incautious! That you will give me no liberty while I have life I perfectly understand, and that King Francis and the Pontifical States alike treat the love of freedom and of justice as a convict's crime, all Europe is well aware. If you allude to my riches, imagining that I will purchase my safety, you err; I will not swell a tyrant's treasuries to gain a personal indulgence."

Rage, hot and lowering, flushed Giulio Villaflor's brow as he heard; yet something of that unwilling homage which had been wrung from him when he had said, "She has the daring of the Cæsars!" was wrested from him now in an admiration that was half amaze, half intolerance; wholly sudden and very ferocious passion was controlled beneath the suave mellow hypocrisies which by long usage had become to him as second nature.

"Madame," he said, with a wave of his long deli-

cate hand, "there are enormities and conspiracies of
such magnitude that the wealth of the world could not
purchase condonation or escape for them. Those of
the Countess Idalia must be expiated; they cannot buy
absolution either from the church she has blasphemed
or the throne she has shaken. Captivity awaits you—
captivity till death. Has it no terrors for you—for
you, in your beauty, your youth, your magnificence,
your reign of love and of pleasure?"

She looked him full in the eyes:—

"Monsignore, you use strange language for a priest.
Whatever my fate be, I merit it; not for the things
which you quote against me as crime, but for luring to
their graves the lives you and your murderers slew
last night."

The nerves of his cheeks quivered with agitated
wrath; not for his bishopric would he have had it known
that he had looked on at the slaughter, and given the
death-word at the Villa Antina. She laughed, in the
aching bitterness of her heart, and in her dauntless
scorn for the foes who had netted her in like a wired
bird.

"Ah, that was a noble exploit, *beau sire;* a gentle
and holy duty of an Anointed of Christ! The cross has
led the van of the slaughterers of life and of liberty
many a time; you but followed the mission of priests
in all ages,—to sow broadcast war and desolation, and
to pile dead bodies by fire or by steel for the glory
of God in the mission of peace! Go and kneel with
Viana's blood on your head!—go and fill the throne
of St. Peter with the murder of patriots heavy on your
soul! Go—you have done no more than the men of
your office have ever done since Hypatia was slain by

Cecil, and the early Christians tore and fought for rivalry in Alexandria, and Rome, and Byzantium!"

The light of the sun had died out, there was only the silvery gleam of a lamp which Giulio Villaflor had brought in in his hand, and set down on the narrow stone table; in the mingled radiance and shadow she stood before the omnipotent churchman, in whose hands her destiny was held, as though she were a feudal monarch who lashed a disobedient vassal with her displeasure and disdain. He stood, doubting his own senses; he, the superb priest, he who aspired to the triple tiara, he the friend of emperors and the ruler of palace consciences, to be arraigned by a revolutionist, by an adventuress, whom his will could consign to the Vicaria, to linger there for life! He was convulsed scarce less with amaze than with wrath; and yet through all something of homage was wrung to the majestic courage which thus defied him.

"*Per fede!*" cried the prelate, the fury and the amazement in him breaking through the ever-impenetrable masking of his dulcet graciousness. "*Per fede!* you are bold indeed!"

"I leave cowardice to ecclesiastics, who net brave men like foxes, and who menace a captive when she can no longer revenge!"

A flush of shame and irritation came on his cheek; he was intolerant, cruel, cunning, an intriguer, a liar, a man of unscrupulous ambition, of intense and overweening pride and vanity; but he was withal a gentleman, and he felt the sting of the rebuke.

"I came—not to menace, but to persuade," he said, restraining the ardour she had roused in him, and bending on her the full lustre of his soft eyes. "My daughter, you cannot suppose but that it is with the utmost repugnance, and only at the last extremity, that force will be resorted to by those you have so justly incensed against you. Your years, your sex, your brilliance, all render the task of chastisement, the exercise of severity towards you, a most painful duty."

She smiled.

"Neither royalty nor priesthood are likely to suffer much from compunction; and as for the things you name, I take no refuge in the shield of my sex's weakness. I believe few men have merited your hatred and your rigour, or the vengeance of any tyranny, more than I have done."

Again she broke his patience, again she rent aside the courteous, polished suavity which never until now had failed him.

"You speak idly," he said, with a jarring anger and insolence in his voice. "You toy with words you know not the meaning of; you little dream what our 'rigour,' what our 'vengeance' can be to those who brave us!"

Her eyes rested calmly and contemptuously on his:—

"Do I not? When my best-beloved friend Virginia von Evon was scourged in the streets of Pesth because she would not yield up a Hungarian 'rebel' who had trusted his life to her keeping; when Pauline Lasla perished under the ice and the irons of Siberia because she had carried despatches for a Polish liberator; when the Countess Rossellio, at eighty years of age, was thrown into a dungeon by your order because she had lost her two noble sons in the cause of her Italy; when the wife of Manuel Canaro was shot down before his eyes by the soldiers of the Pope for no sin save that of loving liberty and him too well; when I have seen those and a score more martyrs like them, do you think I know nothing of how your hierarchy and your monarchy can revenge themselves on women? It is you, Monsignore, who speak idly; I am well aware that you will essay captivity first, and if that do not break me into betraying my friends to you and assigning you my wealth, why, then, that you will try—torture! It may be as well to spare you the probation, and to let you know that, though you have fettered me, you have not vanquished me, and never will. Others have died silent, and so can I."

The words were spoken tranquilly, with no haste, with no excitement in them; only beneath their repose of utterance was that fine, keen infliction of scorn, that proud, unyielding patience of resolve, which goaded and incensed him as no torrent of reproaches or of lamentations could have done. And yet, even in his wrath, even in his amaze, even in his outraged majesty as priest and autocrat, he could not but yield her admiration—admiration that stung and fanned the passion in him to fire. He stood before her, as a Papal Legate might have stood before an Empress who defied his mission and the might of Rome, rather than as before a helpless and rebel captive.

"True!" he said, with that grandeur of dominance which made the iron priests of a dead age the scourge and terror of empires. "True! the church must cut off and root up, even with steel and flame, the unworthy and·the accursed who deny her supremacy. Pity can have no place where *her* holiness is menaced, where her kingdom is denied, where her reign is outraged. True!—even your sex cannot spare you from the chas-

tening that she must, in the fulness of her divine love,
bestow on you for the purification of your heresies and
your rebellion——"

She stayed him with a gesture:—

"Nay, Monsignore! we are not in the Cinque Cento,
and you cannot burn me, though you can slay me more
slowly and more cruelly, perhaps. A truce to this
melodrame! We are both of the world; let us speak
without tragedy. You say the Secular Arm will deal
with me for my 'crimes,' why then are you here?"

The direct question staggered him slightly, but
Giulio Villaflor was very rarely at fault; he bowed
with grace.

"Because I would fain save you, were it possible,
from the fruits of your own misguided recklessness."

"I thought so," she said, calmly, while his eyes
fell beneath her smile. "I have said, I betray no one;
and I give no bribes."

"In gold—no. And I seek none."

He leaned nearer to her, and his voice sank very
low; the flush burnt darker in his olive cheek, and his
eyes gazed on her beauty with a boldness that gleamed
out under their veiled and velvet softness with a tiger-
like ferocity, that those knew well as their death-doom
who dared cross the will of Monsignore.

"In gold—no!" she echoed. "You seek my political secrets. Well, you will never have them."

"What!" His voice was very low still, and vibrated
with the intensity of restrained passion through the
silence of the cell. "You will renounce your pomp,
your wealth, your pleasures, your ambitions, your freedom, for the toil of a convict, the chains of a felon,
the solitude of a dungeon, the slow, festering, hopeless,

endless existence of a prisoner whom no power can release save the warrant of death!"

Her face was still, set, colourless as marble, and as firm:—

"Yes, if liberty be only to be bought by the shame of treachery."

He looked at her, forced out of himself, as it were, by the tribute she wrung from him:—

"Mother of God! What a man you would have been!—you would have ruled the world."

She smiled with a disdainful weariness.

"Who knows? I might have been a court ecclesiastic, and sold my soul for power to a sacerdotal lie!"

The satire pierced him to the quick, and all the darker and more cruel impulses returned on him. He stooped and laid his hand, with the amethyst ring that glittered like a basilisk's eyes, down upon hers; his voice stole very low on her ear.

"Idalia! women of your beauty can bribe more potently than by gold or state-lore. You shall buy your freedom if you will—from me."

She understood him; the blood flashed back into the colourless weariness of her face; she flung his touch off as though it had pollution; she faced him there in the dimness of the lamp-light with a look in her eyes before which he, all fearless, steeled, and omnipotent though he was, cowed like a lashed hound. Even Giulio Villaflor lacked the boldness which should dare twice tempt her with that alternative to purchase back her liberty.

"Monsignore," she said, briefly, and each word cut like ice, "if I refuse to be a traitress, I shall scarce consent to be your mistress.   It were a poor choice of dishonour!"

He could have killed her in her haughty beauty, in her unsparing answer that laid bare the shame and evil of his own heart, that spoke out so mercilessly the meaning of his veiled words, of his hinted tempting! She had dared him, she had refused him, she had unmasked him—well, she should know of what fashion was the vengeance of Neapolitan blood, of ecclesiastical dominion! He bent to her, his lips close to her hair, his eyes looking into hers, his brown smooth cheek darkly stained with the purple flush of passions which nothing but that calm scorn of her fixed gaze, which never left him, which never drooped beneath the fierce menace of his own, held in any check.

"Madame de Vassalis, you might have given your beauty for your freedom and your wealth; you have refused.   So be it!   It is in my power without terms or concession.   You might have reigned my mistress. You shall be now, instead, my toy for an hour, and languish, later, till the grave, in the king's prisons or the galley's shame.   You were unwise, my brilliant revolutionist, to make a foe of me; you are *mine*, body and soul, in life and in death—mine to take when I will, to give where I choose!"

And, with these words, he flung his violet robe closer about him, and, without a glance at her where she stood, swept across the stone floor of the convent cell and left her presence; his keen ear had heard the footfall of a monk without.

"I come, my son—I come!" he said, gently, in his sweet lingering voice.   "'The captive is contumacious still, but, with discipline and persuasion, she may still be reclaimed to the august faith. Draw the bolts well—so! so!—and deal gently with her; she will see her error."

Alone, where the silver lamp shed its lambent flickering light, Idalia thrust her hand within the folds of the rich scarlet and weighty broideries and sweeping lace of the masquerade dress she still wore, and drew half out from its resting-place in her bosom a delicate gold-sheathed Venetian stiletto, a jewel-studded toy slung by a chain round her throat. She looked at the slender, glittering, lithe blade, and smiled as she put it back.

"*His!*—while that steel will release me the moment his lips dare touch mine!"

For she had in her the temper of Lucretia.

CHAPTER III.

"Rien que Toi."

In the warm light of the summer morning the yacht steamed her way once more into the harbour of Capri. The Venetians were safe, and Erceldoune returned—to suffer, as he knew, and suffer hopelessly, yet no more able to hold himself back from it than the mariners were able to turn their prows from the magic music of yonder Siren Isles. Groups of fisher-folk were talking together gravely, and with an unwonted sadness on their ruddy, sunburnt faces; as he waded through the knee-deep surf he noticed it—his thoughts leapt to her in an instant—he asked the sailor nearest him what ailed them. The sailor was the man whose brother he had once rescued from the churning seas below Tiberio.

"It is the Comtessa Idalia, Signore."

"What of her?"

"They have arrested her!"

"Arrested her?"

He staggered against the brown timbers of a boat resting on the sands, and clenched them hard to keep himself from reeling like a drunken man. For the moment, old usage in many countries gave the word no meaning on his ear save in its criminal sense.

"So they say, Signore," answered the sailor, while his strong teeth set. "If I had been there, they should not have touched the hem of her skirts! It was done at the Villa Antina, in the interior; the soldiers shot many, I've been told."

"Many! Who?"

"Conspirators, Signore—so they say," replied the Capriote, who scarcely knew the meaning of the phrase, and thought the world governed to perfection if it proved a good fishing-season, and many visitors came to the coast. "Some tell that his Highness of Viana was killed. I don't know about that; but Miladi Idalia is a prisoner of the King's."

With an oath, mighty as ever rang over the marches from the fierce lips of Bothwell, Erceldoune strode from him well-nigh ere the words were ended, and plunged down into the thicket of vegetation that led to the beetling cliff on which her villa stood. The sun was scorching, the ascent on the slope that faced the sea perilous to life and limb; there was no more than a perpendicular granite slab towering many feet above the water, covered with foliage and rock-flowers. But he was a trained mountaineer; he knew the ice-slope of the Alps as well as he knew the Border-land; he was up it with

the swiftness of thought, swinging himself in mid-air
from the tough coils of the tangled creepers till he
reached the summit, and forced his way, without pause
or ceremonial, into the court of the forsaken dwelling.

"No one passes!"

A soldier on guard stood within the arched entrance.
Then he knew that it was true, and that she was lost
to him, lost to the fangs of the Church, to the dungeons
of the Bourbons.

"By whose order are you here?"

The words were hoarse and faint; he felt his lips
parched with a dry white heat.

"The order of the King."

"The King's! Stand off!" cried Erceldoune, as
though the very name of her tyrant maddened him.
"What right have you, for all the despots who curse
Europe, to invade her privacy, to violate her home?"

The sentinel said nothing, but lowered his bayonet
till the blade was levelled against the intruder's breast.
At that instant the deep howl of the hound moaned
down the silence. Erceldoune shook with rage as he
heard it. Was not her dumb beast even spared! He
wrenched the weapon by the gun-barrel from the soldier's hand, flung himself on the slight frail form of
the Neapolitan, and, tossing him aside lightly as a
broken bough, dashed across the court to where the
dog was chained. It was the work of a second to
unloose and free him. Ere even that was wholly done,
however, the three soldiers left on guard of the villa,
which had been rifled by governmental order of all
papers, plate, jewels, and articles of value, roused by
their comrade's cry, poured into the square court, and
levelled their bayonets at him.

"Stir, and you are a dead man!" said the corporal in command.

A laugh was the only answer Erceldoune gave. His blood was up, and in his misery and his fiery rage he cared nothing, and almost knew nothing, of what he did or said.

"At them, Sulla!" he cried in Servian, lifting his hand.

With a bound the giant hound sprang on the soldier of Francis, and hurled him down as if he had been a dead boar. Erceldoune, with the single blow of his left hand, levelled another to the ground, and before the last sentinel could take aim or raise his fallen fellows, he sprang through the gateway, and, with the dog at his side, dashed headlong through the gardens and down the mountain road, without pause, without heed, well-nigh without sense.

The glow and colour of the world of summer blossom, the fragrant stillness of the morning, the swinging of matin-bells from a chapel far above, the golden fruit that he tossed aside or trampled out as he rushed down the steep incline, all seemed dizzy, unreal, intangible; only one remembrance stood out clear before him—she needed him. He felt giddy and blind, a sickening oppression was on him, the intense odours of the myrtle and orange-flowers were intolerable to him; he felt maddened and senseless with pain; but he was not a man to yield to misery or dread while action was possible, while daring and skill could avail aught. Fire burned in his eyes, his lips shook, his teeth clenched like a vice; he grasped the wolf-hound's mighty mane in a gesture that Sulla understood as though volumes had been said in it.

"We will save her—or kill *them*."

The dog seemed instinctively to know that in his liberator was the avenger of his mistress. He accepted the lead, and followed passively.

Repeated peril and dangerous emergencies, often met and vanquished by himself alone, had given Erceldoune the energetic vigilance, the knowledge and the patience of a soldier; his own nature was rash, impulsive and hotly impetuous, but the habit of long and arduous service had taught him the value of coolness and of self-restraint. His passions and his fiery chivalry of temper could have led him now to any madness, could have led him to seek out Francis in his own palace, and strike him down before all his nobles and all his guards, as her tyrant and her abductor. He had the blood in him of Border chiefs who had fought for Mary Stuart, and Scottish soldiers who had served with Gordon's archers, of haughty Castilians who had died for a point of honour, and steel-clad Spaniards who had conquered with the Great Captain; and a vein of the old dauntless, reckless, fearless, romantic knight-errantry of a dead day was in him, little as he had known it. His rival had not erred when he said that the "Border Eagle" should have lived in the Crusades. But not the less did he know now that discretion and self-control were needed to serve her; not the less did he bend to their curb the violent longings of his own wretchedness.

He paused a moment where a deep leafy nest of rock and foliage screened him from all sight, and tried to still the throbbing misery of his thoughts, and search out the nearest clue to find her. She was in the power of her foes; royal soldiers held her villa; that she was deeply compromised in political matters was evident; where she might now be taken the gaolers who held her alone knew. He shuddered as he remembered all the histories he had heard of the vengeance of the monarchists on those who had defied them! Her dog was with him; the sentinels would tell the story of his onslaught on them; if noticed, he would be suspected and watched, possibly even arrested. To go to Naples was to risk arousing suspicions that might render every effort to save her useless. He must be unknown, untracked, or he could do nothing; yet he must keep the hound with him, for no aid could be so sure to track her as Sulla's scent and unerring instincts of fidelity. The dog stood now beside him, the fine nostrils quivering, the ears pointed, every nerve on the stretch, and every now and then a piteous anguish in the brown lustrous eyes as they were turned on him with a low heartbroken moan.

He stood and thought some moments, then rapidly, and keeping even under the deep shelter of the leaves, he made his way by winding paths to the hut of the sailor whose life he had saved long before on San Constanza's-day. It stood near the beach, hid under a great ledge of rock, like a sea-gull's nest. As it chanced, the fisherman sat without in the sun, singing and mending his nets; he was only just back from a long sail to Calabria. Erceldoune went up to him and held out his hand.

"Nicolò, do you remember the night under Tiberio?"

The nets fell on the sand in a heap, all sea-stained and clogged with weed. The marinaro, with tears of delight in his bright black eyes, and a thousand cries

to the Madonna dell' Mare, thanked him and blessed
him and worshipped him, and would have knelt down
at his feet had he been allowed. Life surely was no
great matter there in the Piccolo Marina, getting scant
bread from the depths of the waters, spreading the nets
on the low flat shingle-hut roof to dry, and going out
in peril of storms for sake of a piece of dry fish for
hungry mouths to eat; yet it must have had its pleasures too, for the fisher Nicolò was as grateful for
the saving of it as though he had been crowned with
gold.

"You will do a thing for me, Colò?" asked Erceldoune, as he arrested the torrent of gratitude.

"I will risk body and soul for you, Signor!"

"I believe you would. I only want you to sell
me a fishing-suit such as you wear, and some of your
fishing-nets and lines."

"I will *sell* you nothing, 'Lustrissimo," said the
sailor, doggedly, and with a certain wounded pride.
"I will give you everything my poor hut holds."

"And I will take it as willingly. Forgive me for
using the word of barter!"

The Capriote's eyes beamed with delight at the concession and the comprehension.

"Come within, Eccellenza."

Erceldoune bent his lofty head, and entered the
low, square, sea-scented hut, with the half-naked children, handsome as young seraphs running wild, and
the yellow gourds, and dried herbs, and onion-ropes
hanging from the rafters. As it chanced, there was a
suit, unworn except on saints' days, and of full size,
for the marinaro was of high stature and powerfully
built. In a few moments his own white yachting-dress

was changed for it; he set the scarlet-tasseled cap on his head, wore nothing over the loose striped shirt that left his arms so free, and flung some nets over his shoulders. With the bronze hue of his skin and the sweeping darkness of his beard, no casual glance would have detected him to be other than a Capriote.

"Shall I pass as a marinaro?" he asked the sailor. Nicolb smiled.

"You look more like a king in disguise."

"I am sorry for it. Now, while I wait here, will you pull out to the yacht, give the captain this ring from me as credentials, and bid him send me, by you, all the gold and circular-notes I have on board, my pistol-case, powder-flask, cartridge-case and shot-belt, and a pocket-flask of brandy? Say nothing of my disguise, and be as quick as you can, for God's sake."

The Capriote obeyed, got his little boat out rapidly, and pushed off from the shore with hearty good will. Erceldoune sat at the hut door with the hound crouched at his feet, and his eyes fixed on the waste of waters. All the glories of the bay were spread before him, but it might have been a sand-desert for aught that he knew or saw; the fishing-skiff flew light and swift as a bird over the sea, but to him it seemed scarcely to move; every moment was a pang, every minute appeared eternity. While he waited here in the noontide glare, how might she not be tortured!—while the hours flew on, how might not her foes be wringing her proud heart! Time was passing so fast: three days, they said, had gone by since the arrest at Antina; Heaven only knew how many leagues she might have been borne since then, to what remote inaccessible recesses of Alps or Apennines, monastic prison, or mountain-shut morass, she might have been taken ere now! The fever of an intolerable agony possessed him. While he was in action he could bear it; it was something at least to be in search for her, to be in her service, to be on her track; but to sit here while those eternal matins tolled the passing seconds away, and the fishing-boat seemed to glide snail-like over the width of the sea! The swinging monotone of the chapel bell, the measured dips of the oars, seemed to beat into his brain and drive him senseless. What was it to him that she had told him his passion was hopeless? If he could give her back her freedom and her happiness, he felt that he could die in peace.

Nicolò returned very rapidly, laggard as the time had appeared, bringing all for which he had been sent. The money was the whole, or very nearly, of his three months' pay just drawn — some two hundred pounds or less of circular-notes in a chamois-leather pouch. He left, unseen, several gold pieces of it in a wooden bowl from which the fisherman was used to drink his onion-soup, then slipped the pistols in his sash and the pouch in his shirt, and turned again to Nicolò.

"Now take me across, some way off Naples if you can, and let me land unnoticed in the nearest route for Antina."

The marinaro, with all the alacrity of his craft, had ready his sailing-boat, a small lugger, awkward but seaworthy, in very little time, and, with his eldest son at the helm, pushed off once more into deep water. Erceldoune sat silent and deep in thought, the hound at his feet, couched on the bottom of the vessel, watching him ever with deep, keen, mournful eyes. The day was beautifully still; the bay alive with innumerable craft, and gay with sails of tawny stripes and flags of all nations' hues. Naples lay white and matchless in her sunlit grace; he saw no more of the glory about him than though he were blind. He thought they sailed slowly as a death-barge; in truth, the lugger danced over the light curled waves and through the snowy surf as brightly as a monacco on the wing.

Nicolò knew every inch of the coast, and landed at length in a small lonely creek, hidden in profuse vegetation, where there was just depth enough to steer the vessel in, and let the beach be reached by wading.

"Yonder lies Antina, Signor," said the fisherman; "a league to the left by that road where the cypresses are. You see?"

Erceldoune took the man's brown hand in his and wrung it hard.

"I see! I cannot thank you now, Nicolò. Later on, if I live—"

The Capriote fixed his large black eyes tenderly and wistfully on him.

"Eccellenza, you go into some danger. Let me be with you."

Erceldoune shook his head.

"Why not, Signor?" pleaded Nicolò, entreatingly. "When *I* was in peril you came to me, down into the churning seas, at risk of your own life. The boy can take the boat back. Let me come!"

Erceldoune put him gently back.

"Not now, Colò, though I could wish for no better comrade. But what I do, I must do alone."

He broke from the man's entreaties and conjurations, and went up through the tangled thickets of arbutus and through the fields of millet rapidly, and never looking back; every moment was so precious. The fisherman stood watching him sadly.

"It is *she*," he said. "It is so with them all! She is a sorceress. I am glad I crossed myself whenever I met her, though old Bice calls her an angel, because she promised Fanciulla a dower. I am glad I crossed myself!"

A league brought him to Antina—a league that lay through olive-grounds, and green fields of maize, and vineyards, and sunburnt grass-land, which his slashing stride, that was the walk of the mountaineer, covered rapidly. To anything like fatigue he was insensible. Since the hour when she had found him in the pine-woods his life had been spent in one vain pursuit—the search for Idalia; yet never had he sought her as he sought her now.

He passed into the villa grounds: nearer the building he dared not venture; it would be occupied, in all likelihood, also by soldiers, and the sight of a fisherman loitering so far inland would of itself excite suspicion. But towards the entrance the hound paused, tore the earth up in mad haste, snuffed the ground, ran round and round again, threw his head in the air, then gave a deep-mouthed bay of joy, and looked back for a sign to Erceldoune. He stooped and laid his hand on the dog's mane; his own heart was beating so thickly that he felt sick and reeling; here his one hope had centred—that Sulla would find her trail.

"Seek her," he said, simply.

The hound needed no other command; with his

muzzle to the earth he tore it up by handfuls, searching hither and thither; then settled to his work as the
pack settle to line-hunting, and dashed off—not inward towards the gardens, but out to the open country.
Stooping an instant ere he followed him, Erceldoune,
whose eye and ear were well-nigh as trained as an Indian's, for they were those of one of the first deer-
stalkers of Scotland, saw the mark of wheels, very
faint on the parched arid turf that was dry and bare
as bone, ,but still there. Hope rose in him;—if he
were not too late!

Onward he went in the burning sun-glare, with
the weight of the nets on his shoulder, and the heat
pouring down into the scarlet wool of the fishing-cap;
onward, where the dog led through the long heat of
the day, through the shades of evening, through the
stilly starlight, as one succeeded the other. It was
tedious, arduous, wearying work; bringing so little
recompense, needing such endless patience. Often the
hound lost scent, and had to try back to where he had
lost the sign of the wheels, as though it were the slot
of a stag; often the dry crisp grasses or the baked
white dust of the roads bore no scent at all, or the
crossing and recrossing of other tracks blurred the marks
and confused the trail; often the impress of a mule's
hoofs or the heavy footprint of a contadina had struck
out or overlaid the faint traces which only guided the
dog. Often, also, for a priest, or a peasant party going
to an *infiorata*, or, worse yet, for a set of soldiers
scouring the country, he had to seek shelter in some
dank dell of woodland, on some sandy pine-knoll,
under the grey twisted olives, or beneath a tumble-down
shed, and hide, as though he were himself the prisoner

hunted, forcing Sulla to lie still beside him. But he had spent many a long day in the patient toil of deer-stalking in the Highlands at home, and he brought the same wariness and the same long endurance here. If he had once abandoned himself to the misery of thought, to the fierceness of vengeance, he could never have borne the intolerable slow-dragging bitterness of this endless search; but he would not give way to them, and he would not let them urge him into the madness which could have made him dash down into Naples and demand her at the hands of the Bourbon. He knew that if it were possible to save her, thus only could it be done; and he gave himself to the toil without pause, and with a self-restraint that cost him more than all.

Three days and three nights were spent thus; he began to think in his agony that he should only find her—if ever he found her—dead. His search was chiefly made after the sun was down; the day, when he had not to secrete himself and the hound from those who might have thought their aspect suspicions, and from village authorities who might have challenged his appearance away from a seaport, he spent in questioning the country people, as far as he could, without exciting wonder or counter-inquiry. Happily he could speak the Neapolitan patois to a miracle, and he supported his character of a fisherman well enough with most; some thought, like Nicolò, that he looked more like a prince in disguise, but he was frank and comrade-like with them, drank with them, ate their own coarse food, could give them a hand in mending their roof after a storm, in digging a trench round their olives, or in reaping their maize, and lived so like one

of themselves, that he soon conciliated them, and per-
suaded them that he was a paid-off mariner who had
sailed to far distant places, and liked now to wander
at will over the country.

From them he gleaned various news; nothing that
told him, however, the one great thing—where Idalia
had been taken. When the sun set each day, and he
was free from observation, he put Sulla on the track
again from the spot where they had last left it, and
worked on the line unwearyingly through the nights.
The hound had been perfectly trained, and understood
what was needed of him to a marvel; he had attached
himself to Erceldoune with a strange sagacity of instinct,
seeming to lay aside the jealousy he had hitherto shown
him for sake of their mutual love and service to the
one both had lost. Such sleep as he was obliged to
take he took in the hottest hours of the day under the
screen of millet-sheaves, or in the cool shade of deep
ravines filled with chestnuts or cypresses; with the fall
of evening he resumed the search, and through the
clear lambent light of the Italian moon, or in the
gloom of frowning hills and woods, the two shadows
of the man and dog glided unceasingly, bending down
and seeking hither and thither. Some who saw them
crossed themselves, and took them for the shades of
some ghastly huntsman and his phantom hound; others,
more practical, took them for truffle-seekers, despite
the gigantic size of the animal. Not one ever ventured
to stop them; a rough muleteer once tried a parley in
the midnight on a lonely hill-side path, and said something, with a menace, of his fancy for the brandy-flask,
whose silver head he saw under the folds of the waist-
sash; but a blow with the butt-end of one of the pistols

soon silenced him by levelling him with the brown-
burnt moss, and Erceldoune was molested no more.
Slowly—very slowly—and with an infinite toil and
patience, he worked his way by the guidance of the
hound's lead, till the dawn of the fourth day brought
him into the rugged, desolate, morass - intersected
country, where, dark and sullen above the miasma-
haunted lake at its foot, the square castellated building
of the isolated monastery stood among its stunted trees,
with the bare grey cliff towering at its back. It was a
red, stormy, misty, oppressive morning, very hot and
poisonous in its heat as the steam rose up from the
black still waters and the wastes of swamp, while
beyond stretched the grey of the monotonous olive and
the still more distant black peaks of cypress-topped
hills, as the hollow booming matin-bell of the monks
swung wearily through the heavy air. "There is no
fortress here; is the dog in error?" he thought, as he
entered on the dreary desert of the level marshy land,
with no sound in it except the echo of the tolling bell
and the noise of the moor-fowls startled from their rest
among the reeds and sedges. But the hound held on,
growing keener and hotter as the scent grew stronger
and the wheel marks plainer in the damp sodden
ground than they had been on the dusty roads and the
traversed highways. With his muzzle to the ground,
he dashed onward mile on mile across the country at a
speed that taxed the Border fleetness of his companion.
There were quagmires, morasses, hidden pools, sponges
of mud, small lagunes hidden under treacherous grasses
or rushes, unseen pools where the water-birds brooded
by hundreds, swamps where a single false step would
be death for any sinker under the yielding, soaking,

nauseous mass; but the hound never missed his footing or erred in his going, and Erceldoune followed him through the grey of the morning; his heart beat to suffocation, the brown lonely waste reeled before his eyes, the hot noxious air seemed to weigh down his breath and stifle him, but a delirium of hope came on him;—the dog must be near at last! Straight in his level chase, straight as though he were running down a stag across an open plateau, fleet as the wind, and with his mighty crest bristling and his eyeballs red with flame, Sulla led on, across the marshes, across the shallow ponds, over the trembling mass of water-sodden earth, through the steaming vapour rising from the lakes—led on till he stood under the broken granite crags on which the monastery was raised above the still, black, reedy surface of the lake.

Then, with one rolling bay like thunder, he woke all the echoes of the lonely silent dawn. Afar from on high, through the gloom of an arched casement, through the swaying flicker of dank leaves, through the transverse lines of iron bars, eyes dark as night, weary as pain, looked down on him;—they were the eyes of Idalia.

She sat in the monastic cell which was her prison-chamber, with the bare hot glare of the sunlight, that burnt all nature black and barren, and made the disease-laden vapours rise up from the swamps below, scarcely entering through the narrow lancet-chink that was the sole casement of this cold stone cage, in which they had shut their brilliant-plumaged bird. Her hands rested on the slab of granite that was her only table; links of steel held the wrists together: they had allowed her no change of raiment, and the lustrous colours and gold broideries of the masque dress still swept the damp flags of the floor, though all jewels had been taken from her. She had been here six days and six nights a captive of the Bourbons; what was yet worse, a captive of the Church.

Food of the coarsest and the scantiest was all that had been allotted her, and once—"for contumacy,"—her priestly gaolers' hands had been stretched to tear down the silks and lace from her shoulders, and bruise and lacerate them with the scourge,—once, when the dignity that they were about to outrage so foully had made the monk, who was bidden to the office, drop the lash, aghast and trembling, and his superior, who had directed the infamy, feel too much shame in the moment to hound him on to his work. They had desisted for twenty-four hours more. "By then," they had muttered, "the rebellious subject might have broken her silence, and become less obdurate to the due demands of Church and King."

The twenty-four hours had well nigh gone by, but Idalia had given no sign of yielding; she had scarcely spoken since the day that Giulio Villaflor had quitted her presence. She knew that the lightest word might be construed into confession, or used as evidence against those whom they wanted her to betray; and she had strength in her to endure torture unflinchingly, without breathing one syllable that should sound as an entreaty for mercy, or be translated into a hint against her comrades in adversity. She knew well what she had to anticipate; she did not seek to palliate to her own thoughts the horror of the doom that awaited her; she knew that only by death, self-dealt, could she escape the passion of the libertine who held her in his gripe; she knew that when that had had its way, and grown sated of its own violence, she would, if she lived, drag out existence in agony, in shame, in felon companionship, in hopeless bondage; she never veiled from herself the depth and the despair of the wretchedness that awaited her, and she knew that not even her sex would shelter her from the barbarity of physical torture, till that torture should kill her bodily strength, or her persecutors learn that it was powerless to destroy her resolve and break her silence. She knew the fate that awaited her, but never for one instant did the thought glance by her that she could purchase freedom from it all by betraying those whose lives she held in her keeping, or by going willingly to the loathed love of her ecclesiastical captor. Such weakness as that was not possible to her nature; she had a virile courage, a masculine reading of all bonds of honour; this woman, bred in luxury, in self-indulgence, in power, in patrician tastes, and epicurean habits, had the nerve in her to endure all things, rather than to purchase her redemption by a traitor's recreancy.

She had been successful hitherto in concealing from her gaoler the slender shaft of the stiletto, and she was prepared in extremity to use it; she had too much of the old Greek heroism to fear such a death, and had too many of the old, dauntless, pagan creeds not to hold its resource far nobler than a long dishonoured life of endless misery.

Where she leaned now, with her chained hands lying on the stone, and the darkness and the silence of the stone cell about her, her face was colourless, but it had on it no fear, no weakness: it was only grave,

and very weary. Her thoughts had gone to many
scenes and memories of her past—the past which, in
eight brief years of sovereignty, had been fuller and
more richly coloured than a thousand drawn-out lives
that never change their grey still calm from the cradle
to the grave. Endless hours of those dead years rose
before her to haunt her in this black solitude, in these
chill iron-bound walls, in which the magnificence of
her life had ended—hours in the lustrous glare of
Eastern suns, under the curled leaves of palm, and the
marble domes of ruined temples; in the laughing riot
of Florentine nights, when the carnival-folly reeled
flower-crowned adown the banks of Arno; in the gaslit
radiance of Paris, when the fêtes of the Regency revived for her; in summer evenings in Sicilian air,
when the low chants echoed softly over Mediterranean
waters, and the felucca, flower-laden, glided through
the starlight to music and to laughter; in palaces of
Rome, of Vienna, of Prague, of Venice, where the dawn
found the banqueters still at their revels, and no wines
that flushed purple and gold in the blaze of the lights
and the odours of perfume intoxicated the drinkers
like the glance of her eyes, like the spell of her smile
—all these scenes rose up above her, and filled with
the hues of their life and their splendour the barren,
bitter, stone-locked loneliness in which she was im-
mured.   She had loved her reign; she had loved
her sceptre; she had loved those years so crowded with
triumphs, with pleasures, with mirth, with wit, with
radiance, with homage, with peril that only lent them
keener zest, richer flavour; she had loved them, though
beneath the purple, fetters had held her, and amidst
her insouciance remorse had pursued her; she had loved

them—and they were dead for ever. She was chained here a prisoner of captors who never spared until their brother-tyrant, Death, claimed their spoil and their prey at their hands.

"It is just—only just," she thought, while her head leaned on the cold steel clasping her wrist, and the black moisture-dripping blocks of the cell enclosed her as though already she were in her grave. "I sent them to their graves; it is only just that I should have a felon's doom."

A shiver ran through her like a shiver of intense cold, though the close air of the cell was oppressive and scorching! It was not for her own life, but for the lives that had fallen around her, like wheat beneath the sickle in the banqueting-halls of Antina.

The silence was unbroken; one burning ray of the outer sun stole through the loophole and flashed on the gyves enclosing the hand, whose lightest touch had thrilled men's veins like fire and impelled them where it would; the dank, noiseless, grey gloom was like the gloom of a charnel-house. Suddenly on that stillness broke the challenge of the hound's bay.

Idalia started; she knew the familiar sound that rolled out like the roll of a clarion. The colour flushed her face, she moved rapidly to the casement; through the glare of the sun, beneath the shelving precipice of rock, she saw the dog, and saw who was his comrade.

She knew him in the first moment that his longing eyes looked upward, and knew his errand there —knew that he had come to save her, or to die with her.

"O God!—he, too!"

The words escaped her involuntarily where she

stood alone, leaning against her prison bars, as the hound shook all the echoes from the rocks around with the impatience of his summons; she had seen so many perish, she would fain have saved this man.

Through the space of the sultry white sun-glare that severed them his eyes met hers, and spoke in that one look all the force of the ardour, all the fidelity of the devotion, that had brought him once more to the woman who, for good or evil, had become the ruler of his life. At that gaze her own eyes filled, her lips trembled; such love had been oftentimes lavished on her, yet never had it moved her as it moved her now. She had told him that no other thing save misery could come to him through her; she had forbidden him even the baseless solace of hope; she had bade him fear, scorn, hate, flee from her; and nothing had killed his loyalty, nothing had burnt out his passion.

A glow of warmth passed over her; an infinite tenderness made the tears gather in her eyes as she saw this faith against all trial borne to her, this chivalry through every ordeal staunch to her.

"If a straight stroke and a lion heart could deliver me, how soon I should be free!" she thought. "He comes too late—too late!"

Too late; not alone to unloose her bonds and rend her from her gaolers, but too late to wake her heart to his, to find her life unusurped, to be sufficient for her in the lotus-dream of love.

The step of a monk was heard without as one of the brethren passed to fetch water from a well that was built under the shadow of a few cypress-trees some score yards from the convent. She left the

barred casement, signing her lover towards the deep
shade where the blackness of overhanging rocks made
a refuge into which not even the noon-rays could
penetrate.

He comprehended and obeyed the gesture to secrecy and silence; his heart was beating to suffocation,
his blood felt on fire, wretchedness and rapture rioted
together in him. He had found her! So much was mercy;
but she was in the gripe of those who never spared;
she was in the power of those who never unloosed
their prey; the battalions of an army could scarce avail
to wrench her from the united hate of Bourbon and of
Rome. He knew it; he knew that he was but one
man against the whole force of a government and a
hierarchy, but the Border boldness in him rose the
higher for that; the reckless romance of the old Spanish
Paladins that slept in his blood awakened as wildly as
it ever awakened in the comrades of Campeador or the
knights of Ponce de Leon.

"I will deliver her, or die for her!" he swore in
his throat: and he had never yet broken an oath.

Forcing the dog to quietude, he drew back from
the monastery into the shade of the stunted cypresses,
and threw his lines into a lake-like pool that lay at
the foot of the rocks; an angler's pursuit went well
enough with his *barcarolo's* dress. The water was
reedy, yellow, stagnant in places, with islets of river
grasses, in which water-fowl herded by thousands; but
the care of the monks, who made their sole repasts
from its treasuries, kept it well stocked with fish, and
in a brief time he landed both dace and roach, though
his strong wrists trembled as they had never done
when a Highland salmon had dragged him miles down

the length of a moorland river in a wrestling duel that lasted from noon till evening.

The monk, returning with his buckets from the well, saw the sacrilegious raid upon the heaven-dedicated food, and as the angler had relied on, drew near him in wrath and in rebuke.

"Nay, good father," said Erceldoune, lifting the fish to him, "I am an idle fellow; grudge me not a chance of doing a trifle for Holy Church. I am more used, maybe, than your brethren to filling a creel quickly."

"My son, you are welcome to our charity," replied the monk, a little confused at finding a robber offer him so willingly the spoils. "All I meant was, that, of a truth, such varlets and ruffians poach on the waters that we are obliged to guard them something strictly. You have a supple wrist and a marvellous strength; we," added the friar, with a sigh of envy, "angle all day sometimes, and catch nothing."

"Let me fish for you, father," said Erceldoune. His heart throbbed with hope and dread as he preferred a request on which all his future fate would hang; but he had control enough to speak carelessly, and his Neapolitan accent was so perfect that the monk never doubted his country. "Let me fish for you, and give me in recompense a night or two's lodging. I shall be well paid."

"You are poor, my son?"

"Poor enough."

"And a wanderer?"

"I have been a wanderer all my life."

"In truth? You are a fine fellow, and if you really want the Church's alms—"

The Cistercian hesitated; a monastery could scarce refuse its charity, yet the orders of the superior were strict to treat all strangers with circumspection, and, if possible, to admit none.

"See, here, father," said Erceldoune, rapidly. "I want no man's alms, lay or clerical; but if you like to strike a bargain, here is one. You are not much of sportsmen, I fancy; now I have all that lore by heart. I am a wild *barcarolo*, but I know none could beat me in river-craft or in shooting. You have ospreys and cormorants in these sedges that eat half the fish in the lake; you have wild swans that would make you savoury messes to sicken you for ever of maize and of lentils; you have shoals of small fresh-water fish that I will snare by thousands in my nets, and, salted, they will last you the whole winter through;—let me work for you on the water, and give me in payment a lodging for myself and my dog. I will warrant you you shall have the best of the bargain."

His voice shook a little with an eagerness he could not repress; the monk, a comely, good-humoured, elderly man from the Umbrian marshes, a poor brother who did servile offices, and was at once porter and angler and hewer of wood and drawer of water for the monastery, felt his eyes glisten and his lips taste savoury things as he thought of the wild swans in a potage, and his own labours lightened by the stalwart arm and the fearless skill of this adventurer. He looked a moment curiously in Erceldoune's face; its frank, bold, proud features won his trust instantly, as they won the trust of all who looked on them; he glanced longingly at the fowl-filled sedges.

"Wait a moment, my son. I have no power to

grant your request myself, but I will go speak with the almoner, and see what we can do. If the Father Superior will listen to your wish, I shall be glad enough for one, for Holy Mary knows it is hard work and thankless to find food for seventy hungry mouths and lean stomachs in these barren lands. Wait a second, and I will be back."

He heaved up the water-buckets, and went his way with bent shoulders and plodding steps. Erceldoune stood by the lake-side, with his eyes fastened on the barred loophole whence the eyes of the mistress of his life had looked down on him. He thought he saw the gleam of her hair in the shadow on high; he thought she gazed on him, though for both their sakes she dared not do so openly; he felt his cheek change colour like a woman's; he felt his limbs tremble as with a woman's tremor;—all chance of aid to her, of deliverance for her, rested on this one hazard he had tried of obtaining entrance to the convent that was her prison-house.

It seemed to him an eternity while the monk was absent; anxiety made his eyes blind and his head swim as he saw the brother at last returning;—if his request were denied! if his disguise were penetrated! The first words he heard made him feel giddy with their joy.

"My son, be it as you will," said the monk; "and I pray you kill a swan quickly. The Father Superior is pleased to grant your prayer; and we will lodge you and give you food; if you will shoot and fish and labour in the marshes, as you have said, till our buttery be stocked and our waters be well netted."

Erceldoune bent his head, so that the rush of vivid joy that flushed his face should not betray him.

"I will labour for you, father, night and day if you will," he said, briefly.

Would he not have laboured like a galley-slave through summer drought and winter chills if, by his labour, he could have bought one smile from her or spared her a moment's pang! Then, without more words, he loaded, fired, and brought down a wild swan on the wing. "Fetch it," he said to Sulla; the hound had been bred to retrieve, and the bird in ten seconds was laid at his feet.

"Chee-e-e!" murmured the Benedictine, ruffling the snowy plumage and thinking longingly of the savoury stew that would vary their refectory fare that night, while he stared at the *barcarolo* as at a stranger from some unknown world. "You are a wonderful shot, my friend. If you go on like that, we shall have the best of the bargain, as you said, for you will find but sorry lodgment with us. Can you sleep on a shake-down of dry grass?"

"I have slept on bare earth and bare decks many a time before now."

"Truly? Yet you look of noble blood?"

"Good blood is scant use if our fortunes be low."

"Ah! You have fallen on evil days?"

"Very evil."

"And you were of proud stock once?"

"Good father, I thought in the eyes of the Church all men were equal."

He spoke curtly, to rid himself of the Cistercian's restless curiosity, and flinging his fishing-shirt open at the breast, he set himself to fixing the stakes and tho nets at the head of the great pool. Every sort of wood and water lore had been familiar to him from his earliest boyhood; every secret of the loch and heather ho had learnt from the days of childhood. With all the skill and strength that were in him ho went to the toil of working for the monastery fare, of reaping such a harvest from the marshes and the sedges and the lakes as should make the brethren give him lodging with favouring cordiality and without questions. Ho worked like a slave, in the scorch of the Italian sky, conscious of no fatigue, sensible of no pain; he worked for her, and on him her eyes might rest from her prison-chamber. It gave him a Samson's force, an Indian's patience. Wading knee deep through the pools, he stretched his nets across the head of the water, as ho had known the poachers to do many a night across the weir of Highland rivers. Afraid of wasting such powder and shot as he had with him, he made a sling from a strip of his sash, and slew with unerring aim the wild teal that flocked among the osiers, till they were flung in scores to the arid banks. He mowed down the reeds where the fish-destroying birds were sheltered, so that they should haunt the monastery waters no more, and bore the rushes in great sheaves to land. Ho laboured without rest, and doing the work of twenty men, in the full downpour of the vertical heat, and all through the length of the day, while his friend the Umbrian brother sat luxuriously, with folded hands, staring at him like an owl lazily blinking in the sunlight.

Ho laboured without ceasing, and with a hot joy at his heart; afar, where the grey walls towered, the eyes of Idalia watched him, and with sunset he would have earned the right to sleep under the roof that made her prison. It sufficed, with his high hope and his high courage, to give him almost happiness. He could not believe that love like his would ever be powerless to defend and to release her.

All through the long day he worked unweariedly among the reedy waters, under the frowning shadow of the monastery-crowned rocks. And from her cell she gazed on him,—on the bold heroic cast of the head, and the sun-warmed brow from which the waves of hair were dashed; gazed on him where, under the cypress shadows, through the sere rushes, through the sullen waters, he toiled as peasants toil, for her—for her, though she had bidden him forsake even her memory for ever, though she had told him that suffering alone could be his portion through her.

Out of the gloom and silence of her stone-locked cage she gazed down on him at his labour through the long hot hours of the southern summer day, and her eyes were heavy with a regretful languor, her lips parted with a sigh of weariness.

"Too late!" she thought—"too late!"

The sun sank down, a globe of red flame in an angry sky; the day was done, and with it the day's travail. More had been gathered in it out of the wastes around than the laggard tempers of the slothful Brethren gathered in a month. Erceldoune stooped eagerly, and drank long draughts of thin crimson wine out of a half gourd-rind that the Umbrian monk held to him, looking at him the while with a curious, compassionate, wondering, envying glance.

"You are tired, my son? Ah! what limbs, what strength! Come within; you shall sup with us, and have such a dormitory as we can give you. Bring the great beast too, if there be no danger in him; cortes, he is a giant like you."

Erceldoune, as he lifted his head from the wine felt his face as flushed as the stormy sunset light that fell on it; a wild, senseless joy was on him—he should be within the walls that held her. He laid his hand on the hound's collar, with a gesture to silence well enough understood by the animal, and followed mutely the brother.

Jagged precipitous flights of steps, rough hewn in the rock itself, led up to the monastery. The entrance-door was a low-browed iron-studded arched barrier of oak, impregnable as granite. It yielded slowly, un-willingly, with a grating jar as the monk pushed it open.

"Enter, my son."

Erceldoune stooped, and passed through it into the vaulted stone passage-way within, dark as twilight; the door swung weightily back to its place, the great bolts rolled into their sockets, the dying day and the living world were alike shut out. Thus far one desire of his heart had fulfilled itself; he shared her prison-house with Idalia.

"This way, my son," said the Umbrian, as he turned down a tortuous vaulted passage which led to the monks' dormitories, small stone cells one in another, with dried grasses shaken down, as he had said, for pallets, and the moisture dripping from the naked walls. The Cistercians of this place were very poor; and Giulio Villaflor loved vicarious mortification, and was very stringent on his monks' asceticism and devotion, visit-ing the slightest laxity with a fearful rigour.

The poor brother, at whose girdle hung the huge keys of the ecclesiastical fortress, motioned to one of the little chambers.

"This is yours, my son. I will come to you in half-an-hour. We sup then in the refectory."

Erceldoune, left in solitude, closed his door and drew its massive bolt; then stripping off his clothes, dashed the cold water that stood in a pitcher over him, re-arranged his fisher-dress as best he could, slung the pistols again in his sash, dropped beside the dog on the hay, and let his head sink on his hands. He was beneath the same roof with her; the knowledge made his heart beat thickly, and his temples throb. But—how to save her?

It would be as dangerous to wrench her from the jaws of the Church as to rend an antelope from a panther's jaws and talons. Yet his teeth ground together under the sweeping darkness of his beard, his hand felt for the butts of his belt-pistols. "I can die with her at least," he thought, "and send some of her foes to damnation first."

His love was too fervent and too true not to be pagan in its longing and his vengeance.

The half-hour soon passed as he sat lost in thought, feverish, tempestuous, conflicting; the Umbrian brother came to him.

"Our supper is ready, my brother; it is richer than common, thanks to your woodcraft and your angling."

Erceldoune followed him, leaving the hound at guard.

A long arched stone corridor led to the refectory, a desolate, dimly-lit hall of the same rough-hewn stone,

with a few feeble oil-lamps flickering in the great sea
of gloom. The board was simply spread with fried
fish and a simmering soup, in which the wild swan and
some of the water-fowls were stewed with lentils and
capsicums. Some seventy monks sat round it, breaking
black bread, and scenting longingly though with down-
cast eyes and immutable lips the unwonted savour of
the fare. As his ringing step sounded on the stone
floor, the recluses looked with a dreary, dull wonder at
this man with his superb manhood, with his luxuriant
beard, and his stalwart build, and his mountain freedom
of glance and of movement, who seemed to bring a
draught of wild, strong, fresh, forest-breeze into the
darkness and solitude of their prison.

He made his reverence gravely to the white-haired
elder whom they pointed out as the Superior, then
seated himself at the lower end of the board, and took
the food proffered him. Many eyes studied him in-
quisitively, but no questions were asked; an unbroken
silence prevailed as the meal wént on. The Order was
sternly ruled—sternly in especial when any wayfarer
or stranger was present; it had a great fame for sanctity,
and that odorous reputation went far to cover any whispers that might steal abroad of other and less holy uses
to which its highest director might turn it. "Great
Heaven!" thought Erceldoune, as he glanced down the
long table at the close-shaven, silent guests that surrounded it, while his hand went instinctively to the
abundant falling masses of the silken hair that covered
his chest, "can living, breathing men—men in their
youth and their strength—exist like that?"

His thoughts swept over the many varying years
of his own life, so full of colour, of peril, of adventure,

of change; of wandering in divers lands, of danger in deserts and on seas, of pleasure in countless cities, of world-wide range of travel, of communion with every nation, of gay nights in western palaces, of wild rides through eastern heats;—and then men lived like this, while all the earth was free to them!

He spoke to none of them; he bore them a fiery hate because they were her priestly gaolers, and even so much needful reticence as lay in breaking the bread of these men under a false semblance, while the intent to deliver their captive was hidden in his heart, savoured too much of a taint like treachery not to be bitter to him, imperative as it was in her service, and just as it was in its employ and errand.

To Erceldoune it were far easier to deal a straight swift stroke, such as that with which men of his race had felled Paynim foe or Southern invader, than to carry through anything that involved a touch of what looked to him like deception. His life had brought him into many critical moments when silence, acuteness, and caution had been as compulsory as hot action and reckless daring; and he had never been found wanting in them. But the rush of a lion, the swoop of an eagle, were more his instinct and his warfare; and he chafed feverishly under this part that he played for her sake in the Italian monastery.

The supper was brief; he had hoped the monks might be, as he had known many, laughter-loving riotous brethren, gossips in their cups, and not averse to heavy libations, from whom he might have gleaned some hint or knowledge of her. They were not; a cold, still, harsh asceticism brooded over them; they were chiefly saturnine, worn, impassive men, whose faces were chill and unreadable as masks of stone; there was nothing to give a suspicion that anything, save the severest form of religious devotion and abstinence, reigned there—nothing to hint that there was a prisoner within their keeping. There was not one from whom he could expect to extract any hope, except the poor porter and water-carrier, on whose round jocund face not even the silence and the hard labour of his life could impress either spirituality or resignation.

The monks filed slowly out of the dark, narrow, vaulted hall; the Umbrian and one other remained to clear away the remnants of the meal.

"Will you take this to your dog?" said the priest, as he heaped up the remnants. "You did well not to bring him here; the Superior would not have loved so big a brute."

"Thanks," said Erceldoune, as he took some broken food; "and do you come to my cell, good father, I have something more cheering in my flask than your water and goat's milk."

The Umbrian's eyes glistened with delight, though a shadow of grievous disappointment stole quickly over his features.

"Another night, my son—to-morrow night I shall be free," he whispered. "This evening I must attend the offices. You know your way back, and you can undress by moonlight? We have no other light, save in the chapel."

Erceldoune, wearily enough, nodded assent, and with a brief word of thanks paced through the long passages to his dormitory. He could do no more; he must wait and watch, and be content that he was near her. He could not tell in what part of the building she was lodged; he must await time to learn that, and learn the means to reach her. With the morrow he might bribe, or stupefy the Umbrian with drink, till he reached his confidence; for the present there was nothing for it, without exciting suspicion, except to remain in the sleeping-place allotted him, and labour afresh for them with the dawn.

The little slit, unglazed and narrow as a hand's breadth, through which the luminous silver moon poured down, was high above his head; he swung himself upward and looked out; the waters and marshy plains, with the dark belt of cypress afar off, slept calmly in the white and glistening night; all was very still, only broken by the cry of a water-bird, the rush of an aziola, or the hoot of an owl. As he gazed, the outer bolt of the stone door of his cell was drawn sharply and swiftly; he dropped to his feet with an oath.

"Do not blaspheme, my son," said the Umbrian's voice through a chink. "It is only our custom with strangers."

He was a prisoner for the whole length of the summer night.

Well—the prison was hers; it was something to share it.

He undressed, laid his pistols ready loaded by his side, drank thirstily of the cool water with which the pitcher had been re-filled, and threw himself on the dry grasses, with his arm flung round the hound's neck; they were comrades—they were both here to save her.

He lay long gazing at the glimpse of starry sky that gleamed above, while the chimes tolled slowly from the bell-tower of the Benedictine monastery, and the moonlight poured down on to his mighty limbs stretched there in rest, and the gladiator breadth of the vast uncovered chest; only to know that he was beneath the same roof with her through the long silent hours, made his brain giddy, his heart on fire.

It was very long before at length a fitful, restless, dreamy sleep came to him.

CHAPTER IV.
Lion and Leopard.

With the first break of the dawn, freed by his Umbrian friend, he went back to his work on the waters; the cool long hours were precious for labour, and he desired so to gratify and serve them, that the Brethren should be loth to lose his services. He was thankful that he was given liberty at all with the sunrise. When the bolt of his cell had been drawn, a horror of dread had stolen on him that his errand was suspected, and that he was trapped, like a fox in a keeper's gins.

The morning was balmy, clear, and beautiful; even the naked wastes and smoking marshes looked brighter in its light, and he went forth with the scythe, and the nets, and the lines across his shoulder, and the hound following close in his path. He had strapped his gold about his waist, and he brought the dog with him. The hound's eyes asked, with as much eloquence as human lips ever famed, to be allowed to seek out his mistress; but he was perfectly trained, and he understood at a glance that the time for his search of her had not yet come. As Erceldoune descended the steep

incline of rock-steps, he glanced up at the lancet window
at which yesterday he had seen the woman who was
the single thought and idol of his life; she was not
there. Though he knew nothing of it, her prison-
chamber had been changed for one in which there was
no casement—one to which light and air only strayed
through by a score of circular holes pierced in the
stonework, high above the reach of her gaze; a chamber
on which no eyes could look, from which no cries could
be heard. His heart sank at the dark vacancy which
was alone seen through the bars, whence a few
hours before her eyes had dwelt on him, from which
she had watched him all through the length of the
previous day. It was bitter work so to rein in his impulse, that he did not rush blindly into the den where
she was hidden, and see what a sure shot and a merciless blow could do to free her. He choked the longing
down as best he could; he knew there were eighty men
there who would swing the ponderous gates to on him,
and shut in with him for ever every chance of rescue
for her; he knew that the only hope for her, or for
himself, lay in the course he now pursued; and he went
out to his toil. There was abundance both of sport
and of labour in those wild marshes and ill-preserved
pools to have occupied for months one who brought to
them the lore and the skill of Scottish moorlands, and
he returned to them with unflagging pertinacity, mowing
down the osiers, slinging the teal, and widgeon, and
mallards, reckless of season so long as they served to
fill the monks' buttery; stretching the nets and thrash-
ing the sedges till the frightened fish swam in by the
score; working through hour on hour till the Umbrian
brought him his mess of breakfast-soup, and some tough

cakes of rye, and sat down beside him under the
stunted cypresses, gazing with devouring, delighted
eyes at the stores of food laid upon the banks.

"Thanks, father; but that is a poor breakfast for
either of us. See here; I have done better than you,"
said Erceldoune, as he stooped over a fire he had lit
with the touchwood, and broke the clay covering off
two succulent water-birds and half-a-dozen dainty trout,
that he had baked in a sportsman's fashion, practised
many a time in Canadian woods, and Kansas wilds,
and Thuringian forests, and Australian deserts. The
eyes of the monk glittered with glee; he dearly loved
savoury food, and abstinence was a sore trial to
him.

"Eat of them as you will," said Erceldoune, as he
laid them on the slab of rock that served as a table.
"They are better than rye bread, at any rate; and if
you fear the Brethren, not a soul can see you here.
You seem very strict in your Order?"

The Umbrian sighed, and shook his little brown
bullet head, while he betook himself to the precious
banquet in silence.

"Yet you have a woman in your holy walls?"

He spoke abruptly; it was fearful to him to speak
of her, and he could have better loved to force the
answer out by a sterner mode than words.

The Umbrian started, and flushed guiltily.

"Nay, my son, you make a strange error. By all
the saints of the calendar, nothing feminine ever——"

"Spare your perjuries, father. I saw her yonder."

He motioned his head backward to the frowning wall
behind them; his pulses beat like sledge-hammers as he
spoke.

The Umbrian hung his head, and hastily gobbled up a liver-wing.

"A delusion of the eye—a snare of the senses, my son. Maybe your thoughts run too much upon women."

Erceldoune swept the board bare of all the untasted fare.

"By my faith! you are a good comrade. I have brandy that will make you dream yourself in paradise, and we would have had a carouse with it to-night; but since you tell me such lies, when my own eyes saw her yonder, you shall have no drop of the cognac as long as you live, and every fish I have heaped on these banks I will fling back in the lakes again, and leave you to fill your own buttery as you best may!"

The Umbrian, terrified and aghast at what he had lost, seized the ends of his companion's sash imploringly:

"Oh, my son! do not be so rash. Set down the good food; to waste it is a sin. You did see her; you are right. But, for pity's sake, never breathe it."

"What is she, then?" asked Erceldoune, as he gave back the birds and trout, that had served him so well, into the eager hands of the monk. "And why should you deny it? except that priests always deny any truth."

"She is a prisoner, and a rebel; and you should not blaspheme."

"Whose prisoner?"

"The king's, my son."

"The king's! Has he no prisons of his own, then, that he must borrow your convent?"

The Umbrian hesitated; he was sore afraid to answer the question, but he was more immediately afraid that his impetuous questioner should sweep his meal away again.

"Monsignore Villaflor is interested in her recovery to the One Faith, my son," he said, slowly and unwillingly.

"Giulio Villaflor!" The words leaped from his lips ere he knew they were spoken; the blood rushed into his face, his hands clenched; the name confirmed his worst horror, his worst dread. He knew the temper and the repute of the mighty Roman; he shivered where he stood in the hot sun.

"What do you know of our holy father in God, my son?"

Erceldoune turned his eyes full on him.

"What do *you* know?"

The other flushed shamefacedly; he was an honest peasant in his way, to whom the mask of sanctity was very irksome, and the great ecclesiastic, and the uses to which the monastery was put, had alike cruelly gone against his simple instincts of a just life.

"You must not question me, my son; I know nothing—nothing save to obey the little I am ever told."

"What are you told of this captive, then?"

"That she is a sceptic and a revolutionist; a very evil and fatal woman."

"And his Holiness of Villaflor, out of his divine love, wishes to reclaim her into the bosom of the Church!"

The words were hot and acrid as they were hurled through his set teeth: it was all he could do to keep any chain on them.

The Umbrian winced under their sting.

"Surely, my son. It would be well that she should be reclaimed. But, of a truth——"

"What? Can a priest speak truth?"

"Hush, my son; you must not be so bitter upon the appointed of God. I was going to say"—the monk played restlessly with the savoury bones he had been crunching, and the colour burnt in his yellow cheek, as his voice sank low, and his eyes glanced around furtively—"whether it was sorcery given her by the Evil One or no I cannot tell, but there was such a look in her eyes—ah, Madonna, she has a fearful beauty!—that when they bade me scourge her for contumacy, the lash dropped from my hands, I was as one paralysed. I could not. I could not!"

With a cry as though the scourge fell on him, cutting into the livid flesh, Erceldoune sprang to his feet; his hands fell on the Cistercian's shoulders swaying him to and fro.

"Scourged her?—scourged her? O God! they never dared——"

"I dared not," muttered the Umbrian, sorely in fear; "they were bitter upon me, but they did not force it—then. She will have the punishment to-morrow, if she have not yielded——"

"Yielded to what?"

"Yielded to the persuasions of the Church, my son."

Erceldoune flung him off with a force that made the Umbrian's blood run cold.

"Yielded to the passions of Giulio Villaflor, you mean! You hell-hounds!—you fiends!"

His voice choked in his throat; the muscles of his

chest, where the fishing-shirt was open, swelled convulsively; he felt blind with rage and agony;—the monk watched him in wonder.

"The sight of her beauty beyond those bars has stirred you strangely, my son. Verily, she is a sorceress, as they say. You feel marvellously for a strange woman."

Erceldoune shook in every limb with the effort to control what, betrayed, must betray both her and him.

"That she *is* a woman, and you are brutes, is enough! What man that had not the heart of a cur could hear such infamy and keep his peace? It is well the lash dropped from your hands, or I would have shaken life out of you where you stand!"

The Umbrian gave a shudder.

"'Truly you could do it, for you are a son of Anak! I must leave you now; I am due with the Almoner; and as for that little matter of the brandy, I will come to your cell after supper, if you be still in the mind."

He made his way back with speed, anxious to get out of reach of this unchained lion; and Erceldoune stood alone in the hot sun-scorch, with shivers of fire and of ice, turn by turn, in his veins.

Whatever could be done for her must be done swiftly, or it would be too late.

Across the pitiless clearness of the transparent air there was alone in the arid wastes about him the figure of a pifferaro, a mere lad, singing a barcarolle, whose burden was borne musically and wildly over the marshes as he toiled on his way with his monkey on his shoulder. With lightning quickness, Erceldoune, keeping out of

the sight of the monastery-casements, waded through
shallow pools and dashed through thickets of osier,
till he reached the boy, a bright-eyed, bright-witted
Savoyard, with a dirty, tattered sheepskin for clothing,
a little ape for a comrade, and a light childish heart
that made him happier than a king. Erceldoune
glanced at him, and saw both intelligence and frankness in the arch, brown, ruddy face of the little
bohemian; he stopped him as the boy was leaping from
tuft to tuft of the rank grass that studded the shaking
quagmires, and stretched his hand out with a broad
gold coin.

"Had you ever so much in your life?"

The Savoyard opened wider his keen, dancing,
black eyes.

"Never! Of a truth, *signor barcarolo*, if that is the
fish you angle out of these pools, your craft's a thriv-
ing one!"

"You shall get just such fish yourself if you
choose. Will you go on an errand for me? You
shall have this coin as you start, if you will, and ten
like it when you come back and show me the errand
is done."

The pifferaro stretched out his little tanned hand.

"Give it here," he said, laconically. "The errand
is done."

Erceldoune tossed him the gold.

"The errand is this. Do you know Ferratino?"

The boy nodded assent.

"Go thither, then; quick as a lapwing, straight as
a crow flies. Run, as if you ran for your life. Take
a paper I will give you to the villa, and say it is for
his Excellency the Baron; he will send word by you,

yes or no. Bring the word to me here, truly and instantly, and you shall have ten of those pieces, I promise you. Can you do the distance? It is far?"

The Savoyard laughed, his bright eyes all glittering with eager zest.

"I have done farther for a dozen bajocchi! You shall have your answer as fast as a pigeon could bring it. Give me the paper. I shall find you here?"

"Yes. On these waters. Wait a second while I write, and then be off like the wind."

As he spoke, he tore a leaf out of a pocket-book in which his circular notes had been sent from the yacht, and wrote with its pencil a few rapid lines; they were simply, in German:

"DEAR ANSELM,—I am in pressing need. Send me at nightfall two of the fastest horses you have; let some boy ride them who cannot speak a word of Italian, and wait with them, unseen, in the cypress grove under the monastery of Taverna—wait all night till he sees me. Do no more than I ask, for God's sake. I know I need not say grant my request; our alliance is too old and too sure. Forgive all that sounds strange and vague in this, and send me simply word, 'yes' or 'no,' by the Savoyard.

"Yours ever,
"FULKE ERCELDOUNE."

Men of his temperament make firm and warm friendships amongst men. The Hungarian noble to whom he wrote, and who, as he had remembered, occupied a villa some dozen miles from the wastes in which he stood, was a generous, reckless man of pleasure, who, he knew well, would have done far greater things than this at his entreaty, and would have the sagacity to do as he asked, and no more. Ernst von Anselm and he had once passed through a mad night together on the burning decks of a ship in the midst of the broad Pacific, when mutiny and drunkenness in a Lascar crew had added their horrors to the pandemonium; and together, back to back, against a legion of devils, and in the red-hot glare of leaping flames, had sent their bullets through the ringleaders' brains, and saved the vessel alike from fire and from anarchy. From that hour they had been friends, true and close and tried, in that noble friendship of brethren, which is worth all the love of women.

The little pifferaro, flinging his ape over his shoulder, where it gripped a sure hold, darted off, over the dreary plain, as he had promised, as fast as a pigeon could fly: that broad gold coin locked in his hand, and the promise of ten more like it, lent him the speed of a desert pony. "I shall go back a millionnaire to my people!" thought the child in his glee. There was hardly so much money in the whole of the little hamlet that had given him birth, where it nestled in a sleepy hollow under the brown hills of Savoy.

Erceldoune looked after him a second,—the careless child was a frail little basket-boat to launch on such stormy waters weighted with the fate of two lives! Then he went back to the work of the monastery, labouring all through the noon-heat among the sedges and the still, shallow, yellow lagunes—working as men only work when in that ardour of physical toil, that restless bodily exertion, they give vent to the thoughts which, if they paused to muse a moment, would unman and madden them. He felt as if the hours would never move; the sun seemed to stand still; the blazing radiance of the day had a sickening oppression;—what might she not be bidden to suffer in it!

He knew the temper of Giulio Villaflor, that leopard of the velvet skin and of the unsparing fangs. He shuddered as he looked on the rugged silent pile, that kept her chained for such a tyrant. He had never fancied that the world could hold such agony as those burning, endless, intolerable hours brought him, as he plunged down eagerly into the coolness of the waters to chill the torture in him, and laboured to kill thought under the burden of corporeal fatigue, under the fever of ceaseless activity.

The day grew on; noon came and passed; the glow of light lay clear and golden over the plains, and the breadth of the sheeted water; the hours were tolled monotonously from the campanila, ever and again the drone of the monks' voices rising in regular diapason, in chant or office, swelled through the narrow apertures of their chapel casements, and echoed with melancholy rise and fall over the silence. When he heard it, deadlier oaths than his lips had ever breathed were hurled over the slumbering pools at the priestly formulas that sheltered a Nero's cruelties, a Borgia's lusts. Once or twice a peasant or a muleteer passed across the horizon line: otherwise there was nothing to break the eternal sameness of the glittering sunlight, the scar country, the cypress points cutting so sharply against the intense blue of the sky. He knew what men had felt who had lost their reason through a captivity that made them dwell in one unending solitude—look on one unchanging scene.

The deep radiance of colour that precedes the sunset was just flushing earth and sky, as the shrill hoot of an owl's note pierced his ear—a night-bird's cry in the sunshine. He guessed at once that it was a signal of the little pifferaro, and followed it. Under the reeds, some half mile or less from the monastery, the boy was crouched, panting like a tired dog, but glowing with life and zest and eagerness as he lifted his hot brown face.

"I have done it," he cried, with all a child's exultation. "Here is your answer—written. Stay here, lest the crows yonder should spy on us. Let priests smell gold, and it's all up with him who owns it."

Erceldoune took the paper and read it, lying there under the shelter of the sedges. It was in German; the Baron was from home, but an old lacquey, who had chanced to be the first to greet the Savoyard, seeing an open scroll, and, pressed by the boy's urgency, had read it, had hesitated at first what to do in his master's absence, but, knowing how well Anselm loved the writer, had known he should run no risk by compliance, and might by refusal risk much displeasure. He wrote now in reply, with sagacity and foresight, promising that the horses should be in waiting at nightfall with a lad to hold them, and that as they would be something worn by the transit, another pair should be in readiness at the gates of Ferratino in case Erceldoune's errand should bear him near, which in all likelihood it might, since all things must pass by there to reach the road to the shore.

His hand shook with joy as he read, and scattered the old man's tremulously-written characters in fragments lest they should tell tales. So far the means for flight were secured, could her freedom be compassed. He had not much gold about him, but he gave double the fee to the little pifferaro, while the child stared in amaze at the twenty shining yellow pieces. He caught them greedily, yet when he had them he was half stupefied with the enormity of his possessions.

"The pastor, and the bailiff, and the innkeeper never had more than that all put together!" he murmured, his thoughts drifting to the village of his birth, with its little steeple hidden under chestnut leaves, and its mild-eyed herds browsing on the green breadths between the rocks. "That is no *barcarolo;* and, whatever the mischief is, I will be bound there is a woman in it," considered the shrewd little lad as he went on his way, the gold safe in the bosom of his sheepskin shirt.

With the dead mallards and teal flung over his shoulder, and with a great osier-basket of fish filled to overflowing, Erceldoune passed, unsummoned, from the lake side up the rock, and to the monastery gates. He thought they might make question of letting him enter for a second night's lodging, and without entrance all hope of her rescue was ended. The Umbrian, however, who through the grating saw the abundance brought in for the larder, admitted him instantly, with many praises of his industry and adorations of his skill.

"You have a heavy door there?" said Erceldoune, turning to glance at the ponderous mass of iron-clamped oak that swung slowly behind him.

"Ah—heavy indeed!" sighed the Benedictine, as he stooped to draw the huge bolts, which were only drawn stiffly and with effort into their sockets. "It is heavy enough, but it is these are the misery."

"These? I will soon make them run smoother. I have something of a smith's skill. Fetch me a file and a little oil."

The Umbrian fetched them gladly, marvelling what manner of man this was who knew every craft under the sun. A little while, and the rusted iron bolts ran noiselessly and smoothly in their massive channels; the monk's lament had given him an opportunity more precious than any other could have been in that moment, and in easing the run of the bolts for the gatekeeper's indolence, he paved the way to a facile exit by night from the monastery, if by any means he could also obtain the great key that swung from the Umbrian's girdle.

"You have a wonderful science, my son," said the Cistercian, with musing amaze. "You can do all things that you turn your hand to it seems!"

"I have lived in many countries and with many men."

"You must have been more than a mere *barcarolo*, my son?"

"I told you I have been a 'wanderer' from my birth," said Erceldoune, with a smile at the play on the Celtic meaning of his nationality. "'The career is a bad one for gold, but it is the best in the world, I fancy, for learning self-help and other men's virtues."

"But you must learn much vice too, my son?"

Erceldoune shrugged his shoulders.

"What of that? Vice is a good teacher too, in its way, and one must take the warp with the woof."

"But, you know, one cannot touch pitch, my son, and keep undefiled."

Erceldoune laughed a little.

"Good father, where is the man that ever did keep so? And as for that, the pitch will not stay long unless the surface be ready for it. But, for Heaven's sake, chatter no more; I love speech little at any time, and now—I am famished."

"Truly you have earned your supper; and—as for that little matter of brandy? I have not tasted a drop since I was in Naples, seven seasons ago!"

"All right, I have the best cognac in a flask here; if you come to my cell after supper, you shall be heartily welcome to a draught of it."

The monk's eyes sparkled with glee; he nodded a hasty assent, and, relieving his guest of the fish and the birds, took him for the second time to the refectory. The same silence, the same rigour, the same fare prevailed; the same double line of lean, immutable, saturnine, emaciated faces were in the dim light of the stone hall; tho same swift upward glance was cast on him as he entered; the same abstracted severity of repose was observed throughout the meal. He had no wish to break it; only for her sake could he so far restrain the hatred in him towards the men who were her torturers and her captor's tools, as to share their bread, justly as he had earned it, and to sit in such semblance of amity with them as lay in this compulsory companionship. Some among them noted that there was a dark shadow on the strange *barcarolo's* face that had not been there so deeply on the previous day, and the monk nearest him heard a heavy oath muttered under the waves of his beard when the blessing before the refection was chanted;—it was a curse on those who covered the lusts of a velvet-voiced priest with the savour of sanctity, with the odour of rituals. Often, moreover, his passionate eyes flashed over the countenances around him, seeking to read by instinct which amongst them was the brute who had dared bid the lash be raised against her: had he known, scarce every memory of the prudence and the abstinence needful for her sake would have availed to chain back his arm from a blow that would have felled the offender level with the flags of the stone floor.

The meal ended, a fresh torture waited him; the Superior summoned him to the head of the table, and held a long converse with him, the rambling verbosity of old age combined, in the incessant vagaries of his interrogation, with the subtle veiled promptings of curiosity and cunning. There was that in the bearing and the glance of the stranger they harboured which made the priests uneasily suspect that this was too bold a lion for their episcopal lord to welcome were he aware of the shelter they gave. Erceldoune saw the suspicion, and saw that he must allay it, or all hope of sufficient freedom for the purpose he held would be for ever denied him. With an effort which cost him far more than any physical toil or bodily strain could have ever done, he forced himself into the part it was imperative to play. Lie he would not, not even for her; and reserve, he saw, would confirm all the doubts rising in the breasts of his gaolers and auditors; he cast himself into a bolder venture. "These men," he reckoned, with a swift glance over them, "must be of two classes only—those who have forsaken the world, and those who have never known it; to hear of it will enchain equally those for whom it is a lost land and those to whom it is an unknown one."

On that rapid inference he acted. In answer to the Superior's questions he told his life frankly; changing it in little, save that they deemed his travel had been the travel of a restless bohemian—a man poor enough to have been glad at times to serve before the mast.

Though he was averse to many words usually, he could speak with a vivid and impressive eloquence when the fire of it was struck alight in him. He forced himself to speak so here. He answered, as one who would tell his adventures, without pressure or comment; and after the brevity of his previous curt replies, the monks heard the picturesque flow of his swift Italian with the same amaze with which they regarded the stature, the strength, the sweeping beard, and the careless royalty of bearing of this athlete, who came amongst them as though to show them all that this manhood, which they had crucified and buried in their own lives as an unholy and accursed thing, might be and might enjoy. His past had been full of ever-changing scenes and experiences; hair-breadth escapes, desperate dangers, wild adventure, and keen perils, had been continually his portion in the distant and intricate missions on which he was sent. A struggle of life and death in the heart of Persia had been followed by dreamy barbaric luxury and magnificence in the midst of Mexican palaces; a death-ride through Russian snow-storms, with the baying pack of starving wolves on his track through the whole of a bitter icy night, had been succeeded by months of gaiety in the capitals of Europe; a shipwreck in the midst of the Indian Ocean, with a Malay crew ripe for murder, and an open boat living for days on tempestuous seas in the glare of a

tropic sun, with men around him dying like dogs for
water, had been effaced almost as soon as endured by
the brilliant fiery pleasures of a volunteer service with
the French cavalry in a campaign against the Arabs;
or a desert quest for desert game over the wild Libyan
tracts in the sultry glories of autumn days and nights,
by a season's sojourn in some friend's summer-palace
among the roses of Damascus, or in the ruby glow of
the Nile suns, painting, shooting, swimming, boating;
finding ever and everywhere the happiness of fearless,
fetterless, vivid life, oftentimes nomadic, and glad in
the mere gladness of strength, in the mere desert chief's
sense of liberty, with

> "the rich dates yellow'd over with gold-dust divine,
> And the locust's flesh steep'd in the pitcher, the full draught of wine,
> And the sleep in the dried river channel, where bulrushes tell
> That the water was wont to go warbling so softly and well."

The memories even of a single year supplied him
with a thousand sources from which to draw pictures
of varied scenes, whose recital entranced imperceptibly
and unconsciously first one and then another of his
auditors, till the whole circle of the monks stood
around as men in the East will stand around the nar-
rator who tells of far countries and of strange fortunes,
while the narghilé vapours out, and the coffee steams
fragrantly in the open divan, and the grave Mussul-
mans stroke their beards in silent wonder.

It entranced them, this recital of worlds unknown,
and of joys as of dangers undreamed of by them.
When he paused, the Father Superior pressed him
eagerly for more; those bold, terse, picturesque words
that drew them sketches of different lands and un-
imagined pleasures with the same rich vigorous sweep

as that with which his hand would paint tropic foliage and mountain outline, the stretch of seas and the burning warmth of sun-tanned prairie, held the priestly circle spell-bound. Those who had known no existence save that of the cloister from their youth up, heard with an entranced, stupefied amaze, as children hear tales of genii; those who had come to the cloister only when every hope of life had been bruised, and wrung, and killed, heard with a terrible pained look of hunger on their faces, as exiles hear a strain of melody which brings them back the songs of the land they have lost for ever. Both alike hung on the swift flow of the descriptive words, only more warmly coloured by the Neapolitan idiom he still employed, as on some tale of paradise; the worn sallow cheeks flushed, the deadened lustreless eyes flashed, the dropped veiled glance was lifted eagerly, the thin and silent lips were parted with rapid breaths, and once a sigh broke from a monk still in the years of youth—a sigh so bitter, so intense in its anguish of vain lament, that a whole broken, wasted life seemed spent in it.

Never again would they be as they had been ere this wanderer had come amidst them; through him they saw all that they had lost for ever.

He had conquered them. When they parted, and he went on his way to his cell, there was not a doubt of him lingering in any heart, there was not a man who had one thought left with him save of that glory of manhood, that splendour of liberty, that beauty of unknown worlds, which they had voluntarily surrendered and buried from themselves till the death of the grave should release them from the death of the monastery.

"Come," he whispered, as he passed the Umbrian, "and if you can bring lemons, sugar, and spices with you, you shall dream yourself in paradise to-night."

"Hush, my dear son; do not be so profane!" murmured the other, while his eyes danced in expectant ecstasy. "I will come, and bring the things, if I can, from the buttery. Your tales were beautiful, but I thought the Superior would never have let you go!"

"Great Heaven! to save my own life I would not stoop to dupe and bribe these brutes as I do for hers!" thought Erceldoune, where he leaned on the stone ledge of his cell-window awaiting the monk. It was very bitter to him, this truce with her enemies, this false play with these ecclesiastics. The soldier-like frankness and the proud honesty of his nature rebelled irrepressibly at the dissimulation he was driven to match them with thus. To lead a charge through the heat of battle, as he had done in Mexico and Algeria more than once, when the chiefs had been shot down, or to imperil his life against all odds in a deadly contest with overpowering numbers, as had chanced to him in Persian defiles and Argentine revolutions, was far more suited to his temper and his instincts than the part that, for her sake, fell to him in these cloisters of Taverna. Yet played out the part must be, or she would be beyond rescue, beyond hope.

It was not long before the Umbrian made his stealthy entrance, with the treasures of the buttery hidden under his frock.

Erceldoune in silence took the things from him. His own flask was large and full of brandy, strong as

fire and mellow as oil; he emptied out half the water
of his pitcher, tossed the whole of the cognac in instead, and with the spices, lemons, and sugar, made a
fragrant and intoxicating drink. The Umbrian, squatted
on the dry grasses of the bed, watched its preparation
with thirsty, devouring eyes.

"He will be dead drunk before this is half empty,"
thought Erceldôune.

"There, tell me if that is not better than sour wines
and rancid goat's milk," he asked, as he poured some
into the little drinking-horn the monk had brought. It
was swallowed in an ecstasy; the Umbrian had no need
to dream of paradise, he was in it the moment the
strong, odorous draught touched his lips. As fast as he
stretched the horn out, so fast his host filled it; the
pitcher held more than a quart, and Erceldoune scarcely
drank himself, though he made a feint of so doing; he
did not yet know how much or how little would be
needed to steep the Italian in the slumberous intoxication he required to produce. As he had imagined, the
first few draughts rose straight to the brain of the recluse, who, well as he loved it, had not tasted any alcohol for years; the luscious, fiery, highly-spiced liquid
quickly flushed his face, and whirled his thoughts, and
loosened his always loquacious tongue; he sat with the
jovial content of a Sancho Panza, laughing, chattering,
heeding very little what replies he had, and very rapidly
forgetting all things except the tender of his horn for
its replenishing. Erceldoune sought first to make him
garrulous, so that he might glean intelligence from his
drunken verbiage. The Umbrian's idle tergiversation
of speech soon wandered off to the captive of their
clerical bondage—wandered to such ardent maudlin

ecstasies on the subject of her beauty that his hearer
suffered tortures as he listened perforce to the profana-
tion. Erceldoune flung himself down on the flag floor,
resting on his elbow, in such enforced stillness as he
could command, while the rambling fervour of the
gluttonous Brother desecrated her name and catalogued
her charms; happily, the drinker was too giddy with
his potations to notice the shudder that every now and
then at his hottest epithets of descriptive admiration
shook his listener's limbs, or the flash that darted over
him from his hearer's eagle eyes when he betrayed, in
his unconscious loquacity, the purpose of her imprisonment in the Cistercian sanctuary.

It needed no questions to elicit all he knew; the
brandy fumes rising over his brain undid all caution it
had ever been taught, and spread out all its shreds of
knowledge as a pedlar spreads his wares. Erceldoune
heard enough to convulse him with horror as he was
stretched there on the naked stone, with the lustre of
the Italian night finding its way dimly through the
aperture above;—enough to know that he must rescue
her to-night, or never.

"And I will tell you more," hiccuped the monk,
laughing low and cunningly, too blind with drink to
have much knowledge left of whom he spoke to, or of
where he was. "Monsignore comes to-night—he often
visits us, you know; we are his special children, and it
has a fair odour for so great a man to leave the world
for such holy, rigorous retirement!"

"'To-night!"

Erceldoune sprang to his feet as a lion springs from
its lair; the priest's villanous chuckle rang like a rat-
tlesnake in his ear; in his cups the Umbrian was but

an animal—a very low one to boot—and the better
instincts which had moved him when the lash had dropped from his hand were drowned and dead.

"Ay, to-night!" laughed the monk, while his head
hung on one side, and his eyes closed with the fatuous
cunning of intoxication; "he comes for the last time—
do you mark me?—for the last time!"

The oath that shook the stone walls thrilled even
through the mists of drink and the imbecility of his
dulled brain, as it was hurled from his hearer's lips; an
agony was in it such as mere grief never spoke yet.
The Umbrian, sobered by it for the moment, shuddered and strove to rise, looking about him with blind,
terrified eyes.

"What have I said? What have I done?" he
muttered, piteously. "Ah, Jesu! Monsignore—Monsignore!"

And with that last dread name on his lips he fell
back stupefied, rocking himself to and fro, and sobbing
like a child.

Erceldoune neither saw nor heard him; he stood like
a statue, his hands clenched, his face dyed crimson, the
black veins swollen on his forehead and his throat, his
breath caught in savage, stifled gasps, his bared chest
heaving like the flanks of a snared animal.

"To-night!—to-night!"

The words rattled in his chest with a curse that
would have chilled even the bold blood of his mighty
rival.

The Umbrian sat motionless, staring at him with
distended, senseless eyes; he was filled with a great
terror, but the terror was vague, and his mind seemed
to swim in vapour. Erceldoune cast one glance at him,

and by sheer instinct forced the vessel, still half-filled with the liquid, into his hands.

"Drink!" he said, fiercely; "drink, and be a beast at once."

The monk, with whom there was but one sense left, that of desire for tho alcohol that destroyed him, seized it thirstily, and drank—drank—drank—till the fiery stream flowed down his throat like water. Erceldoune watched him with eager, aching eyes; every moment seemed an eternity, every thought maddened him till ho felt liko a desert brute; he could not stir till this priest lay senseless before him.

He paced the narrow limits of his cell like a caged lion, his face dark as night, his heart panting till its throbs sounded through the stillness, his breast heaving till the loose light folds of tho fishing-shirt felt like a case of iron, his gaze never leaving tho obese wavering figure of the stupefied Italian, who followed his movement with a dizzy, blinded sight that grew dimmer and dimmer with every moment that the brandy rose over his brain like waves that washed all lingering sense away.

At last the pitcher dropped with a crash from hands that lost all power; a vacuous laugh sounded a moment in the Umbrian's throat; his eyes stared senselessly at tho slender silver cimeter of the young moon that shone through the slit of the casement, then their lids closed, his head fell back, he lay like a log of wood on the pallet—unconscious, sightless, dead drunk.

Erceldoune stooped over him, and forced his eyelids up; by the look of tho eyeballs beneath he saw that this was no feint, but the deep-drugged sleep of intoxication that would be unbroken for a score of hours,

whose stupor made the man it had enchained powerless
as a stone, brainless as a hog, deaf to all sound, insensible of all existence;—he wanted no more.

With his knife he slashed noiselessly the band of
the great keys that swung at the monk's girdle, and
fastened them on his own, so muffled that they would
make no sound as he moved. He looked at his pistols,
and put them back in his sash ready sprung; they were
double-barrelled revolvers, that carried sure death in
their tubes. Then he laid his hand on the hound's
collar, let him without, closed the door, and drew its
bolts, locking in the Umbrian.

The dormitory was quite dark; not even the moon's
rays strayed into its narrow black aisle of stone, with
the double line of cells flanking its length; a single
footfall overheard, a single echo sounding down the
silence, and the sleeping monks would pour out of their
lairs upon him. While waiting, he had bound his feet
with withes of hay, so that they fell noiselessly on the
pavement; and the hound stole softly on, as he had
been bred to steal on a roebuck's slot or a brigand's
track. The first thing Erceldoune sought was to make
the road free to leave the building; he found his way,
that he had carefully noted as he came, back to the
great entrance. The whole place was still; there was
not a sound; he passed uninterruptedly to the vaulted
gate-passage. Here a single oil-lamp burned, its light
dully shed on the broad low oak door, with its iron
cramps and fastenings. He drew back the bolts gently,
and turned the keys in the two ponderous locks; the
door would open now at a touch. He motioned to the
hound to wait and guard it; the dog understood the
trust, and couched motionless as though cast in bronze;

a truer or a bolder sentinel could not be placed there, and it was not for the first time that the brave sagacious Servian monarch had been trusted in a crisis of life or death. Then rapidly, and with the light swift tread of a deer, Erceldoune retraced his steps; he had but the shadowy, rambling information of the monk to guide him to where Idalia was, but he knew, by that, that she was in the westward wing of the monastery, and he made his way there through the thick darkness about him, and down the stone passages winding one in another. It was all so still; he thought the story of the drunkon Italian must have been a drink-inspired dream.

And yet—men who came for shame would come in silence and in secret; his hand was on his pistols as he went, his limbs shook as he traversed the interminable gloom, a hot joy, a terrible torture, were on him; he went to save her—and he might be too late.

He had found his way into what, as far as he could judge, was the western part close on the chapel which the Umbrian had spoken of as the place of her fresh lodgment. Here, also, the darkness was unbroken; he could not pierce it to see a yard in advance; he felt the rough cold stone of the wall against his hand; ho felt by the greater chillness of the air that no ray of daylight ever penetrated; he paused a moment, tempted at all risk of discovery to return and fetch the dog to track her. At that instant his eyes caught a faint narrow thread of light, pale and close to the floor—the light, doubtless, of a chamber within glimmering above the door-sill; he made his way towards it, careless what hand might be stretched out to arrest his course; before he reached it, the sweet imperial tones of a voice that thrilled him like an electric touch rang through the solitude:

"Back!—or your life or mine ends. It matters little which!"

The voice was clear as a bell and rich as music, but it vibrated with a meaning that struck like steel to the heart of the man who loved her;—it told him all.

With the force of a giant he threw himself against the door, guided to it by the light that gleamed beneath against the stones. Passion lent him herculean strength; the bar within was drawn, but the weight of his pressure suddenly flung on the panels sent both bolts and sockets back, wrenched from their fastenings, while the wood was shivered beneath the crash, and a dusky yellow light flared in his eyes from the cell within.

Across the broken half of the door, still jammed by its staples to the floor, he saw Idalia; such light as there was, was on her where she stood close pressed to the bare stone wall, upon her face loathing and scorn unutterable, yet even now no touch of fear; the rich-hued draperies of her masque-dress were torn, as though she had just wrenched herself free from some polluting grasp; her hair was loosened, and against her bosom she held clenched the blade of the Venetian stiletto, its point turned inward against her heart. Above her stood her great tyrant's lofty form.

As the bolts broke, and the splintered beechwood flew in fragments, Giulio Villaflor swept round, his forehead red, his eyes alight with a Borgia's fury of baffled and licentious love—an amazed rage on him at the stranger who dared stand between him and his

captive, between him and his will. With one glance,
in which his gaze met hers, and with a lion's spring,
Erceldoune was on the mighty Prelate, his hand at the
other's throat, as a forest hound's fangs fasten in a
wolf's; the shock of the sudden collision dragged the
Italian back staggering and breathless ere he heard or
saw his antagonist. Then that sheer blood-instinct
woke in Villaflor which wakes with the first sense of
conflict in all men not cowards from their birth; he
closed with this unknown foe, whose gripe was at his
throat, holding him powerless.

Not a word was breathed, yet both knew—strangers
though they were—that they met thus but for her
sake. It was the work of an instant, yet to the Neapolitan it seemed long as half a life, that struggle in
which the lightning swoop of his unseen enemy swept
him from his prey, and bore down on him with the
might of vengeance, in the silence of the night which
he had thought had veiled his tyranny and his crime
from all eyes. No living man had ever crossed the
will or the passions of the great prelate until now that
he was seized as lions seize in the death-grapple.

They were almost perfectly matched; equal in
strength as in stature, though in one a life of adventure
and hardihood had braced all that in the other a life
of effeminate indulgence had enervated. Giulio Villaflor beneath his sacerdotal robes had a warrior's frame
and a warrior's soul, many a time, hearing of battle-
fields and soldier's perils, he had longed to gird a
sword on his loins and go down in the van to the
slaughter; and as the gripe of Erceldoune's hand
fastened on his throat, and the gleam of his enemy's
eyes flashed suddenly into his, the desert rage, the de-

sert courage, roused in the silken soft-footed panther of the Church. In the lamp-lit cell, under the black vaulted roof, in the hush of the midnight-silenced monastery, they wrestled together in that wild-beast conflict, which makes the men who are maddened by it savage and bloodthirsty as the beasts' whose ferocity they share.

Such feeble flickering light as there was in the dungeon shone on the majestic figure of the priest clothed in the dark floating robes of the Church, and the athletic form of his foe, in the white loose linen dress of the Caprioto sailors, as breast to breast, face to face, with their lofty limbs twined like gladiators, and their hands at each other's throats, they swayed, and reeled, and rocked to and fro, in that deadly embrace. It was the work of scarce twenty seconds; yet in it they rent and tore at each other as lion and leopard may do in the yellow dust of a tropic dawn, when long famine has made both ravenous for blood, and each beast knows that he must conquer and kill, or feel the fangs plough down into heart and flanks, and his own life pour out for ever. The prelate, who, ere now, had never even known a hand too roughly brush his sacred person, sought only to fling off the grasp that strangled him; his foe, rife with revenge and burning with a rival's hate, could have torn his heart out where they wrestled in as mortal a combat as ever was that with which retiarius and secutor reddened the white sand of Augustan amphi-theatres.

A moment, and the hardier strength, the leonine force, of Erceldoune, so often tested in victory under the red foliage of Canadian forests and the scorching suns of African skies, conquered; he crushed the priest in his sinewy arms till the chestbones bent, and the breath was stifled, as in the gripe of the Arctic bear; then, with one last effort he swung the Italian off, and raising him by the waist, flung him with all his might downward on to the stone floor, the limbs falling with a dull, crushing, breaking sound as they were dashed against the granite.

Thrown so that his head smote the flags with a shock like iron meeting iron, Villaflor fell insensible, the force with which he was tossed outward stunning his senses, and throwing him a bruised, motionless, huddled mass in the gloom of the dusky cell. The proud and princely ecclesiastic lay powerless, silenced, broken, helpless, like a dead cur, in the heart of the monastery where his word was law, and his will absolute as any sovereign's.

His foe stood above him, his foot on the prostrate throat, that swelled and grew purple with the suffocated breath, the stifled blood. He had lost all memory save the sheer animal impulse to slaughter and avenge; and his heel ground down on to Giulio Villaflor's neck, treading out life till the rich lips of the Neapolitan gasped in unconscious torture, and the olive tint of his bold smooth brow grew black as the full veins throbbed and started beneath the skin.

One pressure more, and the last pulse of existence would have been crushed out where he lay, with his teeth clenched and his senseless eyes staring upwards: —the touch that could lead him where it would, as a child, fell lightly on her avenger's arm. Idalia's voice thrilled him with its sweet brief words:

"Wait! *You* are too brave for that. He is fallen; let him lie."

Her gaze dwelt on him, full, humid, eloquent,
speaking her gratitude far more deeply than by words.
Breathless, victorious, with the war-lust in his eyes,
and his heart panting under the bruised muscles and
the aching sinews of the chest to which his enemy had
been strained in so deadly an embrace, Erceldoune
turned and looked at the woman for whose sake he had
fought, as a hound, called off from the throat of the
thief he has pulled down, looks at the master whom he
obeys, even whilst he longs to disobey, and serve him,
and revenge him, with the death-gripe.

He took his heel off the neck of Giulio Villaflor.

"As you will."

His voice shook over the simple words; his face
flushed hotly to the very temples as, for the first time,
he met her gaze; his eyes searched hers, thirstily wistful, wildly eager.

"Come, for the love of God! You trust me?"

"As I never trusted any."

She stretched out to him, as she spoke, her fettered
hands that, even chained, had found strength in them
to hold the slender blade that would have sheathed
itself in her heart or her tyrant's. There was that in
the action which, even in such a moment, made him
feel faint and blind with hope. It repaid him all—
would have repaid him his death-stroke, had he laid
dying at her feet.

For all answer he crushed the steel links that hung,
holding her wrists powerless, in the grasp which had
stifled Giulio Villaflor, and bent and wrenched and
twisted them with the same force as that by which he
had once torn off an Indian boar from its writhing
human prey; the chain broke and fell asunder.

His eyes, as they looked up to hers, spoke a meaning to which her own heart answered as flame leaps to the touch of a torch.

"We will have *one* freedom—the freedom of death, if not of life!"

She knew all that the whisper meant; knew that he might be powerless to give her the liberty of existence, but that he would give her the liberty of the grave—and share it.

As the links of her fetters broke, a rush, an alarm, a tumult, were borne down the silence from the distant corridors; the monks had awakened, and found, either their stranger-guest absent or their bolted gates unloosed. Those doors once freshly closed, those sleepers once aroused from their countless cells, and every avenue of escape would be sealed, every chance of flight ended for ever.

Without a pause for breath, without a glance at the fallen form of the great churchman, without sense or memory of the aching sinews and the bruised nerves that throbbed in heavy pain across his own breast, where the strength of his foe had dealt him blows that had rained down like an iron hammer on an iron plate, he drew his pistol with one hand, while with the other he held her close against him.

"We will beat them yet!" he said, in his teeth, that were clenched like the strong fangs of a mastiff. He was a soldier at the core; all a soldier's daring, all a soldier's war-fire, rose in him, as with him alone lay her defence, her liberty, her life.

With the swiftness of a moorland deer he plunged out into the passage beyond, and dashed down the windings of the narrow ways. The darkness was like the depth of midnight, and the first false step might fling them like broken birds upon the wall that towered on either side, or down the sheer descent of the granite stairs that ever and again at intervals led into the unknown horrors of the underground crypt and vaults. Yet, as he bore her onward through the rayless, treacherous blackness, fierce joy was on him: for her pleasures, and her riches, and her brilliance, half the world might be her comrades and her candidates, but he alone shared her danger. In her prosperity so many had been round her; in her extremity he had no rival.

The rush of feet, the clamour of voices, the tremulous utterance of vague alarm pierced shrilly and incessantly from the farther end of the building the dead silence of the night. From the broken cries which reached him, he could tell that the priests knew nothing as yet of the fall of their great leader, but had been awakened by the noise of the far-off conflict, and had discovered his absence and the Umbrian's drunken sleep. But one chance remained—the single chance of reaching the entrance-hall before they searched there for him.

"Can you fire?" he whispered, as he bore her onward and outward to where the feeble lamplight gleamed yellow and faint in the passages he had traversed.

In answer, her hand glided over the barrel of his weapon, and closed on the butt firmly.

"My life has hung on my own shot before now."

There was no tremor in her own tones as she replied to him; there was only the calm valour that thrilled him as a clarion thrills the soldier who hears its silvery melody command him to face death and to deal it.

"Promise me one thing?" she murmured.

There was light enough now, grey and dusky as it was, for him to see her eyes as they looked up to his, the gold gleam of her hair against his breast, the glisten of the steel blade against her bosom.

"All things."

"Then, if we are outnumbered, keep the last shot for me, and *take sure aim.*"

A mortal anguish quivered through him; he knew it might well prove that this boon, and this only, would be all that he could do to rescue or obey her.

"The last but one," he answered. "The last shall bring me to you."

The words were brief, and had the noble simplicity of his own nature in them; blent with a high devotion that held her honour dearer yet than all her beauty, and would obey her will even unto this last night of all. He had loved her ere now as dogs love, as slaves love, as men love whose passions can make them madmen, dotards, fools; but with that hour he loved her more grandly, more deeply, with a passion that sank into her heart, and stirred it as the storm winds stir the sea; that, for the first time in all the years in which this insanity had been roused by her and lavished on her, moved her to reverence what she ruled, to feel the strength, the depth, the force of this life that she, and she alone, could break as a child breaks reeds. She was silent; she let herself be borne by him through the twilight; she, too, felt a lulling sweetness, a subtle charm, in that breathless passage through the gloom, whose only goal might be the grave. She, too, felt something of that dreamy sorcery which lies in the one word—"together."

Nearing them came the clamour of the shrill Italian voices; behind them, from the cell where Giulio Villaflor was stretched senseless, the shouts of those who found their lord lie dying as they deemed, rang the alarm through the whole monastery, till the stones echoed with the outcry. From the stillness of slumber and the drowsy monotone of prayer, the whole silence teemed with noise and tumult; the whole building was alive with men, who started from their first stupor of sleep in vague terror and senseless excitation, while above all thundered the roll of the hound's bay, attacked at his post and giving challenge to his menacers.

"If he can guard the gates, we are free!"

The cry broke from her with the agony of a prayer as they pressed on into the great hall, where the single swinging entrance lamp burned dully through night and day. Hope almost died in him as he saw the crowd of monks that filled it, while before the unbarred door the dog couched like a lion ready to spring, with his mane erect, and his eye-balls red with fire, and his mighty teeth gleaming white under his black-bearded muzzle, holding them so at bay that none dared be the first to pass him and swing to afresh the unloosed bolts and chains. They forgot the hound as they saw the prisoner of their Church, and rushed on to her with a shrill yell. There were men among them who had flung the priestly robes over lives of foul crimes and unsuccessful villanies; and men who had hated her for that mere feminine forbidden loveliness that here, in their stone-locked den, they never looked on; and men who would have killed her, were it only that such service might find them fair favour in the eyes of the great dignitary, who held their fates in the hollow of his hand. These threw themselves headlong towards Erceldoune as he came out of the darkness of the corridor into the entrance-square, low-roofed and broad, with the arch of the door filling its farther end.

He paused, and levelled his pistol full in the eyes of the foremost.

"Let me pass, or you are dead men."

CHAPTER V.

"Stoop down and seem to kiss me ere I die."

The flash of the steel tube in their sight, the pressure of its cold circle on the forehead of the nearest, staggered the monks a moment; they recoiled slightly one on another. They had measured the height and the girth of this stranger's limbs as they had sat with him at their meal, and they dreaded the tempest of his wrath. Erceldoune, holding her to him still with one arm, and covering the foremost with his aim, thrust himself against the mass and strove to pierce his way through them to the gates. A voice from behind cut the silence like a bullet's hiss.

"Cowards! Bolt the doors and trap them; we can pinion them then at our leisure!"

The speaker, as his figure towered in the shadow, was a gaunt Abruzzian giant, fierce-eyed, hollow-cheeked, eager and lustful for slaughter; in a long dead time he had been a chief among ferocious soldiery, who had imbrued his hands deep in blood, and the old savage instincts flared alight, and the old brute greeds breathed free again, as for once after long captivity they broke the bondage of the priesthood. He took the leadership among the herd of half-awakened and bewildered monks, as the long-stifled impulses of war and murder rose in him, and glared wolf-like from his eyes, reddened with a light that was well-nigh insanity. He lived once more in a thousand dead days of battle, of rapine, and of cruelty, as he strode downward into the hall, heaving aloft a great iron bar with which he had armed himself, in default of other weapon.

Erceldoune, as he turned his head, and saw the lamplight glow on the lean ravenous face, knew that here lay his worst foe; the rest might be driven like a flock of sheep if once terror fairly mastered them, but in this man he read the bloodthirst of the tiger, the fiercer and the more ruthless for its long repression. With the keen glance of a soldier the warrior-monk sprang forward to secure the doorway; once netted, he knew that the prisoners could be dealt with at pleasure. The weight of the iron bar was lifted, to be hurled on to the hound's head, where—no more to be moved in fear or in wrath than the sentinel, who perishes at his post for sake of honour and obedience —he might be slain so with ease, though not passed or approached except at cost of life. The iron swung above the Abruzzian's head, swaying lightly as a flail, to descend with another instant on to the dog's bold brow; as it was raised, his arm fell paralysed, Erceldoune's first shot broke the bone above the wrist. Maddened with the pain, the monk shifted the bar to his left hand, and, forgetful of the hound, rushed on to his antagonist, head downward, with the blind infuriated onslaught of a wounded boar. Erceldoune, watching him with quick, unerring surety, was ready for the shock, and, sparing his fire—for he knew not how much more yet he might need it—caught him with a blow on the temple as he rushed on, which sent him staggering down like a felled ox. As he dropped, his brethren, catching that contagion of conflict which few men, priests or laymen, can resist when once launched into it, threw themselves forward to revenge his fall, rough-armed with the hatchets, the clubs, the pickaxes used in out-door toil, which hung or leaned against the wall.

Brigands of Calabria, tigers of the Deccan, would not have been wilder in their rage than were these sons of peace, who took in one brief hour payment for all that had been silenced, and iced, and fettered under the weight of the Church's rule. The sight of a woman's loveliness lashed like a scourge the futile envy roused beforehand in them by the stranger who had broken their bread, and who had showed them all that they had lost in losing for ever their freedom of will and act. What was at riot in them was not a gaoler's rage or a hireling's terror of chastisement; it was their own heart-sickness, their own rebellion, and despair, which made them savage as murderers.

For the only time in all his life a deadly fear came on Erceldoune—fear for her. He glanced down once on her, and her eyes gave him back a smile proud, serene, resolute, sweet beyond all tenderness—a smile that said, as though her lips spoke it, "Remember!" It nerved him afresh, as though the courage of Arthur, the power of Samson, poured by it into his veins and limbs. He had sworn to give her the freedom of death, if that of life were beyond his reach; the memory of his promise made him mad with that desperate strength whereby men, in their agony, reach that which, told or heard in the coolness of calm reason, seems a dream of impossibilities, wild as those of the deeds of the Red Cross.

"Fire with me!" he said in his teeth. "Our lives hang on it."

She heard, and raised her weapon steadily as the priests rushed at them, while the Abruzzian lay like a mass of timber at their feet; the two shots echoed together, aimed at the mass of stretching hands, of brawny arms, of gleaming hatchets, of lifted clubs, that was within a hand's breadth of them in the twilight of the lamplit hall. The mass wavered, quivered, staggered back; in that one breathless pause Erceldoune, with his arms round her so that she was held close against his breast, dashed forward with a rush as the lion will dash through the *cordon* of hunters who have fenced him in for the slaughter, hurling them back and front, left and right, by the impetus that bore him through them as swiftly, as resistlessly, as a scythe clears its way through the grasses.

One Cistercian, more rapid than the rest, swerved aside from that terrific charge which carried all before it like the sweep of cavalry, and threw himself against the door to swing the oak close ere the fugitives could reach it. "Seize him!" shouted Erceldoune in Servian. The hound had waited, panting and agonised, for the command; he sprang on the monk's breast, and threw him prostrate, his fangs clenched in the man's throat almost ere the words that loosed him from his guard were fairly uttered. The fair, still, lustrous night gleamed soft and starlit through the narrow space of the opened portals; the world and all its liberty lay beyond.

Blows were rained on him, yells hooted in his ear, hands clutched his clothes, his limbs, his sash, to wrench him back; an axe hurled at him struck him, grazing a wound an inch deep in his shoulder; a herd of devils shrieked, cursed, wrestled, and pursued behind him. He heeded nothing, felt nothing, heard nothing; he only guarded her from the weapons that were flung in his rear, so that none should touch her save such as struck first at him, and bore her like the wind through the half-opened door, out into the night air, and down the flight of rock-hewn stairs; the hound, coursing before him down the slope of the black rugged precipitous steps, slippery with moss, and worn uneven by the treading feet of many centuries. One step unsure, and they would be hurled head downward on to the stones below; there was no moonlight on the depth of intense shadow that shelved straight into fathomless darkness; behind, the rush of the priests followed, and the clamour of their shouts shook the night silence;—yet on he went, fearless, reckless impervious to pain, and feeling drunk with the sweet freedom of the fresh night wind, with the beating of her heart upon his own. To have held her thus one instant he would have given his life up the next.

Of that downward passage he had no knowledge, no memory in aftertime; he followed it as men in a nightmare follow some hideous path that ends in chaos; he touched the earth at last, clearing the three last granite rungs of the rock-ladder with a leap that landed him on the breadth of turf that stretched beneath. He rushed across it at the speed of a wild deer, making

straight for the cypress knot where he had bidden the
horses be waiting. A monk held him close in chase—
so close, that the priest reached the ground well-nigh
with him. He did not see or dream his danger; Sulla
did, and, with one mighty bound, was on the Italian's
naked chest, as he had dealt with wolf and with bear
in his own Servian woods. The monk fell well-nigh
senseless, and the dog tore onward through the moonlight with a loud bay of joy.

They were alone; the pursuit could not reach them
for seconds at least—seconds, precious in that extremity as years. The clamour and tumult of the
monastery pealed from the height above; but few of
the brethren he reckoned would dare to risk the peril
of descent in the blackness of midnight, the few that
would must be some moments yet before they could
be on him. In the shadow of the cypresses stood the
horses, held by a German lad, and eased by rest till
they were fresh as though they had not left their
stalls.

Without words, she threw herself into the saddle;
she had ridden stirrupless ere then across the brown
dark desolation of the Campagna in an autumn night,
with the Papal troops out against her. Idalia was of
that nature to which danger is as strong wine. Her
face was pale to the lips, but resolute as any soldier's
on the eve of victory; her hair shaken down rested
in great masses that gleamed golden in the flickering
light; her right hand still held the pistol as though
it were some love-gage that she treasured close, and
the fairness of her face was set calm as death, resolute as steel, even while her eyes burned, and glowed,
and dilated with the ardent fire of war, and with a

look sweeter than that which swept over him like a
sorcery.

"Off! Every second is life!"

While she spoke he was in the saddle; the horses,
young and wild, broke away at a touch in a stretching
gallop, with the brave hound coursing beside them,
mad with the joy of his liberty. The hoofs were noiseless on the moss that was damp and yielding by the
moisture from the swamps, and the belt of the cypress
screened their flight from the monastery; the monks
would search for hours, till their torches flared out, in
every nook and cleft of the rocks around, ere ever
they would dream how that midnight ride had borne
away their prisoner.

Out of the cypress-grove and beyond the beetling
wall of the crags the moonlight lay in a broad white
sheet, clear and soft as dawn, across the open country,
scarcely broken by a tree or hut. Afar the still green
fields of rye and maize were scarcely stirred by a
breath, and the twisted boughs of the olives were veiled
with a soft mist, the steam of the marshes and the
plains. Through the luminous half-light the horses
dashed at racing speed, while the water-threaded earth
trembled beneath them, and the rank grasses were
crushed under their fleet hoofs.

Through the shallow pools, with the water splashed
to their girths, and circling away in eddying rings as
they broke its slumbering quiet; through the vaporous
haze that hung over the black expanse of the morass
and the plain till they seemed to hunt down the white
wraiths of its smoke that curled and uncurled before
them; through the tall reedy grasses that broke as
they crushed them, and sent dreamy odour out on the

air as they bowed their broad ribands and their feathery clusters; through the intense silence, till the water-hen flew with a scream from her rest, and the downy owl brushed by with a startled rush, and the landrail woke with his shrill cry from his sleep in the midst of the millet-stalks; through the balmy southern night they rode as those can only ride behind whom yawn a prison and a grave, before whom smile the world and all its liberty.

All through the night they rode on, till the slender arc of the young moon was sinking towards the west, and countless stars were shining larger and clearer towards the dawn, burning through the blue-black darkness of the sky, veiled ever and again by sweeping trails of mist.

Under the grey dim colossal arches of the Ferratino gates fresh horses waited. The tired beasts were changed in haste and without question, and the young unworn ones raced on through the gloom as fleetly as wild horses sweep over prairie plains.

Behind them hunted Death; with the morning light the whole land would be as one host risen against them, as one snare spread to trap them; the bloodhounds of a Church were on their track, and the hate of a king and a priest ran them down; yet scarce a touch of fear, scarce a breath of the chillness of terror were on them; they had drunk deep of the rich wine of danger, and one at least was blind with the blindness of passion.

The world was still about them; all things slept. The earth was hushed and without sound, as though the deep tranquillity of death had fallen everywhere. Only through the calmness came the low sigh of the air through grasses, and the liquid murmur of unseen waters foaming down from height to height, or stealing under the broad leafage of arum-shadowed channels. Nothing awakened around them, save the downy-winged *aziola*, or the changeful bands of the fireflies gleaming like gold among the grey plumes of olives, or above the tender green seas of ripening millet. The summer was still young, and the night was divine, as the nights of the south alone are; the barren plains and the vaporous pools were passed with the swiftness of a dream, and beyond the olive belts, and the outer woods of cypress, lay the richness and riot of Italy, all shadowed and softened, and steeped in the moonbeams. Vineyards where the budding grapes were thrusting their first life through the leaves; great chestnut woods, where no ray pierced the massive fans of foliage, and the ground was white as though from snow with the heavy fall of the dropped flowers; fields where melon and gourd, and the fantastic shapes of the wild fig-tree coiled one in another, fragrant as gods' nectar, when the hoofs trod out the fruit and bruised the amber skins, and broke through the filmy, silvery webs of weaving insects, glittering with the dew; black, silent groves, noiseless and cavernous, with the hollow moan of earth-imprisoned torrents, and lofty aisles of cedars shutting in the broken ivy-covered ruins of the deserted altars of dead gods; vast piles of rocks, and stretching plains and hills covered with ancient strongholds mouldering to dust, and nestling dells where sheeted water mirrored in the starlight slender stems of sea-pines and marble shafts of classic temples. Through them all they went, never drawing rein, with the hound coursing beside them, through the changeful light of the calm late hours, guiding their flight by the stars, and holding ever straight for the sea. With sunrise the soldiers of the King, the mercenaries of Church and of State, would be out over the land; the night alone was liberty. Liberty, for the breath of the wind on their brows, for the splash of river-spray on their lips, for the wild joy of fearless speed, for the fragrance of trampled flowers, for the limitless glory of sight free to range over the width of the earth, for the nameless rapture of living when every sense and pulse of life is hot as with wine, yet is lulled as with sleep, and holds the pain of the world well endured for the sake of one hour of joy;—Liberty, in whose sweetness lies all the ecstasy of life, and in whose loss lies all its anguish.

Through the shallow foam of half-dry water-courses, through the long sear grasses where the cattle couched, through the odorous thickets of wild myrtle, through the withes of osiers where the bittern, wakened, rose with his sullen booming cry, they rode on towards the sea. Down the perilous slopes of ravines, where the loosened shingles shook in showers into yawning depths; down naked breadths of stone where no mosses broke the polished incline, and one uncertain step was death; across bridges high in air, spanning the white smoke of boiling torrents, while the timbers shook and bent beneath them; under mighty aisles of oak and cypress, where no path led save such as the rush of their gallop forced between the breaking boughs, they held their way through the twilight haze that deepened to blackest gloom where the woods closed above, and lightened to silvery lustre where the plains stretched out unbroken. All memory of danger, all sense of danger had fallen from them; on her the dreamy night silence and the passionate sweetness of freedom rested; with him there was no thought remaining save that he alone held his place by her bridle-rein, that he alone had delivered her out of her bondage.

In the calm around them all was at rest save their own hearts, save their own flight that held on for the same goal; all human life except their own seemed banished from the world, and the slumber-hushed earth left only to them; through ravine and woodland, through vineyard and valley, under the overhanging brow of lonely cliffs, and across the swaying bridge of giddy heights they rode together; and while the flickering light flashed down through parted leaves upon her beauty, and ever and again as he swept on beside her he met the gleam of her eyes through the shadows, he who loved her felt drunk with his joy. What cared he though he should fall dead at her feet when that midnight ride should have reached its end? He should have passed to his grave with her.

Where the jagged iron had been hurled against him, the rent nerves throbbed, and the linen was stained with blood; where his rival had strained him in that deadly embrace, the breadth of his chest was bruised as though weightily struck by a mace, and compressed as though tight bound in bands of steel; but he felt none of its pain, he knew none of its suffering; he only knew that she rode beside him, that through him she was saved, that once his arms had held her, that still in all the width of the world there was none with her in her extremity save himself,—whose love she had forbidden, yet whose love, she had seen, outlasted all,

and only asked of her a place with her in her danger,
a place near her in her death.

No words passed between them; the breathless
passage of their flight left no space for speech, and
the soft hush of the darkened world was too solemn to
be broken. They had passed away from the beaten
track, lest any should see and mark their course, and
had borne straight across the country westward to where
the bay lay—breaking through the blossomed vines,
the sheets of maize, the nets outspread for birds in
southern mode, the deep-grown screens of myrtles
fencing villa lands, and the wild growth of rocky
channels, where hidden streams ran below earth, and
made the vegetation riot rank and thick, where the
snake found its lair, and the mosquito swarmed in
hundreds, and the hot heavy vapour uprose like clouds
of steam. Now and then her eyes turned on him in
the darkness of cypress shadows, or where some yawning
river-bed, yellow and reed-choked, and unfathomed in
the gloom, was crossed with a measureless leap, their
horses close abreast. For all except the echo of the
ringing hoofs trampling through ripening corn, or
sounding loud on rocky pathways, there was utter
silence between them.

The night was fast waning, the stars growing larger,
till the whole skies seemed on fire with their brilliance;
the hours were passing swiftly—the hours which alone
were safety. Here and there, from lonely marshes, the
bittern's booming call sounded, desolate and mournful;
or, as the trodden millet-stalks muffled the noise of
their gallop, the cry of the cicala could be heard from
under the maize. The world went by them vague as
a dream, mist-like as a cloud; ruined temples, shadowy

landscapes, waters glistening white, monastic piles darkly looming down from rocky heights, sullen depths malarious, impenetrable, death-laden, divine beauty gleaming vine-crowned under southern moonbeams, all passed by them like the fleeting, changeful phantoms of a feverish sleep. They rode on and on, without thought, without refuge, with one impulse only, to leave league on league between them and the abhorrent dens of the Church; the burning breath of the past hours was on them, driving them forward as the curling prairie flames drive the lives they course after; and the riot of liberty was in them both, with every breath of wind that tossed the foliage from their path, with every current of air that drove sweet, and wild, and warm against their faces, as they dashed down by the pole-star's guide straight to the sea, yet southward first, ere they bent round to the shore, since Naples, where she lay amidst her loveliness, was the tiger's lair of priest and king, was death and worse than death.

The horses coursed like greyhounds; their feet scarcely touched the earth; the shallow brooks, the parched soil, the reddening osiers were scattered as they went; neck and neck, their heads stretched like racers, their flanks heaving, their bits foam-covered, they held on at that mad pace, without pause, without stint, now forced through screens of netted boughs, while the great chestnut fans blinded their eyes, and the branches snapped with a crash, and the vipers slid from under their feet—now scouring swamps where the earth quaked beneath them, and the heron's wings, startling, brushed them, as the brooding birds rose with a rush —now keeping footing, as best they could, down narrow ledges of slippery rock, where the mosses glided, and the stone crumbled under the crush of their thundering gallop. Mile on mile, league on league, were covered with that breathless racing speed, that reckless course on giddy heights, that headlong plunge through tawny waters; when any risk, darker than the rest, was in their way, his hand closed on her bridle-rein, so that the peril which might menace her should by no chance swerve by from him. She was his in these hours at least—his in her need, in her solitude, in her jeopardy, in her flight; his now, for this one night so far as bonds of mutual danger could so render her, so far as his arm alone to shield her, his heart alone to beat for her, his strength alone to stand between her and her foes, could lend him right to hold her so; his, while the net and the withes were about her, and the sleuth-hounds were tracking her down, even though —if she ever again reached her freedom and her sovereignty once more—she should forget that he once had served her thus, and bid him go and see her face no more. He loved her with an exceeding love; not less would he have brought her from her misery, or less have laid down his life to save hers, though he had known that, dying thus, he should never have seen even one look that thanked him.

Passion was stronger than pain, and gave him unconsciousness of it, as it had given him the thews and the sinews of giants in the contest whereby he had freed her; though the monk's blows had been rained on him like a smith's blows on his anvil, and his breast had been bruised and dinted and swollen by the grip of his priestly foe when they had strained and stifled each other like wrestlers in the death-fling, he had no feeling of suffering, no feeling of exhaustion.

The glow of triumph was on him; the fragrance of the sultry night seemed to steep his senses in voluptuous delight; the fierceness of contest and slaughter were still hot in his veins, and the lulling charm of a dream fell upon him while the world lay sleeping in silence and darkness.

At every leap to which their hunters rose, the wound that the iron had slashed opened as though the rusted axe afresh was hurled at it; at every convulsive bound with which the beasts cleared some riven chasm of stone or some high aloe fence that lifted its sharp folinge right in their course, the weight on his chest caught his breath, and the bruised muscles ached to bursting; often the stars grew giddy above him, and the *lucciole* glittering among the leaves looked a confused heap of sparkling fire, till he could scarce tell which was earth beneath and which was sky above him; often faintness came over him from the loss of the blood that had soaked his fishing-shirt through, and the weight of the blows dealt upon him which, at the time of contest, he had felt no more than he felt now the gentle rain of syringa flowers as they were showered from boughs they broke asunder. Yet he had barely any knowledge of this; he flung it off him, and was strong as he rode—strong to watch every danger that threatened her in their passage—strong to lead their flight with a mountaineer's keenness of vision, a desert-hunter's instinct of guidance—strong to let her see no paleness on his face save the pallor of moonlight, no look in his eyes save the love that had dared all things for her, and would do so unflinchingly on to the end, whatsoever that end might still be. A wild, senseless, fiery intoxication of joy was upon him; he knew no pain, he knew no weakness, he fled with her alone through the night. Come what future there would, no fate could wash this out, no fate could steal this from him; —that once his arm had thrust dishonour and death back from her, that once his heart alone had been her shield against her foes.

The first grey gleam of dawn was breaking where the morning star hung in the deep mystical blue of night, when their. horses, panting, worn, steaming, covered with foam, and staggering in their gallop, tore down through forest glades of oak and bark into the heart of woods where once the altars of Dionysus had arisen, and the print upon the thyme where the wild goat had wandered had been kissed by shepherds' lips as sacred ground touched by the hallowing hoof of Pan. The wood stretched up a hill-side's slope, dark even by day, so thickly woven were the old gnarled boughs, so heavy was the foliage even in summer drought, from the hidden streams that ran beneath its soil, sun-sheltered and making cool liquid music through the gloom, rising none knew whence, flowing, none knew whither, but telling to all who chose to hear of the dead days when their song had mingled with the vine-feast chants to Bacchus, and had borne their cadence in companionship with the thoughts of Virgil or of Martial. No heat could reach, no season parch, those subterranean waters that here and there welled up to sight, rushing brown and bright under the moon, but soon were lost again in the recesses of the earth, and only traced by the rich herbage that grew wherever they wound, or—when the stillness was intense as Alpine solitudes—by the murmuring hollow ripple that told where they threaded their way through secret channels to the sea. Here the sun-rays could not touch

to burn the grasses black; here the twisted leafage was
fresh and dew-laden as though a northern coolness
fanned them; here the silvery arum uncurled above the
screened channels of the brooks; here the white hellebore thrust its delicate head through mosses green and
curling as though they grew under English elm-woods.

And here in the deep loneliness, sunk over their
hocks in the water-fed reeds and grasses, the worn-out
horses slackened speed and strained to reach a freshet
that brimmed and bubbled under an aisle of oaks; and
as the headlong gallop paused, and the swift rush of
the air ceased, as they entered those dim aisles that had
the twilight gloom and calm of some mighty temple to
forgotten gods, a sudden blindness veiled all things—
even her face—from his sight, Erceldoune swayed
heavily forward on his saddle, the faintness of mortal
pain vanquished him at last.

With sheer instinct he threw himself from his stir-
rups and staggered towards her; all was dark and sickly
to his senses, and the iron bands seemed to crush tighter
and harder round his chest, straining out the very life;
but his thought was still for her, and he smiled in her
eyes, though he could no longer see but only felt that,
they were on him.

"Have no fear;—it is nothing!"

But even as the words left his lips his strength at
length was conquered; and senseless from the loss of
blood, he reeled slightly, and fell, head backward, on
the earth.

Almost ere he had fallen Idalia was beside him;
she had not dreamed that he was wounded or even in
suffering, till with those few gentle words he had
swayed downward like a dying man. Then, where the

moonlight strayed in through a parting in the branches
above, she saw that his face was white as the arum
lilies amongst which he fell, and that the snowy crowns
of the flowers and their broad and pointed leaves were
darkened with the stain of blood, soaking through the
linen of his barcarolo's dress. He was stretched there
as when first, under the Carpathian pine-woods, she
had found him laid struck down by the bullets of the
Greek assassin, with the vultures waiting above to
swoop to their feast. For many moments she knelt by
him; no tears rose before her sight, and her lips were
pressed close without a sound, almost without a breath,
but as she gazed an agony came in her eyes greater
than any that the uplifted scourge or the locked fetters
of her prison had wrung from her.

She had seen so many perish for her, perish through
her; she had seen the brave lives at Antina fall like
the ears of wheat ripe to the reaping; she had known
that east and west, far and near, in the wide wastes of
the Magyar-land as in the silent streets of Venice, in
the snow-plains of the Muscovite empire as in the
laughing loveliness of Lombard meadows, men had
poured out their blood like water at her bidding, under
her will, only for sake of that fatal beauty which many
with their last breath in the battlefield or on the scaffold had cursed with bitter reproach, which some—
and not so few—had to the last still blessed. So
many had died for her!—and now he who had found
at her hands but coldness and suffering, and gone
without reward for a loyalty passing all that even she
had ever found, lay to all seeming dead or dying at
her feet; as a noble hound dies for its mistress' sake,
dies faithful to the last, though never may her hand

have given him one caress, though never may her lips have spoken more than careless command or chill dismissal.

She knew then that she loved him; loved him, not with pity, nor with disdain for it as weakness, nor with mere warmth to one who had risked all things in her cause, but with a passion answering his own, with a passion holding the world worthless if he no more were numbered with the living. To-night, when his heart had throbbed against hers; to-night, when his strength had stood between her and her destroyer; to-night, when his promise had been given her to save her with death, if no other freedom were left him wherewith to rescue her; to-night, she had known that she had loved him with the love she had deemed dead in her heart, impossible to her nature; she, with whom love had been but the sceptre with which to sway slaves, the mandragora with which to blind madmen, the supreme folly with which women, otherwise powerless, reach a power that mocks at kings and creeds, and reign over the broadest empire of earth.

She knelt by him, mute, motionless, with a terrible longing in the eyes that had never quailed under Giulio Villaflor's, and had made the Umbrian priest let fall the lash. In that moment, in the silence and the loneliness of the forest, where the shadows closed above them, and in all the width of the land there was not one whom she could summon to his aid, one whom she dared trust with their lives, the anguish she had oftentimes too mercilessly dealt, too lightly counted, recoiled back on her. She learned what it could be to bear, this thing that men call love, this deadly gambling of heart, and thought, and sense, which casts all stakes in fate upon the venture of another's life; she, who had watched that madness so often and so long, with calm, contemptuous gaze, and tempted youth, and manhood, and age into it with a sorceress' smile, heeding the wreck she made no more than Circe heeded those who went down beneath the waves because her white arms waved them to that fatal sea. She loved him now with a great love; passionate, with the fire that slept in her, yet pure so far as remorse could burn it pure, and harrowed deep with a contrition that would have purchased freedom, and peace, and joy for him had it been possible, at any cost, at every sacrifice.

The stillness was intense; the solitude absolute as in a desert, no living thing was near, and had a peopled city been around in place of that profound impenetrable desolation, none could have been summoned to them; she had become as one plague-stricken, she was hunted down by Church and King, she could not ask a draught of water from a peasant, or bid his help to bear her lover under a shealing's shelter, the very reeds and grasses trodden in their flight might tell their course and betray their resting-place, the very moments might be numbered in which she could even watch beside him here unpursued, unarrested. Though he perished before her sight, she could not reach for him even the succour of a beggar's wallet or a charcoal-burner's roof.

The linen of the fishing-shirt had fallen open on his breast, and by the flickering light shed through the leaves she saw where the blows had fallen fast as hail upon his chest, that was strong as any corslet of steel, but blackened and beaten by them like the steel after a long close battle; his head had sunk back, he had reeled down senseless from exhaustion; through the crushed arums tho slender stream of the blood still flowed till the snowy cups were filled with it as though they were purpled by wine; she had looked many a time on death, and death seemed to her on his face now, as it had done when beneath the mountain pines she had first seen the carrion birds waiting and hovering above his sightless eyes.

For the moment she had no strength; no consciousness to seek to save him; she knelt beside him, knowing nothing save that through her he too must be sacrificed, that for her this life also had been laid down, uncounting its own loss, yielding up its breath without reproach, forced nobly on to perish in her defence. She stooped over him, with that look in her eyes with which she had gazed down on the lifeless frame of Carlo of Viana, only that now, beside remorse, there were a grief and a passion deeper yet than remorse alone.

That gaze, though he lay senseless under it, seemed to have power upon him still, as when first under the Carpathian sea-pines it had been bent on him in the glow and fulness of the noon, never again to be forgotten. His eyes, blind and seeing nothing but the swaying motion of the leaves, still instinctively looked upward seeking hers. A heavy sigh heaved his breast, —a sigh in which words brokenly rose to his lips and died.

"Leave me. Save yourself."

His one thought was still of her; his one instinct still was for her. A quiver shook her from head to foot, as fear, and danger, and the pressure of the poisoned steel against her bosom, had had no strength

to shake her grand and fearless courage. He was faithful to her thus—to the last—and she had given him
no recompense save this—to die for her.

Her head bowed its haughty royalty downward and
downward until her brow rested on his breast, and her
hands drew his within them against the beating of her
heart.

"Oh, truest, noblest!" she murmured, "I know it
now. I love you, if love be any worth."

Through the sickening delirium in which his mind
was floating, through the darkness that closed on sight
and sense, and seemed to him, as to her, the presaging
shadows of dissolution, the words reached, the touch
thrilled him, with an electric shock, a sweetness of
hope so wild, so rich, so breathless, that it called him
back to consciousness, as in priestly legends the touch
of the anointing chrism has summoned the departing
soul to earth.

He raised himself slightly with convulsive strength,
a living warmth flushed his bloodless features.

"Say it again!" he whispered, with that terrible
doubt still in his look of one who fears the joy he
touches will vanish mocking him. "Say it once more
—once more!"

Through the mist before his vision, through the
blackness of the forest shades, through the haze of
flickering foliage, and watery moonlight, and stars that
seemed to stoop and touch the earth, he saw her eyes
grow humid, lustrous, gentle with an infinite gentleness.

"Say that I love you? Yes—I say it now."

The words were low and slowly uttered; proud
still, for in them she yielded far, but tender with a
tenderness the deeper for that pride which stooped, not

without lingering reluctance still, to own itself disarmed. The glory that shone one moment on his face she had never seen save in her youth's earliest dreams of the glory on the faces of the gods; for—let the world lie of her as it would—to none had she ever spoken as she spoke now to him, while her voice was sweet as sorcery and filled with unshed tears that would not gather in her eyes, but were driven back to her heart in grief that mingled with the poignancy of softer thoughts and tenderness unloosed at last.

Then, at last, its ecstasy reached him, and he knew that it was truth—truth that rushed through him like the wild potency of some eastern drug, burning, blinding, lulling every sense like opium-mingled wine. He lifted himself from where he lay, he stretched his arms out to her, he strove with futile effort to strain his gaze through the mists of pain, to free his strength from the bonds of exhaustion; and once more it was in vain—once more he fell back, powerless, senseless, yet with his thoughts keeping their hold on their one memory of her, and still with that glow as of light upon his face. His lips moved faintly in words that scarcely stirred the grave-like silence of the deep oak-woods:

"O God!—if it *be* love—not pity—stoop down and kiss me once."

She was silent awhile, looking motionless upon him in the grey, fitful, shadowy haze, that was dusky and darkened by the massive canopy of foliage above; then—with a faint flush rising over the weary fairness of her face—lower and lower she drooped her imperial head, and let her lips rest in the answer that he prayed for on his own.

CHAPTER VI.

"Why must I 'neath the Leaves of Coronal press any Kiss of Pardon on thy Brow?"

THE earliest dawn had broken eastward, where the mountains stretched—the dawn of a southern summer, that almost touches the sunset of the past night—but under the dense shadows of the old woods that had sheltered the mystic rites of Gnostics and echoed with the Latin hymns to Pan, no light wandered. There was only a dim silvery haze that seemed to float over the whiteness of the tall-stemmed arum lilies and the foam-bells of the water that here and there glimmered under the rank vegetation, where it had broken from its hidden channels up to air and space. Not a sound disturbed the intense stillness; that the night waned and the world wakened, brought no change to the solitudes that men had forgotten, and only memories of dead-deserted gods still haunted in the places of their lost temples, whose columns were now the sea-pines' stems, and on whose fallen altars and whose shattered sculptures the lizard made her shelter and the wind-sown grasses seeded and took root. Of the once graceful marble beauty and the incense-steeped stones of sacrifice nothing remained but moss-grown shapeless fragments, buried beneath a pall of leaves by twice a thousand autumns. Yet the ancient sanctity still rested on the nameless, pathless woods; the breath of an earlier time, of a younger season of the earth, seemed to lie yet upon the untroubled forest ways; the whisper of the unseen waters had a dream-like, unreal cadence; in the deep shade, in the warm fragrance and the heavy gloom, there was a voluptuous yet mournful charm—

the world seemed so far, the stars shone so near; there
were the sweetness of rest and the oblivion of passion.

When her lips had touched his, life had seemed to
return to him; he lay in a trance vague as a rapturous
dream.   He was powerless to answer her; he had no
consciousness, save the one sense of a joy that in its
intensity was half delirium; he had no remembrance,
save that he held himself dying, and felt death, glorious,
welcome as the richest life that ever poured its golden
wine out in the sunlight of youth—felt like the lover
who, slaughtered at his mistress's feet and learning by
his fall her love, murmured with his latest words,

> It was ordained to be so sweet, and best
> Comes now, beneath thine eyes and on thy breast,
> Still kiss me! Care not for the cowards! Care
> Only to put aside thy beauteous hair
> My blood will hurt.

Stretched there motionless, strengthless, seeing only the
gaze of her eyes in the dimness, and feeling the depth
of the solitude in which their lives were alone, as in
the awful stillness of a desert, he knew not yet whether
this was truth, or whether dying visions mocked him—
whether this spiritual stillness round him, this madness of
incredulous hope, this breath of whispered words that
fanned his hair, this caress that burned one moment on his
lips, were not the mere phantoms of vain desires dreaming
of the joys denied to them for ever.   For a while she let
him lie thus, with his head sunk back against her heart,
and his eyes alone speaking as they gazed up with
their dog-like fidelity: she had no thought now that
this was death which had come to him; she knew that
he would live as surely as though with that answer to
his prayer she had breathed back the certainty of ex-

istence upon his lips; and she knelt there silent and immovable, letting the moments drift on, forgetful alike of time, of danger, of flight, and of pursuit; remembering no more than if they had never been, alike the agony that was of the past, and the jeopardy that was still of the future. On the dauntless courage—the courage of Marathon that had revived in her—peril had frail and passing hold: and in the deep bosom of these untracked and classic woodlands all sense of mortal fear seemed lost in their profound peace, their nameless melancholy, their ethereal lulling charm.

At last, as though smitten suddenly with the sharp iron of recollection, she moved from him, rose, and went from the great oak shelter where he lay.

"Love! love! What have *I* to do with love?" she murmured, as she leaned her arms on the broken slab of the old stone altar, and let her head droop downward on them. A flood of memories, a tide of thought rushed on her from the years of her past; on the impulses of a gratitude touched to the core by the fealty and devotion of his defence, she had let words escape her that pride had silenced, and weightier chains fettered for so long, that she would have taken her oath no pity for him would ever shake, no yielding in herself would ever lead her to revoke, the decree of severance from her for ever, which she had uttered unfalteringly on the night by the Capri sea. It was done;—he knew now that she gave him back some measure at least of that passion wherewith he adored her. She gave him love — she who had held it with so superb a disdain as the dalliance of fools, or the sensualism of libertines; she who used the whole power of its empire but as a weapon, a mask, a snare, a means scorned in itself for ends nearer her heart and worthier the consecration of her thoughts than she deemed that any single life could ever become to her. For the first time—whatever calumny might say, or vain jealousy upbraid her with—for the first time the softness of this passion had touched her, and its caress been given by her. She had made a slave of its madness many a time, or lashed it into fury when she needed, as the priestesses of oriental altars tamed or enraged the beasts which they crowned with flowers only, later on, to lead them out to sacrifice. That she would ever render it back, that she would ever feel to it other emotion than a half contemptuous compassion, had seemed impossible to her for so long. Moreover, when of late some sense of its tenderness had stolen on her, some echo in her own heart been awakened to the strong vibrations of his, she had known that the bonds which bound her could never be loosened, and she had told herself that she had no title to, no fitness for, a noble and unsullied homage.

Where she leaned now against the ruined altar-stones, remorse, keen as though their love were guilt, weighed on her. He had justly won his right to all of joy, of honour, and of peace, that she could give the liberator and defender of her life; he had been willing to purchase liberty for her at loss of all things to himself; he had merited the tenderness she had yielded to him by service which no gratitude rendered could repay:—and she knew that, in all likelihood, the sole reward her love would bring to him would be a violent death by shot or steel: a fate as merciless as the blow his Abruzzian foe had dealt at him that night. An exceeding bitterness came on her—a heart-sickness of regret.

Why had not he come to her in the early years of her
youth? Why had not this thing, since at last it reached
her, been wakened in her while yet it would have sufficed to her, while yet it would have had no shadow
cast upon it from the past, while yet no self-reproach,
no weariness of doubt, no fever of reckless ambition,
and no darkness of untold bondage, of fettered action,
of dead memories, would have stretched between them?
The poignancy of that cruel remembrance, "too late,"
which had passed over her when she had leaned against
her prison casement, and seen him look upward in the
tawny torrid heat of the monastic marshes, was with
her now.

She had told him that he was dear to her, and she
knew him to be so; knew that she could go to his side
and promise him a love that should be no mockery
and no treachery, but a living truth, deep and warm,
and rooted fast in honour.

She had known many who, in other things, equalled
or far surpassed him; she had known every splendour
of intellect, every dignity of power, every brilliance of
fascination in the men of every country who had been
about her in so many changing throngs, but none
amongst them had touched her as the singleness and
the self-sacrifice of Erceldoune's devotion touched her,
and none had roused in her the mingled pity and reverence which the hopelessness of his passion and the
chivalry of his character had roused in her almost from
the first moment of their intercourse. There was a
bold free carelessness of manhood; there was a lofty
fearless reading of honour and its bonds; there was a
noble simplicity and an antique grandeur in the cast
of his nature, that had won from her what she had

never felt to those amongst her lovers who had charmed her with an intellect a thousand times more subtle, wooed her with a dominion infinitely more commanding than his could ever have been, even had the fortunes of his race never fallen as they had done, or the pursuits of a statesman's glories ever been possible to the untamed Border blood.

When in the gloom of the monastery's corridors, with a hundred human tigers thirsty for slaughter swarming from their dens, she had been guarded by his arms and shielded on his breast, his heart had wakened her own with its quick beating; when in the darkness of the night she had made him pledge his word to serve her by a death-shot if to give her freedom from dishonour otherwise were forbidden him, she had felt to this man, whose eyes answered hers in comprehension of that loathing of captivity, that disdain of the terrors of the grave, what was nearer akin to reverence than the imperial temper of Idalia had ever yielded to any.

"He loves me! Yes, as no man, I think, loved me yet!" she thought. "But he loves me because he believes in me. How long should I reign with him if he knew?—if he knew?"

That was the iron weight on her, which made her whole frame sink with that fettered worn-out fatigue and desolation against the ivy-covered stones in the motionless musing that succeeded to the breathless, fearless intoxication of danger and of flight. It would not have been possible to her to do as many weaker and less truthful natures do — seek shelter in self-evasion, and turn the very nobility and trust of the man who loved her into the withes to bind him, and

the band to blind him. It would not have been possible to her to stoop and touch his lips with hers, if on
hers there were ever to be for him the shame of falsehood or the disgrace of subterfuge. When once she
had answered him with that caress he prayed for,
when once she had murmured to him, "I love you!"
she had acknowledged to herself his right that there
should never be one thing in her past or her present
screened from him, one truth veiled, one act distorted.
And on her, silence was bound; either way, withhold-
ing all or giving all the records of her past, she saw
herself a traitress to her creed of truth and justice—a
traitress alike to others and herself.

Lost in thought, and weakened now more than she
knew by her captivity, by the scant coarse food and
noxious air of her prison-house, and by the wild speed
of the lengthened headlong midnight ride, she sat there
in the still deep shadows of the oak glades, with the
faint grey hue of the young day serving but to deepen
into blacker sombreness the colonnades of trees. She
had left him on the sudden sting of many memories—
memories which made it deadly to her pride to have
bent thus to passion and to pity—memories which
recalled to her that she had no right to bind in with
her own the fate of one who brought to her the loyalty
of perfect faith in her nature, the defencelessness of
perfect ignorance of her past. She had done him evil
enough; she had saved his life once, only to chain it
so to hers that its doom must be whatever her own became; for her he had risked liberty, existence, everything save honour, ungrudgingly, and with the lavish
largesse of a princely giver, who would have held no
gift as any worth, no suffering as any sacrifice; now

—at the last—she had surrendered her love to him, and listened to his own. She knew that there were thousands who would tell him that this was the darkest evil of all that, through her, had befallen him. And at her heart ached a burning, endless, futile pain, rather for him than for herself, though for herself there was sharp anguish in the knowledge that the world would tell him all love rendered from her could be but a graceful lie to fool him to his peril, an eloquent simulation to cheat him into misery, a mockery, hollow as it was beguiling, to draw him downward, Circe-like, to his destruction.

Her head was sunk on her hands; her thoughts had drifted far in that vague, unreal musing which comes after long fasting and severe exertion; she was unconscious that he followed her wistfully with his gaze, like a dog, as she left him, and slowly, staggeringly, after a while, rose, steadying himself by the boles of the oak trunks, and came towards her with the dizziness of his wound still on him, but the ardent glow and the bewildered doubt of feverish joy warm on his face and eager in his glance. She was unconscious, even, that he was near till his hand touched her; then, as she started at the touch, she once again forgot that the world held any other than his life and hers. Stooping, he looked down into her eyes; a look so longing, so incredulous, so straining with hope and fear, as a man might give into the deep brown depths of fathomless waters in whose light he sees some long-lost priceless jewel gleaming.

"Is it true?"

As his voice quivered on the words he read its truth. Doubt was no longer with him as he gazed down on her face; but with a cry from his very heart, he drew her in his arms as he had held her against the onslaught of her foes; he gave back that one caress with breathless kisses on her lips and brow; he forgot danger, and pain, and all things upon earth, save that this woman he worshipped was his in all her splendid grace, in all her sovereign loveliness; the world reeled round him—he felt blind, and drunk, and mad. And Idalia for the instant made him no resistance, but let her beauty lie in the arms that so well had shielded it, and let her head rest upon the breast that had been as a buckler rained on by a thousand blows between her and her enemies.

This trance of sweet forgetfulness, this momentary banishment of every bitter thing, she at least could give him, and he had earned his right to it. For the moment, also, she too shared it. She felt nothing but the softness, the silence, the voluptuous abandonment of the emotion so long contemptuously discredited and unswervingly repressed as owning any power to sway or move her heart.

Then slowly, and with her old reluctance to yield to so much weakness blent with a deeper and a keener pain, she drew herself gently, from him.

"Do not thank me for *my* love. The world will tell you it is worthless, and can have no strength save to destroy."

For all answer he sank down at her feet, his arms about her still, his hands on hers, his eyes looking upward to her own with such a radiance in them as she had never seen in any human gaze.

"Destroy me as you will, so that you love me!"

Mad words;—she had heard many such, yet they

had never borne the meaning to her that these bore to her now. A shudder passed over her as she heard, a chillness of icy cold. She knew it might well be that nothing save ruin might come to him through her. She stooped towards him, and her lips quivered a little as the answer stole from them.

"Well,—many will tell you that no other fate can ever come to you from me."

"Whoever does will find his lie his last word."

"But—if *I* say so?"

"I have answered. Do what you will, since you have blessed me thus."

"Blessed you? God knows——"

Slow tears welled into her eyes as she saw his own so full of longing eloquence, where he gazed at her in the faintness of the waking day that left the forest gloom and forest hush around them. His trust was sweet to her, and yet so bitter; sweet because she knew that her heart gave it the answer it believed and sought, bitter because she knew that her past could never merit it or meet it. She passed her hand softly over his forehead with a gesture that from her had deeper tenderness than far more passionate demonstrations from natures more yielding and less proud.

"What you have suffered for me!" she murmured. "What you have done and dared! You merit my whole life's dedication for such love—such service. And—that life is so little worthy of you."

The woman who so late had fronted Giulio Villaflor with so superb a resistance, so defiant a disdain; the woman who had laughed at the threats and the prayers of her lovers, as of her foes, with so cold and so careless a contempt; the woman who had been

tranquil before death, pitiless in power, victorious
against outrage, and without mercy in fascination, felt
abased, heart-stricken, smitten with a weary shame, before the loyal gaze of the man who held her life as the
most valued and most stainless gift the world could
hold for him.   To a nature integrally truthful and integrally noble, however warped by circumstance or
error, the deadliest sting, the surest awakener of remorse, will always lie in the perfect faith of another's
implicit confidence.   Steeled to venom, careless of censure, and contemptuous of rebuke, it will bend, contrite
and self-accursing, before the fidelity and clearness of
one regard that vows a simple and unsullied belief
through all and against all.

He doubted that he heard her rightly.   To him it
seemed that he had no earthly thing or claim by which
to win her; and he held his service in her cause no
more deserving of her care than he held the wolf-
hound's at her feet.

"Worthy of *me?*" he echoed, his voice still faint
with exhaustion, but breathless with the incredulous
joy that seemed to make tenfold strength flow back
into his limbs, tenfold force arm him steel-clad to save
her.   "Oh, my love, my life, my empress, my wife!
—what am I that I should ever share one thought of
yours!"

She started slightly; a flush of warmth passed over
the paleness of her face; a half smile came on her lips,
sad yet doubtful; wondering yet reverent.

"You would make me your wife—still?"

She spoke almost dreamily, with a touch of questioning doubt in her words as in her smile, while at
the same time they returned to her something of that

negligence of hauteur, something of that royalty of challenge, which were as inherent in her as though she had worn the crowns of empires.

He started to his feet, staggering with the weakness of his wound.

"You ask it? Do you not know that I feel mad with the mere licence only to touch your hand with mine? And—what insult do you think that I can dare to offer you?"

"None."

She looked at him full in the eyes, with a tenderness infinitely melancholy, a gaze intense in its calm unspoken thought.

"Then why——"

She smiled slightly, with something of her old delicate irony, her own contemptuous, unsparing cynicism, which never was more unsparing than to herself.

"Why? Well,—you may have heard that I have no great belief in marriage, and little favour for it; and the answer was not sure, or would not have been, rather, if you were as other men. What do you know of me? Where have you lived, if you have not heard my name coupled with evil? Why should you deem so much scruple needful with a woman whom you found a conspirator in chains—a prisoner, degraded to the mercy of Monsignore Villaflor?"

A great darkness swept over her face as she spoke her persecutor's name, though through the bitterness and mournfulness of all her speech there ran the vein of reckless, careless, satirical disdain, which had grown to be as her second nature in many things, and had so long been used as her surest veil to every deeper unacknowledged feeling.

The wistful uncertain pain which that tone had ever brought into his look was in it now, as he stooped towards her. He felt that he had no comprehension of her, but he was content—with that magnificent folly which is so noble in its rash unwisdom—that he loved her, and believed in her.

"I know nothing of your life—true. But make it one with mine, and I shall hold it as the divinest gift on earth; and if any dare calumniate it, they will find their reckoning with me. Oh, my love, my mistress, my idol! only give me the title to defend your honour against the whole world!"

The tears stood once more in her eyes as she heard the passionate prayer, to which the tremor in his voice gave a yet deeper pathos—a yet more imploring eagerness. She grew paler still as she heard; a sigh from her heart's depths ran through her. The more faith he lavished on her, the more sublimely mad the blindness of his chivalry, the more heavily self-rebuke smote her, the farther the iron entered into her soul, and the farther she stood in her own sight from any fitness with this man's noble simplicity of trust. She bent towards him, leaning her head one moment on his hands, where he stood above her—that bright-haired pride-crowned head, that had borne itself with such imperial courage above the massacre of Antinn, above the priestly herd of the monastic hall, was lowered with the abasement of a brave and erring nature, struck to the core with self-chastisement, and refusing to accept one shade of worship of which it knew itself unworthy.

"Listen!" she said, softly, while a bitterness, that was to herself not to him, lent a strange thrill and force to the low-murmured words—"listen! I have said I love you—love you as I never thought to love —my noblest, bravest, best! But it is because I do, that I tell you I am unworthy of your generous faith —that I tell you there had better be separation between us now and for ever. I will not urge on you to leave me because while with me you share my danger. You are too brave to be insulted with such a plea; but I do say, forget that I have ever confessed you have grown dear to me, abandon every hope that I can bring you any happiness; do as I bade you when last we parted—hate me, scorn me, condemn me, if you will; do anything, save trust your happiness to me! There are many women who can lay bare their hearts to you like an open book, make one of them the holder of your honour, they alone merit it, and I am not amongst them. Who can know me as I know myself? Believe me, then, when I tell you the greatest cruelty I can do to you is to bestow on you my love."

He heard her silently; but not as he had heard her bid him leave her and condemn her the last night they had stood together above the sea at Capri. He knew now that she loved him; knowing that, he refused to take a decree of divorce between them, even from her lips; he claimed a title that he would never surrender, though through years he should vainly assert his right to it. The strong passion and the staunch patience of his nature were welded together, persistent and invulnerable.

"Let me judge that," he said, simply. "If I preferred misery at your hands, rather than paradise at any other's, I should have the right to make the choice."

"Yes, and I the right to guard you from the fruits of your own madness. You love me with a love that needs an angel to be worthy it; and I—I have thought of late, that if those tyrants yonder had killed me under the worst tortures they could frame, they would have done on me no more than my just due; they would only fittingly have avenged all those who died by shot and steel through me."

"What *is* your life, then?"

His voice sank very low, his face was very colourless, as he leaned over her. Believe even her own witness against her he did not, would not; but he knew that some dark thread ran through her life's golden web—he knew that some deadly remorse underlay the brilliancy of her gifts and of her sway, and beyond these he knew nothing of it, no more than he knew of the track, and the spring, and the destiny of the unseen waters that wound their way beneath the herbage and the lilies at his feet, whether downward to nethermost depths of gloom, or outward to the fair freedom of the sea, none had told, or ever would tell.

"What is it?" she repeated, dreamily. "Well, beyond all, it is a long regret."

"Many regret who are but the prey of others."

"Perhaps; but my regret is—remorse."

"Well, may not even that oftentimes be noble?"

She gave a gesture of dissent, while the smile that had in it more sadness than tears, though it had also her old careless satire in it, passed a moment over her face.

"You bade me once not ask you to turn sophist for my sake. Do not turn so now. You have your own bold broad creeds of simple honour and dishonour;

keep to them; men wander too far from them into subtle windings now."

His teeth clenched on his beard with an agony of impotent impatience.

"O God! do not trifle with philosophies! Answer me straightly, for the pity of Heaven; what *is* your life that you repent it thus?"

"I cannot tell you wholly. It is enough that it has forfeited all right to such a trust as yours."

"Nay, let me judge that, I say again. Let me judge fully—give me your confidence, your history; did I not swear to you that the worst trial would never change my fealty? I love *you*, my sovereign, my sorceress! What matters it to me whence you come, what you bring?"

His voice, that had been grave with a gentle command as he spoke the first words, sank down to the hot, vehement, reckless utterance of a love that was ready to take, risk, suffer, and imperil all things so that only the sweetness of her lips closed once again on his, so that only the gift of her loveliness were yielded to him one hour.

She rose, and looked him once more in the eyes, with a serene, fathomless gaze, in that pity and that reverence which blent strangely and intricately in the feeling she bore towards this man who was at once her slave and her defender.

"No," she said, slowly; "it would matter nothing to you if you sought me as your mistress; but—as your wife? You told me once the stainlessness of your name was the only inheritance that you still held from your ancestors."

He gave a short, sharp sigh as though a knife had

been plunged into the nerves that his wound had laid bare; her words bore but one significance to him. Ere she had time to resist, his arms were round her; he crushed her against his breast, he looked down into her eyes with a terrible longing prayer.

"Answer me; answer me yes or no, or you will kill me; and forgive me if the question is an outrage —you madden me till I must ask it. Is there any shame in your past that forbids you to hold and keep my honour?"

The last words sunk so low that they scarcely stirred the silence as they stole to her; for the moment she was silent; she longed for his sake to sever him from all communion with her, she desired for his sake to bid him leave for ever one who must withhold from him all he had the just right to seek in the records of her past; she hesitated one instant whether she should not render herself up to his utmost abhorrence, that by this means, since none other could avail, he would be parted from her fate for evermore. Almost she chose the sacrifice; she had strength far passing that of women, and she had the generous self-abandonment of a nature which scorned self-pity, and—once bending to love —loved nobly. She was silent; then as she looked up and saw the gaze wherewith he watched that silence which wrote on her a condemnation deadlier to him than words could ever have uttered, her courage forsook her, she had no force to yield herself up to his hatred and his loathing; to let him believe this of her was to let him be made desolate by a lie, and all the regal temper of her race arose and refused to bear falsely the yoke of shame even to save him, even to do towards him what she deemed her duty and his defence. She lifted her head, and looked him once again fully in the eyes, calmly, unflinchingly, though a flush of warmth came over her face.

"Nothing—in *your* sense. But in mine much."

"Thank God!—thank God! Against the world, against all destiny, ay, even against yourself, you SHALL be mine!"

He had never heard the last words; the first sufficed to make the wild joy course like fire through his veins, to light the future with the glory of unutterable gladness, to give her to him then and for ever; his own, let all the earth stand against them, or let her own will forbid him her beauty and her tenderness as she would. The one agonised dread that had stifled him as with a hand of ice through the last moments was gone; he feared no other thing—not even death, since if that smote her it should strike him with the same blow.

He would not release her from his embrace; he held her there, with the loosened trail of her hair floating over his chest and his ceaseless kisses on her lips; he forgot that every hour of their lives might be numbered, that they had just broken from a prison that might yawn afresh for them, and enclose them beyond hope ere even another day had passed; that he knew no more of her past now than he had known when first her hand had held the curled leaf filled with water to his parching lips in the Carpathian woods; he heeded nothing, remembered nothing, asked nothing, since her eyes had told him more surely yet than her words that no shame rested on her to divorce her in the sole sense in which he would accept shame to have the power to part them. It was neither the world's calumnious breath', nor the slander of rivalled lovers, that could have terrors for the man who had pierced his way to her through dungeon walls, and torn off her the leopard fangs of Giulio Villaflor, and fought his passage with her through levelled weapons, and the storm of blows, and the battle of the hot Italian night. It was not for libel or for lie that he would surrender her—he who had thrown his manhood and his life on one reckless venture to secure her freedom, on one uncounted stake to touch her hand again.

While he had believed that he was no more to her than the hound beside them—nay, scarce so much— he had been content to hold his silence, to save her without thought of recompense, to obey her implicitly, and to hold her as high above him as the morning stars that, through the dawn, shone in the blue heights above the forest. But now that once he knew she loved him, it would have been easier to shake off a lion from his desert foe, when once the desert rage was at its height, than to force him to yield up the claim that her love gave him to Idalia.

"I knew it—I knew it!" he murmured, as he stooped his head over her, and wondered even yet whether this were aught but the sweet vain mockery of some mandragora-given dream. "Dishonour with you!—it were impossible. Ah God! why will you belie yourself with such self-condemnation?—you who are noblest among women—who chose death rather than that villain's touch?"

"Hush! that was nothing. I should have been false indeed to all the traditions of my race if I had had fear of that moment's pang which the Pagan world held the signal of release—which Christians alone

have raised into a gigantic nameless terror.　But"——
she drew herself from his arms as she spoke, and stood
with the dignity that had awed even the ruthless Prelate, blent with an infinitely gentler sadness than had
ever been upon her—"do not cheat yourself with
thinking that I have no errors on me.　I have grave
ones, dark ones.　In your sense, it is true, there is
nothing to part us; but in my own conscience there is
much to make me unfit for ever for such love as you
bestow.　See! I tell you that those men died at Antina
through my work; I tell you that many more lives
than theirs have been lost, sent to their graves by me;
I tell you that I have made all men who fell beneath
my sway serve me for one end, not a mean one, indeed, but one to which I sacrificed everything and
every one ruthlessly, and did more ruin than you ever
dream, or I could ever measure.　I tell you that the
chief of my history must remain hidden from you—for
a while, at least; perhaps for ever; and that if you had
lived less in your wandering freedom and more in the
intrigue of cities, you would have heard every evil,
every danger, every unsparing sorcery, and every pitiless unscrupulousness attributed to my name, and—for
the most part—rightly.　Now, knowing this for the
mere outline of a deadly truth, you can scarce call me
'noblest among women,' and you will be mad if into
my hands you yield your future.　Believe me, and fly
from me while you may."

She stretched her hands out to him with a gesture
of farewell, that had in it an exceeding tenderness!
she loved him well enough to do for him what she had
done for no other—save him from his own passions,
spare him from herself.

He took her hands in his, and laid his lips on them in one long kiss; then lifted his head and raised his eyes to her with a regard in which a feeling, far deeper than the mere voluptuous fervour of the senses, blent with a loyalty grave' and calm as that of one who pledges his life, not lightly, but witting what he does—looked at her softly and thoughtfully.

"That is idle; I will never leave you *now* while there is breath in me. It may be that you have that which you repent of; few women have such sorcery as yours, and use it wholly blamelessly; but what I trust is, not your past but your nature, and what I ask is, not your secret but your love. It is too late to speak of our ever parting; I will make you mine in the teeth of all, even of your own will, now that once you have let me know that your heart is with me. And—do you not think that I have tenderness enough in me to pardon much, if there be ought to pardon? Do you not think that I have justice enough to hold you in higher honour for your noble truth than I could ever hold the pale, poor, feckless virtue that should have no stain because it had no glory, and had never fallen in any path because it followed coldly the straight one of self-interest? Idalia!—I can bring nothing worthy you, save a straight stroke to free you and a whole strength to love you; but since you have no scorn for those, take my future now and for ever—I trust you as no man ever trusted woman."

He spoke from his inmost soul—spoke with that vivid simple eloquence which came to him in moments of intense feeling; and it stirred her heart as none had ever stirred it; no qualities could have won the reverence of her wayward, dominant, and world-worn nature, as it was won by his chivalrous dignity of faith, his absolute refusal of the ignoble soil of suspicion. It broke down her force; it moved her to a sudden sweetness and warmth of utterance that he had not heard since that moment when she had stooped and touched his lips with her caress.

"Ah, my love, my love!" she murmured; "it is not *that*. I will never forsake you; I will never betray you! It is that my past, that my present—But, since you will it so, be it so. I will break my chains for you, and lay down my evil sway for ever. Call me your wife if you will; no wife shall dare for any, what I will dare for your sake."

CHAPTER VII.

"By Pride Angels have fallen ere thy Time."

WHEN the morning rose higher, and its light shone full on both their faces, his was warm, brilliant, eager with incredulous delight; hers was grave, weary, very colourless. To him a very Eden opened; on her a thousand memories weighed. The one saw but the future; the other was pursued with the past. He knew that he had gained the only life that made his worth the living; she knew that she had drawn in with her own the only one that she had ever cared to save.

"Ah! I bring you already only ill," she murmured, as the rays of the risen day, half shadowed still beneath the oak leafage, recalled to them that they were fugitives —fugitives from pursuers never yet known to spare. "You are wounded—you suffer now?"

He looked at her with the smile whose sweetness had more tenderness than lies in any words.

"If I do, I have no knowledge of it. A bruise!—
a hatchet-stroke! Do you think I could remember
those?"

"I do, at least. They were enough to stretch you
as one dead but very lately—"

"A passing faintness, nothing more. Believe me,
a thousand wounds like these would never harm me.
I have been half a soldier all my days."

"So have I."

And as she spoke she rent off some of the delicate
white laces of her masque dress, and steeped them in
the little spring that bubbled under the oak stems till
they were cool and soft as lint, and tore asunder a
broad strip of the scarlet silk of her Venetian domino
and laid the wet laces on it.

"Stoop down," she said to him—a singular softness, so gentle that in itself it was a caress, had come
upon her.

He stooped to her as she bade him, but his hands
drew the gold-broidered ribbons away.

"Not so. *You* shall not serve me."

"Why not? You have earned your right to service,
if man ever earned it."

The breath of her lips was on his brow, her eyes
looked into his with the dew of unshed tears glistening
heavily in them, her hands touched him, making the
pulses of his heart throb faster and the current of the
blood glow in his veins, while, with a gentleness that
seemed to him balm enough to heal mortal wounds
themselves, she wound the silken bands over the gash
that the blunted axe had hacked, and the width of his
chest that the rain of blows had covered with livid
marks like the marks where a scourge has fallen.

11*

"God grant that these be the last things you suffer through me."

The words escaped her almost unconsciously, while for the first time since her eyes had gazed in their set anguish on the dead men lying round her in the banqueting-hall of Antina, the tears gathered in them like the gathering drops of a storm, and fell one by one slowly on his hair and on his breast. She had made many endure danger and wretchedness, risk and despair, without pity; it was but fitting retribution that she had no power to ward them off from the only life for which she had ever cared.

He held her hands close against his heart.

"I can never suffer *now!*"

It seemed so to him. Keeping this, her love, he thought that no vicissitude or bitterness of life could have an hour's power to move him; that no fate could approach him which had any shadow on it; that nothing men or fortune could deal unto him could ever move him to an instant's pang. He did not dream that there are gifts, breathlessly, burningly coveted, which are more disastrous reached than lost. Like Faustus, he would have said to the future and its fate, "take

> My soul for ever to inherit,
> To suffer punishment and pine,
> So this woman may be mine!"

And his noble reckless, senseless belief in her had alike the sublimity and the blindness which lie at the core of every chivalrous idealism; blent, too, with something grander and something loftier still—a love that cleaved to her through all and in the teeth of all —a love that could find her human and darkened by human stains, yet never lose its fidelity, but reach high, even high as pardon, if need there were of any pardon's tenderness.

The day was waking; the sun had risen; even here, through the darkness of the oak boughs, the radiance was coming. He started to his feet, made as strong to save her now, as though the force of a score of lives was poured into his own; of pain, of weakness, of the aching fever that thrilled through his bruised limbs, he knew nothing. He seemed to have the strength of Titans, to have lost every sense of existence save those of its deep delight, its wild joys, its dreamy ecstasy.

"My love, my love, forgive me," he murmured. "In the heaven you have brought me I forgot your danger."

"Was it not best forgot?" she asked, with that carelessness and that sadness which mingled intricately in her nature. "In a race for life and death, few would pause to speak as we have done; but it is the surest wisdom to defy fate while we can."

"Fate? There is no fate, save such as a strong hand carves, or a weak hand spoils, in Life."

"Nay, am *I* not yours?"

She stooped to him with her old half-mocking sorcery, her loosened hair brushing his breast, her rich lips near his own, her eyes, deep with thought, humid with tears, yet luminous with that victorious challenge which was without pity, and which had so often defied men to have strength or power to deny her as their destiny. The old evil passed over her for a moment —the old evil of triumph in the unmerciful, unsparing knowledge that a human soul was hers to do with as she would, as a crown of roses lies in a child's wanton hands to be treasured or trodden down at will.

He looked at her with a long wistful gaze, earnest as an unspoken prayer, and once more the darker and the more callous tyranny that had for one instant returned on her was softened and banished and driven back by the pure strength of an undivided loyalty, by the undivided trust of a brave man's heart.

"You know it," he answered her. "Why play with me in speech when you hold my life in your power?"

The patience and gentleness of the rebuke touched her as had never done those florid vows, those ornate protestations, such as she had heard so often until she was as wearied by them as eyes that dwell long on the dazzling hues of jewels ache with their glitter and their profusion. Others had loved her as well as he,. even with this depth, this might, this absolute submission of all existence to her, yet in him these had a dignity and a simplicity that claimed a reverence no other had done—these in him made her worthless of them in her own sight.

"Ah, forgive me!" she said, with that passionate contrition which in a woman thus proud, and of old thus unyielding as she was, had at once so much of poignancy, so much of self-reproach. "I wish only it were otherwise! I wish only that your fate were safely anchored in some pure and peaceful life mine could not touch. Why *will* men ever love where love is fatal?"

He looked at her with earnest thought, grave and infinitely tender.

"Fatal? What is it that you fear for me?"

"All things."

"All!   That is to place but little trust in my strength to endure or to resist.   What is it you dread most?"

"Myself."

She gave him back his look, intent as his own, fathomless, and filled with a pain that was half remorse, half prescience.

His face grew very pale.

"You mean—you will desert me?"

"No.   Not that."

She spoke slowly, as if each word were a pang, then leaned towards him once more with the light of the risen day full on her face, and the splendour of her eyes troubled beyond grief.

"No.   I never broke a trust; and yours is the noblest ever placed in me.   But—cleaving to me— you will have bitter trials for your faith; you will have, most likely, cruel suffering that I shall be powerless to spare you; you will lose me, perhaps, by captivity, by shot, or by steel: you will pay for me, it may be, if ever I be yours, no less price yourself than death. *Now* do you not know why, though it rent my heart in twain, I would surrender you up, and never look upon your face again, my love—my love!—would you but take my warning?"

The first words had been almost cold from their enforced control; with the last a yearning, aching desire trembled in her voice, which would have told him, had no other moment told him, that what she felt for him was not pity nor gratitude, but passion itself.   He heard in silence to the end, as one who has his own resolve set immutably, and listens to the utterance of

counsel that has no more likelihood to make him
swerve from it than the beating of the winds to move
the rocks that they pass over. Not that he heard her
lightly, or believed that undue fear made her count the
peril for him with needless exaggeration; he knew this
was not in her nature, but he was wholly careless of
what price might be exacted from him for allegiance
to her, and he was as firm to cleave it, whatever that
price might be, as a soldier to cleave to his standard
while there is sight enough left in his dying eyes to
watch one gleam of the silken folds above his head
that shall never droop through him till men have killed,
not conquered, him. Then, holding her hands against
his heart, he looked down on her with that graver and
more chastened tenderness which, mingled with the
vivid ardour of his love, born from the darkness of
danger that was still around them, and from the defence
that through it she, so brilliant, so fearless, and so
negligent, had come to need from his strength and from
his fealty. In her intellect, in her ambitions, in her
carelessness and her magnificence, he was content that
she should reign far beyond him, content to know that
she reached many realms which he had barely dreamed
of; but in her necessity, in her peril, in her desolation,
he took up his title as a man to guard her, his right
as a man to shield her, and to save her, if it should
need be, even from herself.

"We will speak no more of that; our fates, whatever they be, will be the same," he answered her. "It
may be that I shall suffer through you, as you say; if
so, it will be without complaint while I can still be
dear to you. If death come—well; it had little terror
for us last night—it will have none for me, if it be

only merciful enough to spare me life without you. As
for faith—believe enough in me to know that no trial
will exhaust it. If silence be bound on you, I will
wait till you can break it with honour. I have no fear
of what it guards from me. Love were of little worth
that could not yield so slight a thing as trust."

"A slight thing? It is a greater gift than the gift
of crowns or kingdoms—and still more rare."

She had heard him, moved deeply by the brave
simplicity of the generous words; her face was very
pale, her head bowed; in her own sight she was unworthy of this sublime unquestioning belief, and the
knowledge entered like iron into her soul.

"Is it?" he answered her. "Then all love is a lie.
However that be, take it as *my* gift to you, then; I
have nothing else in the world to bring."

She looked at him with that long, grave, weary
look of which he could not wholly read the meaning.

"You could bring me none I could prize more, or
—could deserve less."

"That cannot be. If you did not merit it, you
would see no treasure in it. It is not those who value
trust that betray it."

· "Betray it! No; I never betrayed yet."

Her face wore for a moment the fearless look of
royal courage and strength that had ever been most
natural to it; then, swiftly, it changed, and a darkness
fell over it—the darkness of remorse.

"That is not true," she said, bitterly. "Betrayal
—in men's sense of betrayal of comrade to comrade,
of friend to friend, of honour to honour—never yet
did touch me. But I betrayed as women mostly do—
all those who loved me."

He watched her wistfully, but silently; his heart ached that there should be this shadow of unrevealed remorse between them; his knowledge of her told him that Idalia was not a woman to let slight regrets weigh on her, or slight errors stir her conscience into pain; he knew that among the wild-olive crown of her genius and her power some poisoned leaf of the belladonna must be wound, brilliant but life-destroying. It was acute suffering to him; she was to him as luminous, glorious, divine, and far above him as the sun itself; that across this sun of his life there should lie these black and marring shadows, gave him pain deep as his love. But loyalty was with him before all; and beyond the reckless resolve of a blind passion, that would possess what it adored, though the possession should be accursed, there was the noble fealty he had sworn to her—the brave, patient, chivalrous trust which left unasked whatever she wished untold, and was contented to believe and wait.

He stooped to her, tenderly passing over her latest words.

"Weary yourself no more with the past," he said, gently; a gentleness that was sweet to her, like the lulling murmur of calm waters after the blaze and riot of the voluptuous colour of tropic forests. "We have to think of the present and the future. Every moment is precious; I have been too forgetful of your safety. You know better than I where your enemies lie, and how best they may be baffled. There is one who will not spare——"

"There are hundreds who will not. The land is as a net for me."

"Then we must leave it——"

"Is it so easy to leave such close-woven meshes?"

"Easy, no. Possible, yes."

"And how?"

"That we will speak of later; for the present moment you must have food and rest. There will surely be some charcoal-burner's or contadina's hut here somewhere; there is nothing hardly to fear from the peasantry in the forests or open country, and we must wait till nightfall for further flight. Stay an instant while I look around us——"

"But you are not fit for any exertion! Your wound, your faintness——"

He smiled on her; and the light of the smile had a strange, sad beauty, that touched her with a pang, keen in pain and yet not without its sweetness.

"Those were nothing. Such as they were, you cured them. I think I have the strength of lions now."

He left her, and, going up where the earth rose precipitously, looked down the great dim aisles of forest that stretched away on every side, with the far unerring sight of a man who had known what it was to go through the heart of Persia with his life hanging on the sureness of his eye and aim, and who had ridden over the grass seas of Mexico and steered down the lonely windings of the Amazons, when with every moment a spear thrown from behind him, or an arrow launched from the dense screen of foliage, might have ended his years there and then for ever. He stood motionless some instants, not a sign of bird, or beast, or vegetable life in the woodlands round escaping him; he had learned all such forest lore of Indians and Guachos, and he had a traveller's swift sweep of vision,

with a soldier's rapid tactic and decision; the horses
were grazing quietly near, too tired to stray, and
watched, moreover, by Sulla, who had, unbidden, taken
their guardianship. In a few moments longer he returned to her.

"There is some one living a score yards onward,
or I am much mistaken. Wait here while I reconnoitre,
and if you need me, fire; I will be with you at the first
echo of the shot."

He loaded the pistol that had fallen on the grass
by her, and put it back into her hand, then thrust the
boughs aside, and made his way to where, at some
slight distance, the hut of some woodland dweller
stood; a faint low flicker of smoke, curling among the
thickness of the leaves, had told him rightly there was
some human habitation, and though it was but a poor
cabin, rudely built of loose stones and woven branches,
it was more welcome to him than a palace would have
been. He knew the Italian people as well as he knew
the Border peasantry at home, and knew that they
were gentle, kindly, and generous in the main. The
hut stood in a very wilderness of beauty, wild vine,
and the sweet fig beloved of Horace, gigantic pines,
and the wood-strawberry that nestled in the grass, in
their profuse and vivid contrast, making a paradise
around it, while in its rear the high slope of pine-covered
hills rose dark and massive, with falling waters tum-
bling down their steep incline into a broad still pool beneath, that was never stirred unless by the plunge of some
diving water-bird. A young female child, with a rich
Guido face and the step of a princess in her rags, was
the only living thing found there; she answered him
readily, balancing her water-jar as she came from the

torrent like some Pompeian Naiad; her father had gone
to his work at dawn; he was a charcoal-burner, and he
would not return till evening; the stranger was welcome
to shelter; and food—well, there was no food except
some millet-cakes, and a bit of dried fish from the
fresh water; he could have that, if he wanted. Any
one near? Oh no, there was no one for ten miles or
more round, except one or two huts like hers. She
was a picturesque, handsome little forester, bare-legged
and scarce clothed, yet with a wild freedom of movement, and a certain pensive grace thoroughly national;
very like the beautiful mournful models, Campagna-
born, of Rome, who look like living poems, and who
have but one thought—*baiocchi*.

"It is a miserable place for you, yet it will give us
some sort of harbour," he said, as he brought Idalia
to the woodland cabin.

She looked across a moment at the luxuriance of
vine and blossom, and backward at the black pine-
mass, through which the falling waters glanced like
light, and smiled half wistfully as she looked.

"I think it is a paradise! To forget the world
amidst such loveliness as this—what do you say?
Would it be wise? And yet—power is a dangerous
thing; once having drunk of it, one has lost taste for
every purer flavour. You do not know what that is?
You do not know what ambition is, then? I can tell
you; it is satiety *with* desire."

"A bitter thing?"

"Yes. But not so bitter that it is not sweeter than
all sweetness—only the sweetness so soon goes, and
the dregs are so soon all we hold!"

He did not answer; his heart ached that he was not

able to bring dominion to this woman, who was so born for it; that he had no diadem such as that of her foregone Byzantine sires to crown her with; that he had nothing wherewith to achieve greatness—nothing wherewith to content that desire, half disdainful yet undying, which was in her for the sceptre and the sword, for all they ruled and all they gained.

He left her in the inner chamber of the hut, that was roughly partitioned in two by a wall of stakes and woven rushes, and brought the horses under the shelter of a great cedar that shut out every ray of the sun; he could use his left arm but little, owing to the shoulder-wound, but he loosened their girths, watered them, gave them a feed of rye from some corn that the cotters kept for bread, then bathed, and shook his *barcarolo* dress into the best order that it would assume, and thought what food in this wild waste he could find for her. That he was anhungered and athirst himself, that there was fever on him still from his injuries, and that, despite the plunge into the water's refreshing coldness, his bruised frame ached and his breath was hard to draw, he scarcely felt; Idalia was his only memory. For her, he could have not alone the lion's strength that he had said, but a woman's gentleness, an Indian's patience, an Arab's keenness; and nothing was too slight for him to heed, as nothing too great for him to brave, that could be offered in her service and her cause. That he had had no sleep, no rest, no food, weighed nothing with him; in the heat of the early day he sought with unwearying diligence for such things as he thought could tempt her. Wild strawberries on their own mosses; beccaficos that haunted the place, and that he slew with a sling and baked in clay; dainty fish that he speared with the knife from his sash, wading waist-deep in the pool—these were all the woods would yield him. But love for her had made him an artist and a poet; he served them in such graceful fashion, covering the rude table of the cabin with a cloth of greenest moss, and screening the coarse-hewn wooden trenchers with vine-leaves and flowers, that it was rather like such a forest banquet as Theocritus or Ben Jonson loved to cast in verse, than like the meal, in a wretched refuge, of fugitives for whom every moment might bring the worst terrors of captivity and death.

When it was done—that travail of willing, tender service—he could have swept it down again with a stroke of his hand.

"I am a fool," he thought, with a smile that had a sigh in it. "A child might thank me for those trifles; but she—wild strawberry-leaves for one who wants the laurels of fame, the gold foliage of a diadem!"

Yet he stooped down again, and changed the garniture a little, so that the snow-white arums might lie nearer the scarlet of the fruit. He had a painter's heart, and instinct told him that beauty in the lowliest things has ever a sweet psalm of consolation in it; he loved, and his love unconsciously told him that a coil of forest flowers is a better utterance of it than all the gold of Ophir.

It was not wasted on her, this which he deemed so idle a trifle that she would not even note it. As her glance fell on the woodland treasures that the hands, which a few hours before had been clenched in a mortal gripe at her foe's throat, had gathered to cover the poverty of their refuge, Idalia's eyes filled with soft sudden light and gratitude—eyes that had so often looked down with cold, amused, careless scorn on those who wooed her with every courtly subtlety, with every potent magnificence of bribe.

"What depths of exhaustless tenderness there are in his heart!" she thought. "I might gaze *there* for ever and find no base thing! O if he could say that of mine!"

The day went on its way deepening to the full heat of noon, cloudless, sultry, lustrous, as such days of summer-length in southern lands alone can be; to him it was like one long unbroken dream, divine, voluptuous, intense as the radiance around them. They were safe here in the heart of the untrodden forest—safe, until with the fall of night their flight could be resumed. Within, the darkness of the hut, the moss and foliage he had strewn everywhere made couches yielding as velvet, and filled the air with their fresh fragrance, with the gleam of the white flowers flashing in the gloom; without, stretched the vivid light and endless growth of the woodland, the glow of colour, the foam of water, the play of sun-rays upon a thousand hills, and, above all, the deep blue of an Italian sky. Beyond, under the great cedar, tho horses browsed and rested, with broad shadows flung upon them cool and dark; all the fantastic foliage ran riot like a forest of the tropics; here and there an oriole flashed like gold in the sun; here and thero the rich green of a lizard glanced among the grasses; all else was still and motionless, steeped in the sensuous lull of southern heat.

In such a day, in such a scene, danger and pain were forgot, as though they had no place on earth; they were alone; the young peasant-child went hillwards

after her single goat; there was not a sound or a sign
of other life than theirs, and the oblivion of passion
was upon them both; they ceased to remember that
they were fugitives—they only knew that they were
together.

They spoke very rarely; she let the past, with all
its mystery and all its bitterness, drift away forgotten.
To the future neither looked; it might lead to the
dungeon or the scaffold. They lived in the present hour
alone, as those who love do ever live, in the first abandonment and usurpation of their passion.

Once she looked down at him where he lay at her
feet, and passed her hand among his hair.

"Does the earth hold another man capable of such
sublime folly as yours? You give me your life; yet
never ask me once of mine."

"What marvel in that? You have said, you wish
silence on it."

"And how many would heed such a wish?"

"I know not how many would. But it is law
to me."

"Ah! you are rash as Tannhäuser. I told you so
long ago."

"And I said then as now, Tannhäuser was a cur.
She was *his;* knowing that, what wanted he? If he
had had faith aright, and love enough, he would have
wrested her out from the powers of darkness. He would
not have yielded her up—not even to herself. Evil
is black in us all; love, that is love in my reading, does
not surrender us to it, or for it."

The deep glow of his eyes gazed into hers, speaking a thousand-fold more than his words. He knew
that the chains of some remorse bound her; to fear this .

for himself never dawned on the careless courage of that which she had well termed his "sublime folly," but to free her from its dominion was a resolve with him not less resolute than had been his resolve to deliver her beauty from her captor's fetters.

Her face was softened to a marvellous richness, sadness, and pathos as he looked up at her—the gloom of the low-shelving roof above and behind them, the light of the day falling on her and about her, through the hanging leaves, from the burning sun without.

"You like better the passion of the 'Gott und die Bajadere' poem? Well, so do I. It is nobler far. The god had faith in her, and, *because* he believed in her, saved her. Brave natures, defying scorn, may grow to merit scorn; but no brave nature ever yet was steeled and false to trust."

"And yours is brave to the death; wherefore, till death, I trust it."

His words were low, and sweet, and earnestly grave with that depth of meaning and of feeling which made reverence, not less than pity, move her towards the only man who had ever stirred her either to compassion or to veneration, and which gave grandeur, force, and nobility to the love which, without it, might have been but a madness of the heart, and a desire of the senses.

"False women vow, as well as true—I vow you nothing," she murmured to him; "but—I thank you beyond all words."

She did so thank him from her soul; she to whom this faith was precious as no other thing could have been, since she knew at once that she had forfeited all title to claim, all likelihood to gain it, yet knew that very often calumny had wronged and envy stained her

with many a charge of which she had been as guiltless
as the white arums that lay unsullied at her feet. That
strong, undoubting, imperishable trust was the one jewel
of life that she had of her own will renounced her title
to, yet which she could value as no other, perhaps, who
had not lost it, ever could have done so well.

"Listen," she said, stooping over him where he was
stretched on the foliage at her feet, while her hand
strayed still with a caress among his hair and over his
lips. "So much of my life as I can tell you I will—
it is not a thousandth part, still it may make some
things clearer to you. I am of Greek birth, as you
know; and I doubt if there be in the world a descent
that can claim greater names than mine. My race—
nay, both races that were blent in me—stretched far
back into the earliest Athenian times on one hand, and
to the records of Byzantium on the other. A myth
moreover blends in me Halicarnassian descent from
Artemisia;—that is doubtless legend. But I was the
last to represent the pure Greek stock, and it was the
one of which I was the prouder, though it had fallen
into evil fortunes and much poverty. Of the Byzantine,
there was but one besides myself, the brother of my
dead mother, a strange man; a rich, wayward, luxurious
recluse; a feudal prince, where he held his chieftainship
in Roumelia; leading an existence more like an eastern
story than aught else; magnificent, voluptuous, barbaric, solitary, with all the glitter of Oriental pomp and
all the loneliness of a mountain fief. A terrible tragedy
that had occurred in his youth—I can tell it you
some other time—begot his love of solitude; his passions and his tastes led him to make that solitude at
once a palace and a prison, a harem and a fortress. I

have little doubt that his life was evil enough; but I
did not know it, and he loved me with a lavish tenderness that left me fearless of him, though he had a great
terror for all others. So the life I led from my birth
to my sixteenth year was this: sometimes I passed long
months in Greece, in a great, desolate, poverty-stricken
palace, with vast deserted gardens, in which I wandered
looking at the bright Ægean, while dreaming of the
dead glories of my people, with an Armenian monk,
old, and stern, and learned, for my only guide, who
taught me all I would—more, perhaps, of abstruse
lore, and strange scenes, and deep knowledge than was
well for me while so young. Ere I had seen the world
I was steeped in it, from the telling of Roman cynics,
and Athenian sages, and Persian magi, and Byzantine
wits. I believed with all the credulous innocence of
my own childhood, and I disbelieved with all the scornful
scepticism of my dead masters. I had studied more
deeply while I was yet a child than many men do in
their whole lifetime. From that lonely meditative life
in Greece I was often changed, as by magic, to the un-
bridled luxury and indulgence of the Roumelian castle.
Slaves forestalled my every wish; splendour, the most
enervating that could be dreamt of, surrounded me
within, while the grandest natural beauty was everywhere without; if vice there were, I never saw it, but
the most gorgeous pleasures amused me, and my bidding
was done like the commands of an empress, for I was
the adopted heir of the great Julian, Count Vassalis.
Now can you not imagine how two such phases of life,
alternating in their broadest and most dangerous contrasts
from my earliest memory upward, made me fatal indeed
to others, but to none so fatal as to myself?"

She laid her hands ou his lips to arrest the words he would have spoken, and passed on in her narrative.

“No. No denial. God grant I be not fatal at the last to you. Well, it was these two dissimilar lives that made me what I am. I was happy then in both; happy, dreaming in poverty in Greece; happy, dreaming in magnificence in Roumelia; ambitious already, ambitious as any Cæsar in both. In Athens I had the poetry and the purity of glory in me; in Turkey its power and its pomp allured me. Both, combined with the knowledge of my past heritage in Hellenic fame, and of my future heritage in the Vassalis dominion, gave me the pride of an emperor and the vision of an empire wide as the world. Ah Heaven! yet the dreams were pure, too—purer and loftier than anything that life can realise. For I did not dream for myself alone. I dreamed of peoples liberated, of dynasties bound together by love of the common good, of the Free Republics revived by my hand, and shedding light in all dark places where creeds reigned and superstitions crouched, of misery banished, of age revered, of every slavery of custom broken, of every nobler instinct followed, of men made brethren, and not beasts of prey who hunt down and devour the young, the weak, the guiltless. Ah Heaven! what dreams they were.”

Her head sunk, her eyes were fixed on the flood of light without, her thoughts were far from him, far beyond him, in that moment, as the thoughts of genius ever are far from those who love the thinker best, and are best loved in answer.

They were with the dreams of her youth; such

dreams as lighted the youth of Vergniaud and found their fruition on the scaffold.

"Well," he asked gently, "with you they never perished?"

"No, not utterly. But they were tainted, how deeply tainted! So, thus I lived, a fairy story and a pageantry filling one half my years, monastic seclusion and heroic memories holding the rest. As I grew older, Julian Vassalis often spoke with me of many things; he was a bold, magnificent, kingly, reckless man, a chief who answered to none, a voluptuary who laughed at the world he had quitted, a genius who might have ruled widely and wisely with a Sulla's iron hand, a Sulla's careless laughter. He found me like him, and he made me yet more like. It might be—but it is not for my lips to blame him: he loved me well in life, and strove, so far as prescience could, to guard me when his life ended. That was in my sixteenth year. He bequeathed me all his vast properties, with the fief in Roumelia and other estates, requiring only that I took his name, and, wherever I wedded, never changed it. It is through him that I became one of the richest women in Europe; much is gone, but great wealth still remains with me. Can you not fancy what I was nine years ago, with the world before me, untried, unknown, with passion untouched, with ambition still but in its sweet vague ideals, with innocence as soilless as those lilies, and courage fearless as the courage of the young eagles? Can you marvel that I believed I should have the sovereignty of Semiramis? Can you not understand how easily I credited those who for their own ends deluded me to the belief?"

Her face darkened as she spoke, and her voice sank

with a thrill of hate in it. He caught it, and his own voice took her tone.

"'Tell me who they were. If they be living——"

The menace recalled her from the past to the present.

"No. That is one of many things I cannot tell you yet, if ever. From no love of mystery—I abhor it—but from a brutal inexorable necessity, as little to be escaped from as the destiny of the ancients. *We* know that there is no such thing as destiny, but we make as hard a task-master for ourselves out of our own deeds. Of my childhood I can speak freely, but from Julian Vassalis' death dates tho time that I must in so much leave a blank to you. Those were with me who knew how to touch every chord in my nature, and they used their power ably. I was ambitious; they tempted my ambition. I loved sovereignty; they pointed to such realms as might have dazzled wiser heads than mine when I first stood on that giddy eminence of command, and riches, and splendour, and was told that I had the beauty of a Helen, while I knew that I had tho courago of men, and felt even stir in me men's genius and men's force. Do not deem mo vain that I say this. God knows all vanity is dead in mo, if I ever had it, and I think that I was at all times too proud to be guilty of that foible. And it was by higher things than such frailty that they lured me. I loved freedom; I loved the peoples; I rebelled against the despotism of mediocrities, the narrow bonds of priesthoods; I had the old liberties of Greece in my veins, and I had the passionate longing for an immortal fame that all youth, which has any ideal desires at all, longs for with the longing 'of the moth for the

star.' Well, through these, by these, I fell into the
snares of those who draped their own selfish greeds
and intrigues in the colours of the freedom that I
adored; who knew how to tempt me with the pure
laurels of a liberator, while in truth they bound me
with the fetters of a slave."

He did not speak, but looked at her, with his lips
breathless, with his eyes passionate as fire, through the
mist that dimmed them as he heard. Hearing no more
than this, her life seemed known in its every hour to
him; he understood her more nearly, more deeply, than
any man had ever done; more truly far than those
whose genius and whose aspirations had far more
closely been akin with hers.

She looked at him and sighed.

"Wait. Do not think me blameless because in the
outset I was wronged. I tell you that I have great
sins at my score. True, at the time I speak of now,
I was sinned against, not sinning. I was led to ally
myself in earliest youth with those whom later years
have shown me were desperate, insatiate, unscrupulous,
guilt-stained gamesters, who staked a nation's peace to
win a gambler's throw, and played at patriotism as
keenly and as greedily as men play for gold. I was
dazzled, intoxicated, beguiled, misled at once by all
that was best and all that was worst in me; and, too
late, I found the truth, found every avenue of retreat
closed, found myself bound beyond escape, found
that——"

She paused abruptly, shutting in the words, but
the hand that lay in his contracted as though it
grasped a weapon wherewith to requite a deadly, endless wrong.

"So far I was sinned against," she went on, with effort, as though the memories which arose stifled her with poisonous fumes. "But in all else the evil is mine. The sway was guilty that had been put into my hands, but I grew to love it as we grow to love the opium that we hate at first. All power had irresistible fascination for me, and I learned to use mine pitilessly; and I should use it so to-morrow to all save you. The political career into which I had been plunged had its sorcery for me; I delighted in it even whilst I abhorred it. I soon learnt how to play on men's passions until from them I gained what I would. If my instruments were broken under my hands, I never heeded it; they had served my end, and the end was great still, though its means were accursed; the end was still the liberties of the nations. The truth did not come to me till I had gone too far to draw back, too far not to be enamoured of the merciless dominion that I found I could command. When I knew it, I grew wholly reckless. I had been foully, basely wronged, and all that was dangerous in me rose and hardened. I had been stabbed in the dark by hands that were sworn to shield me. I cared little what I did, nothing for what was said of me, after that. I am not justifying myself; I merely show you what fires they were which burned me heartless. I have been associated with every movement of the advanced parties of Europe through the years that have gone by since I first became the Countess Vassalis; I have been the inspirer of more efforts, the guide of more intrigues, than I could tell you in a score of hours, even were I free to tell you them; I have held in my time, indirectly, more power than many a minister

whose name is among the rulers; the world does not
know how it is governed, and it does not dream how
kings have dreaded and statesmen sought to bribe me.
One thing alone I remained true to, heart and soul—
my cause. For the freedom of the peoples, for the
breaking of their chains, I have laboured with all such
strength and brain and force as nature gave me. In
that I have been true, and without taint of selfish desires. God knows that to raise my own land among
the nations, and to gain Italy for the Italians, and to
do—were it ever so little—to crush the tyrannies of
creeds, to bring nearer the daylight of fearless and
unfettered truth, I would let Giulio Villaflor and his
creatures kill me as they would. In that I have been
loyal to the core, but in all else I have been very
guilty. I have tempted, blinded, seduced men into the
love that gave them as wax into my hands. I have
rouséd their darkest passions, that of those passions I
might make the firebrands or the swords my purpose
needed. I have taken their peace and crushed it to
powder; I have taken their hearts and broken them
without a pause of pity; I have sent them out to the
slaughter careless how they fell, so that my will was
done; I have sent them out to perish, far and wide,
north and south, east and west, and never asked the
cost of all that gold of human life wherewith I played
my pitiless gambling. I smiled at those for whom I
cared no more than for the stones of that torrent; I
let them hope I loved them, so long as that hope was
needed to make them ready instruments to my using:
I was stirred no more by despair than I was for compassion. So long as I had my slaves, I heeded nothing
what they suffered, how they were captured. I only

smiled at the fools who thought women had no share in the making of history, no power to penetrate the arcana of life. That was all."

He listened, and a heavy sigh answered her as she paused; it was involuntary, unconscious. He had believed in Idalia, as with a woman's absolute unquestioning belief; it struck him hardly, deeply, to know by her own telling that she had these ruined broken lives, these Circean cruelties in her past; that the witching splendour of her sorcery had been thus steeped in tears of blood, thus bartered for the gain of triumph and dominion. No fear for himself even now crossed him; his courage was too bold, his passion too ardent. It was the knowledge that she should thus have stained the beauty and the genius of her life, which came on him, not unlooked for, since he had ere this known that there were error and remorse upon her, yet bitter as the fall of what is treasured and is reverenced must ever be, however love remain faithful and unshaken to that fall's lowest depth.

"One question only," he said to her, while his voice was low and tremulous. "Through this, was there never one whom you loved?"

She met his gaze fully, thoughtfully, truly he could have sworn, or never eyes spoke truth.

"Not one!"

"Is it possible?"

She smiled a little, with her old weary irony.

"Very possible. Poets have written much about the love of women; I do not think it a tithe so warm and strong as the love of men. Many women are cold sensualists, many are inordinately vain; sensualism and vanity make up nine-tenths of my sex's passions, though sentimentality has so long refused to think so."

"But you must have been surrounded by so many —by all that was most brilliant and most seductive?"

"Yes; yet a tinsel brilliancy, for tho most part. Besides, I did not come into the world ignorant of it, as most youth comes. Julian Vassalis, and my own tastes, and others who influenced me then, had given me the surest shield against the follies of love in studies deeper far than most women, if they had driven away my faith in life too early, with the sneers of Persius, with the scourge of Juvenal, with their own cynic wit and their own manifold knowledge. Ambition was infinitely more the passion to tempt me than love ever was. I luxuriated in the sense of my own power, in the exercise of my own fatal gifts; but I scorned from the bottom of my heart the men who were fooled by such idle things as a girl's glance, as a woman's smile. If the gold gleam of my hair ensnared them, I could not but disdain what was so easily bound; if they were spaniels at my word, I knew they had been, or they would be, as weakly slaves of any other who succeeded me, and as easily subjugated by a courtesan as they were by me, when I chose to use the power, I thought very scornfully of love. I saw its baser side, and I held it a madness of men by which women could revenge a thousand-fold the penalties of sex that shut us out from public share in the world's government. A statesman is great, a woman can make him a wittol; a chief is mighty, a woman can make him a byword of shame and reproach; a soldier has honour firm as steel, a woman can make him break it like a stalk of green flax; a poet has genius to gain him immortality,

a woman can make him curse the world and its fame
for her sake, and die like a dog, raving mad for the
loss of scarlet lips that were false, of eyes divine that
were lies. No power! We have the widest of all!
Well, I but knew that better than most, and used it
yet more unmercifully than most. And I think what
gave that power tenfold into my hands was that one
fact—that the weakness of love never for one instant touched me myself, that the temptations of love
never tempted me for an instant, that my intellect
alone dealt with them, and my heart remained ever
cold."

"And it has wakened for me? How is it possible?
What have I that those had not? I have nothing on
earth whereby to be worthy of you—whereby to have
won you?"

His life was so sweet with its rapture, his passion
was so blind with its victory, he scarce remembered
those who had so vainly suffered before him. Every
happiness is selfish, more or less; and his was so in
that moment. She half smiled, and let her head droop
over him, till her lips touched his again:

"Who can answer for love? Others have done as
much for me as you—others have loved me, even as
well as you; but—"

"None had yours?"

He asked it eagerly, breathlessly, still; this was
all that he doubted in her past—that some other life
had reigned before him in that heart which beat so
near to his.

"No! A thousand times 'No!' if you care for the
denial. Love was my tool, he was never my master."

She spoke with her old imperial dignity of disdain

for those follies of feeling and of the senses which sway mankind so widely and so idly. Then the scorn faded from her eyes, a weariness stole there instead; her voice sank, and lost its pride in the contrition of self-accusing memories, of heart-sick confession.

"But do not honour me for that. It made my crime, I think, the deeper. Those senseless women, whom I have so often contemned, with all the contempt that was in me, for their maudlin romance, their emotional sentiment, which make them see a god in every common-place mortal, and give them idols as many as the roses in summer, are, after all, perhaps, truer and better—fools though they be—than I. Their emotions, at least, are real, however fleeting, vain, and shallow. But I—leave me when you know it, if you will, but know it you shall—never felt one faintest touch of tenderness for any one of those who loved me, yet I was merciless enough, sinful enough, shameful enough, if you will, never to let one amongst them know that, until he was deep enough in my toils to have no power to loose himself from them. I let them hope, I let them believe, I let them think their reward sure until such time as they were mine—courage and honour and body and soul all mine—to use as I would, for the ends and in the cause of my ambitions. I let them think I loved them, and then I used their minds or their hands, their names or their strength, whichever I needed to take; and I never asked once, I never once pitied, when I knew that their hearts were broken. Go—you must think me guilty enough now. Go—for if your trust be dead, rend me out of your life once and for ever at a blow, rather than pass your years with what you doubt."

She put him from her, as she spoke, and rose; her face was very pale, grave with a profound sadness, with a set resolution. The words cost her more than it would have cost her to have thrust the Venetian dagger into her bosom to escape the pursuit of Giulio Villaflor, but they were spoken without a pause to spare herself; she loved him better than herself, and she knew that unless this man's faith were perfect in her, the lives of both would be a hell. And Idalia was too proud a woman either to submit to live suspected, or to allow such faith to be given in error and in ignorance, unmerited.

His breath was sharply drawn, as under a keen physical pain; he stood and looked at her with a look that was revenge enough for all the unpitying cruelties of her past; it was so unconsciously a rebuke, so silently and terribly in its pain a condemnation passing words.

For the first time under his gaze her head drooped, her eyes filled with tears of shame, the paleness of her face flushed; before the integral truth of his every act and word, the bold simplicity of his creeds of honour, her own life looked to her very guilty, very far from the fair light of justice and of loyalty.

"Leave me," she said to him, briefly, though her voice was very low. "But—do not *you* reproach me."

In answer his arms were stretched to her, and drew her to his breast; in that moment he had command over her, in that moment he was not her slave, but her judge. His face was grave and almost stern, for he suffered keenly, but his voice and his touch were infinitely gentle.

"Leave you? You think I know so little how to value a woman who has the noblest virtue on earth—truth?"

"Truth! when I have told you my whole life was, in one sense, a lie?"

"Truth—because you have so told me. Oh, my beloved! know me better than this. Can I not condemn your errors, and yet cherish you but the more because you need some pity and some pardon?"

She was silent, deeper smitten than by any rebuke or execration by the unutterable tenderness of this love that was too true to truth to hold her guiltless, yet too true to itself to forsake her because it condemned her. In that moment she knew how much greatness there was in this man's nature, how much dignity in his passion.

"But your trust, your faith?" she said at last, as she looked up at him.

"Will be with you ever, as my love will be."

He stooped, and leant his cheek on hers, while low in her ear a few words stole; he could not keep them back from the aching and the longing of his heart.

"Tell me but one thing. You say you wore the mask of passion to fool them;—did you ever let another before me tell you of his passion thus?"

His own lips lingered in their kisses upon hers. She drew herself from his embrace with something of her old smile, of her old scorn.

"No. Or no prayer of yours should make me your wife."

"And then you ask me if my faith be perfect still? There are scores of women—women who would censure

you—who think it no shame to bring tainted lips to
their husbands."

"Well," she said, wearily, "give me not too much
praise for being prouder, and it may be colder, than
many women are! If I never bent to the follies of
love, I was but the more blameable, perhaps, for using
them without mercy to my own ends. I tell you I
never spared. If any ever doubted or resisted me, he
had a terrible chastisement; he soon gave his very soul
and conscience up into my hands. Sometimes I think
that Mephistopheles himself never tempted more deftly
and more brutally than I have done. That dead Vanna!
He would be living now were it not for me. He was
half a Bourbon in his creeds; he worshipped pleasure,
and pleasure alone; revolutions might have reeled around
him, and Carlo would never have laid down the wine-
cup, never asked with what side the day went or the
battle turned. But I brought him to give his very life
to my moulding; I moved him to his own ruin by
those very qualities of fearless chivalry and generous
passion that should have been his shield from me. And
—if you had seen him lying dead there as I saw him,
with his brave face turned upward, that he might smile
in my eyes to the last!—"

Her head sank, there was the mute anguish on her
of a remorse that would never fade out while life remained. He stood beside her silent also; he knew that
there were no words that could assuage this bitterness,
he knew that to this self-condemnation justice forbade
any consolation that must have been at its best but a
deceiving sophistry.

"Yet you say your cause was noble?" he asked her,
gently, at the last. "It was not to gain the cruel

empty triumph of a woman's vanity that you beguiled
• them?"

"God knows! There was guilty triumph enough
in me at times. In the main—yes—it was for the
cause of freedom that I won them. *That* had been
harmless; but *my* sin was that I made them stake
their lives on me, yield their souls to me, surrender
their consciences to me because I taught them love,
and then, when they were my slaves, I used them to
their own destruction, as these charcoal-makers thrust
the fresh wood in to burn and feed their fires."

"Still—you believed that those fires were the
sacrifice-fires of the peoples' altars of liberty?"

She shivered slightly in the ardent heat of the
broad noonday.

"At first, with all the youth and passion of faith
that were in me, I *did* believe it. And I clung to
the belief long—long after I knew it had its root in
quicksands. But after I had learned how hopeless the
struggle for pure freedom is, after I had learned that
the absolutisms of thrones and churches are masked
batteries of iron and granite on to which the thinker
and the poet and the patriot fling themselves in combat
only to be crushed and perish, after I had learned that
only one amongst ten thousand of those who had the
welfare of the peoples on their lips had it also in their
hearts, and that fraud, knavery, selfish greed, impatient
discontent, corrupt ambitions, were the natures of the
liberators not less than of the tyrants;—after I had
read the bare truth to its last letter;—I lured them
still. Partly because I was irrevocably bound to the
work, partly because all my old belief would not die;
chiefly of all, because I had grown to love the power

possessed, and could not bring myself to lay it down and own my whole life a defeat. Nor was it one—" •

The warmth flushed her face again, her eyes lit with the light of victory, something of the haughty defiance with which she had challenged Giulio Villaflor, returned then as she challenged the memories of her past.

"It has been a crime, it may be—but not a failure. No Vassalis ever *failed*. I have fed hope into action, when without me it would have died out in darkness. I have armed hands that but for my weapons could never have struck their oppressors down. I have breathed liberty into a thousand lives that but for me might never have drawn in its mountain air. I have loosened the bonds of many martyrs; I have broken the chains of many captives — men who suffered agonies, here in this Italy, simply because they dared to cling to her, and seek vengeance for her violation. No. It has been no failure. Are we not victorious at the last, if the least thing for freedom have been wrought by us?"   •

She spoke not to him but to her past, as though its remorse arraigned whilst yet its conquest crowned her. She pleaded with her own conscience; she raised her cause in justification against the witness of the years that were gone; she had been true—true to the death —to the peoples of the earth and to their liberties, true to truth through all

It is a noble loyalty, one very rare amidst mankind —one that surely may avail to atone for much.

Those words were the last on her lips for many moments. From the gloom and stillness of the hut, where there was a depth of shadow only broken by the

green mosses that strewed the floor and the grey flash
of a tame pigeon's wing guarding its brood in the
farthest nook, she looked out at the luxuriance of
colour and the blaze of sun, whilst her thoughts were
sunk into the past.

He did not break her musings; his own thoughts
were filled with her history, of which he still knew, in
truth, but so little, yet which seemed to him told wholly
in those few brief sentences. Memories also came to
him, revived by her relation—memories vague and
fugitive, as of things scarcely heard before, because
without interest at the time of their hearing, of stories
that had floated to him in clubs and cafés in the cities
of Europe, long ere he had met Idalia, of some beautiful Greek or Roumelian, of whom men told marvels of
loveliness and sorcery, and about whose reputation had
gathered many splendid idle romances, fabulous as they
were contradictory—romances that gave a thousand
magnificent impossible legends to the records of her
life, but stole from her, as such romances ever will, all
"the white flower of a blameless life," and made her
pleasures as guilty, and her charms as resistless, as
those of Lucrezia or Theodora. He had never heeded
them in their telling; he had cared little for women,
still less for the babble of slanders, and they had passed
him without interest enough to linger on his remembrance an hour. But now—with the words of her
story—they recurred to him as such forgotten things
will. Not to sting him with doubts of her, with fear
for himself—suspicion of her was a thing impossible
to him—but to madden him with impatient longing
to reach her calumniators and strike them down. His
nature was too bold for slander to do more than rouse

his passion against the slanderer, his chivalry for the slandered.

"They were all lies!" he muttered in his beard, his face flushing as those distant memories stole on him. "All lies!—where are the tellers of them?"

She started slightly, and her eyes came back from their dreaming speculation and dwelt on his.

"What were the lies?"

"Things that I heard of you—once. I remember now——"

"Ah!" A quick sigh escaped her — she would so gladly have kept her life fair and unshadowed in this man's sight at least. "Well, do not blame the tellers of them; my life laid me open to misconstruction; no one can complain, if their lives do so, of any calumny that may befall them."

Her voice was cold and careless; the evil of calumny had not possessed power to wound, but it had possessed power to chill and harden her, and the venom had left its trail thus for ever.

"But why——"

He paused, not willing even by a syllable to risk trenching on that silence which she thought it fittest to keep unbroken.

"Why did I so leave it open? For many things. First, ere I knew what calumny meant—when I was so young to the world that I yet believed I and Truth could avail to convince and to conquer it!—my name was stained too deeply, all undreamt of by me, for any future career, had it been pure as a child's, to wash the stain away. I was slandered—unjustly. Slandered, I say! It was a thousand times worse than that. A traitor took the blank page of my youth and wrote

it over behind my back with infamous, indelible falsehood——"

A heavy curse broke asunder her words.

"Tell me who he was, and vengeance shall find
him."

She passed her hand over his brow with a gentle
caress.

"No. You shall have no darkness on you from
my past of my bringing. But—you do not fear to
take to your heart a woman whom the world has called
evil thus?"

"The world! What terrors do you think that liar
has for me?"

She smiled—a smile in which there was as much
of weariness as of sweetness.

"It is not always a liar; it was not so always in
what it said of me. But we will leave that! To-day
is our own; we will not poison it. You think we may
make our way to the sea to-night?"

"I do. There is little to be feared in the open
country—almost nothing from the peasantry. The
horses will be fresh, and if we can reach the little
fishing village nearest to Antina, I could send some
barcarolo to bring in my yacht. No suspicion falls on
the vessel; the soldiers I saw at your villa did not know
me, and no one will hear anything from Nicolò. We
have only to fear the sbirri——"

"Wait; tell me all. How was it you heard of my
arrest? How was it you found me?"

He told her; and she listened in the soft lull of the
noon silence, in the leafy twilight of the forest hut, to
the story of his search for her—listened with an exceeding tenderness on the face, whose careless pride so

often had smiled contemptuously on all love and all despair. He told it in very few words, lessening as much as was possible all pain he had endured, all difficulty he had conquered, lest he should seem to press a debt upon her in the recital. But the very brevity, the very generosity, touched her as no eloquence would have done. By the very omissions she knew how staunch had been this endurance, how devoted this fidelity which through good and evil report had cleaved to her, and fought their way to her.

"Oh, noble heart!"—she murmured, as she stooped to him, staying his last words,—"that I might repay you in the future! If I were only sure that I should bring you no misery—if I could only know that no evil from me would fall on you—if I could only feel there were nothing untold between us, and that my life were worthier of your noble loyalty—I would lose every coin and rood of my inheritance, and come to you beggared of everything, yet rich—my God! how richer far than now!"

He had never seen her dignity so utterly abased, her pride so utterly swept away as now, when those broken and longing utterances escaped her; he saw that memories, which were in that moment an agony, shook down all the strength and all the calmness of her nature.

"Listen!" he said, softly and gravely, while he drew her hand in his. "Beggared or crowned, you would alike be my mistress, my empress, my idol. Slandered or honoured, you will alike be the one glory of my life, the one thought in my death. Why let us speak as if we should ever part? You must slay me, or forsake me, ere ever we shall be divided now."

Hor eyes filled, as she heard him.

For some moments she answered him in no way; then, with one of the swift transitions of her changeful temperament, she looked down on him with a smile in which all her most seductive sweetness gleamed as the gold rays of the southern day flashed in the dark lustrous langour of her regard.

"*Anima mia*," she murmured, caressingly, "we will believe so, at least while we can, even—even if you should live to curse me, and I should live for Monsignore Villaflor's vengeance! Let us dream of a Future, then. I have so long thought of the world's future only, and so long not dared to give a glance at my own. Let us dream while we can. Tell me of your old Border castle. We will raise it from its ashes once more if you will. And you shall come and be lord of my great Roumelian fief, all its hills and its plains, and its rivers, and its vast solitudes with their terrible beauty, and its fortress that is a palace, like some Persian vision of the night that we see when we have fallen asleep in reading Firdusi. Ah! there is a life there possible, if we could but reach it—a life fit for your bold chieftainship, a life that might redeem my past. We both know the world to weariness. There, eastward, you and I—we might find something at least of the old ideals of my early fancies; there are a people sunk in sloth and barbarism, there are the domains of a prince, there are grand woods and waters, and mountains to be piled between us and the world, there are human minds barren of every good thing, uncultured, useless, needing the commonest tillage. I should be free there, and you would be a king in your own right. It needs just such a sovereign as you would be, my dauntless, lion-hearted wanderer! We might be happy? We might reach still more yet than merely happiness?"

And they dreamed of the Future, while the brilliant day stole onward, and the stillness of intense heat brooded over the sun-lighted earth; the Future that to him was a treasury of joys so passionate, so measureless, so incredible, that they seemed passing all hope, escaping all reach; the Future that to her was in its fairest vision but as a mirage of that lost land of peace and liberty, which her own act had forfeited for ever.

CHAPTER VIII.

"By Morning touched with Auroole Light; by Sunset stranded."

THE day declined from its noon height, and neither knew or asked how the hours were numbered.

When the sun was touching the lowest cloud, and the amber glow was burning into scarlet, he started to his feet: he remembered that the forester would be coming homeward, and that with evening their flight must begin. As they left the cabin, Idalia looked round it with a long and wistful glance; the day would be dear in her memory beyond all others, and in her own heart she believed that it was the last they should ever pass together. Then she lifted one of the rude wooden bowls to him with her old half-tender, half-haughty smile.

"The child is not here; put some coins in for us both. You must give me your gold to-day; if ever we are free, you shall be lord of all I own. Ah! you only care to be lord of myself? Do you think that I do not know that? But *I* shall care to crown you, and give you such purples as I have. You are royal to the very core of your fearless, kingly heart; and you shall reign over my kingdom, such as it is, if ever we can reach it."

They went out into the stillness of the forest, so still that they might have been alone in an unpeopled world. Here and there through the network of branches the flushed sky glowed as fire; darkness already had fallen on the slopes of the hills, behind which the sun had sunk down; on the foam of the waters opposite gleams and breadths of prismatic colour still sparkled; the evening air was heavy with fragrance, and under the foliage the lucciole began to glimmer. Erceldoune went towards the grazing horses, tethered in camp fashion by a long heel-rope, beneath the cedars; she followed him, stroking the neck of the brave sorrel that had borne her with such unflagging speed through the whole of the past night.

"Carry me as bravely again, *caro*," she murmured to him, drawing the silken mane through her hand. "Take me to freedom, and you shall have such pathless meadows of wild grass to wander in, eastward, at your will!—no curb shall ever touch you, no spur shall ever gall you!"

As she caressed the hunter, the hound at her side dropped his muzzle earthward with a low smothered growl, then lifted his head and looked at her with anxious, eager questions in his imploring eyes.

"The dog scents some danger. What is it, Sulla?" she asked, giving him that sign of silence which the animal had learned so well.

"A wolf, maybe. We will unearth him if he be anything worse," said Erceldoune, as he swept back with one arm the heavy boughs, while with his right hand he loosened the pistol from his sash. The rocks sloped sharply down; the sunset light shone on the dell beneath as he bent forward.

A cry broke from him, loud, wild, exultant as the cry of the eagle swooping to its prey. With one hand still holding upward the matted veil of foliage, he stood rooted there, all the worst passions of his nature roused in an instant into deadliest strength.

There, almost at his feet, far beneath in the curved hollow of a moss-grown, cup-shaped dell, sleeping as he himself had slept on the Capriote shore at his foe's mercy, with one arm beneath his head and the other flung idly outward, in the loose linen dress of an Italian melon-seller, lay the Greek, Conrad Phaulcon. Such disguise as he had given himself could not shield him from the glance of the man he had wronged.

Erceldoune motioned her to him with a gesture that let the leaves fall for an instant back into their places; his teeth were clenched, his words hissed broken through them, his eyes were alight with the blood-thirst of desert animals.

"Look—look!" he gasped. "There—at last—there in my power — the brute who shot me down——"

He swept the boughs backward and upward once more with the dash of his arm, and she bent to look through the twilight of the leaves; her face changed to the whiteness of death as her eyes fell on the up-turned face of the sleeping man, her lips drew their

breath gaspingly; a shiver of unutterable horror ran
through her.

"He!—he!"

That one word seemed all her voice could whisper,
and in it a whole world of loathing, remorse, hatred,
and shame unbearable seemed told.

Erceldoune, with the lifted boughs still held above
their heads, stood and gazed at her in a horror scarce
less than that with which the sight of the slumbering
Greek had stirred her.

"*You* know him!"

She seized his wrist, and, with the convulsive force
that comes to the most delicate women in their hours
of extremity, shook his grasp from the arm of the tree,
whose foliage fell once more between them and the
sight of that bright Athenian beauty that lay there in
the careless rest of the Lykegênes.

"Know him!—do I know him!"

"Ay! Do *you* know the man who sought to murder
me?"

There was the first sternness of waking fury, the
first unconscious violence of stealing doubt, in the
question as it broke from him, while he vainly
wrought to wrench his wrists from the close grasp
she held them in, and be free to fall upon his enemy
as lions fall on their foes. With them her courage
returned, her self-command came back to her, though
her face was bloodless still, and anguish was set on
it; she looked him full in the eyes—eyes for the first
time bent on her with the searching severity of an
accuser.

"Yes. I know him. I did *not* know that he was
your assassin, though—though—I grant I feared it."

"Feared it! What is he to you?"

She was silent.

"What is he to you—this brigand, this brute, this vilest of the vile scum of Europe?"

He spoke with the imperious vehemence, the intolerable horror, that possessed him. She was silent still; over her face a hot flush came and went, the flush of an intense humiliation.

"What do you know of him? Answer me, before I wring it out of his throat!"

She shuddered where she stood; but with a strength scarce less than his own, she held him from the place where the Greek slept, and drew him by sheer force farther and farther outward.

"Let him be! He has been the curse of my fate; he will be the curse of yours."

"Never! I will stamp his life out where he lies. Let me go—let me go!"

"Go for what?"

"To deal with him—justly."

"Justly!"

"Yes. Men kill murderers; and it was through no lack of will in him he was not one. I will not kill him sleeping, but I will wash my wrongs out once for all. Let me go!"

She flung her arms close around him, so that he must have wrenched her beautiful limbs asunder before he could have left her; she drew him backward and backward, her breath against his cheek, her hair showered on his breast, her dignity broken, her self-control forgot, vivid emotion, agonised abandonment, making her a hundredfold more resistless in that hour than she had ever been in her proudest moments of supremacy. She knew her power; under that embrace he stood subdued, irresolute, remembering nothing except the loveliness on which he looked.

"Is that your love?" she asked him. "Is that your trust?"

She felt a tremor run through all his frame—the tremor of the blind rage against his foe, of the blind idolatry of her, that warred within him.

"I break neither because I will deal with my assassin! What is he to you that you should shield him?"

The first taint of jealousy ran through the words. The tremor of shame that he had seen when her glance first fell upon the Greek passed over her; yet her gaze met his, and never sank beneath it.

"I cannot tell you."

There was an accent of hatred deep as his own in the low words; he looked with a terrible eagerness into her eyes.

"*Cannot!* Wait. You say you never loved; were you never wedded where you hate?"

"Never."

"Then what is this villain to you?"

She seemed to shrink and shiver where his arms held her, as though his words stabbed her through and through. She kept silence still.

"Tell me," he swore to her, "or, as God lives, that tiger shall, with my shot through his brain to pay for the confession!"

"Hush, hush! If he wake, we are lost!"

"I will wake him in such fashion that he never wakes again! An assassin *your* care? Let me go—let me go, I tell you!"

He strove to put her arms from him, to fling off him the coil of her hair, to break from the paralysing spell of her beauty; but she would not loosen him, she would not be shaken off—she drew him farther and farther from the Greek, let him seek as he would to escape from her.

"Oh, my beloved—my beloved! where is the faith you promised me? One trial—and it breaks! With such a life as mine, do you not know that there must be far darker things than this to try you? Have you not said that you will cleave to me through all? Have you not refused to believe even my own word against me?"

"God knows it, yes! But——"

"Here is the first test, then; were your oaths empty words?"

He was silent; he stood motionless and unnerved under the brief touch of the rebuke. She knew that she had bound him in those withes of honour that he would never break; and she knew that she had touched him in the one noble weakness that laid him utterly at her will and mercy. She loosened her hold from him; she stood apart, and left him free.

"Go, if you will. Suspect me, if you will. Avenge your wrong, if you will. But if you do, we never meet again."

His lips parted, without sound; an anguish of appeal looked at her from his eyes; he stood consumed by the passions of his hate and of his love that strove with one another in a deadly conflict.

"Choose," she said, simply—and waited.

His chest heaved with a mighty sigh.

"Great Heaven! You ask me to spare him after such a crime!"

"I ask you nothing. Take your vengeance, it is your right; but you will never look upon my face again."

"Because I am his foe?"

"No? Because you doubt me."

With that one word she pierced him to the quick.

He had no strength, no memory, no thought, save of her and of her will; he looked back once to where his slumbering traitor lay, with the mad longing of denied vengeance in the look, then slowly, and with his head bent, he turned away.

"Be it as you will. I yield you to-day more than my life itself."

And as she heard, all her coldness and her imperious resolve died out, as though they had not been; she sank into his outstretched arms, and wept as she had never done in all her haughty womanhood—wept uncontrollably, agonisedly, in such abandonment, in such weakness, as the sovereign temper in her never, ere then, had known.

At sight of that grief he forgot his own wrong, his own doubt, his very vengeance; he remembered nothing, except that the woman for whom he would have laid down his life suffered thus, while to her suffering he could bring no more consolation than though he stood a stranger before her. It was not in him to have one thought of his own cause of hatred against this man, when once he saw that she endured this poignant and deadly pain through his assassin, this unutterable misery at sight of the sleeping Greek, whose face turned upward, with the sunset warmth and flickering

shadow of the leaves playing on it, thus had broken all
their dreams of the future, all the sweetness of their
solitude.

She lay passive some moments in his arms, her
whole frame shaken by convulsive, tearless sobs.

"Oh God!" she moaned. "And I dreamt of a Future, while *he* was living there!"

A gloom like night swept over her lover's face;
the evil spirit was upon him, which in the midnight
chase through the moonlight of the Bosphorus shore
had been on him, thirsting for his enemy's blood. He
stooped his head over her, and his whisper was fear-
fully brief.

"Let me go, and he will not be living long."

He had surrendered to her; he had yielded up to
her this vengeance, which had been the one goal of
such ceaseless search, such vain desire; but though he
had let her for awhile hold his hands from it, his whole
heart and soul were in tempestuous rebellion still; his
blood was hot for war, his conscience was strangled by
hatred.

"Let me go," he whispered, thirstily. "You shall
see him lie dead at your feet—dead, like the brave
horse that rotted to carrion through him."

She shivered, as though an ice-cold wind had passed
over her; but danger had been too long her atmo-
sphere, and the tempests of men's hearts too long the
powers by which she swayed them, not to nerve her to
force and calmness when both were needed. She was
deathly pale, except for those flushes of shame that
had made the blood rush backward to her veins; but
she spoke tranquilly, laying her hand upon his mouth,

and with that command which never, in moments of
need, deserted her.

"Peace.　　Those are not like yourself — those
tiger instincts.　Leave them to him; they are beneath
you."

"They are not.　They are my right."

"Is revenge ever a right?"

"We deemed it so in old Scotland.　A right
divine!"

His face was stern and evil still, with the storm of
his longing wrath, with the pent tide of his loosening
jealousy.

"Divine?　Devilish!　Right or wrong, lay it down
for my bidding."

He was silent.　Under her hands she felt the
muscles of his arm thrill and swell; against her breast
she felt the stifled panting of his breath. To hold him
back, was like holding in leash a gazehound when it
sees the stag.

"Lay it down, or you are man-sworn, and fore-
sworn."

She spoke with a vivid intensity in the words that
left her clenched teeth so low, so slowly; she knew
every chord in the nature of this man, as fine artists
know every note in the diapason of the instrument that
echoes and vibrates to their slightest touch.

He held his peace; he would not break his word
to her—break his word to a woman, and that woman
defenceless, and his mistress, and his life's pledged
law; but his hunger of desire was terrible to fall on
that sleeping panther lying so near, and to deal on him
ten thousand blows.

She saw the struggle in him, and her heart went

out to him in it—went out to the strength and the
weakness that were so blent in it, the strength of honour and the weakness of passion. How often she had
seen these two antagonists strive against each other to
hold and to keep a soul!

"Oh, my love!" she murmured, as she drew him
farther and farther from the place where his foe slept.
"Give me this one thing, and you shall have all my
life. Let him be—let him be. He took all; he shall
not take you. Come, come, come!"

He held back still, while still her arms clung to
him, and drew him onward and onward to leave his
murderer in peace.

"One word only," he muttered, close in her ear,
while his lips, as they brushed her throat, scorched it
like fire. "You deny me my vengeance. Is it for love
of *me*—or pity of *him?*"

The eyes, that he could have sworn were true as
he would have sworn that the stars shone above them,
looked up long into his; there was a depth of pain in
them that smote and stilled his wrath as with a sudden
awe.

"Both. I love you, as I never thought it in me to
love any—the living or the dead; and I pity him, as
the earliest, the latest, the most wretched of all my
enemies, though they are many as the sands of the sea.
Have I answered you now? Come!"

The intonation of the words, rather than their meaning, laid their own solemnity on him; he read that in
her eyes, before which his own wrongs seemed to dwarf,
and pale, and die out.

"Do with me as you will; I cannot reach you—in
all things—but I will follow as best I may."

She seemed to him so far above him with this royal past, that had given her the sway over royalties, with this lofty serene generosity from which she looked with compassion on one whom she declared the greatest enemy of her life.

She started as if the homage stung her like an adder—as if the reverence of his words were some unbearable disgrace.

"Never say that! Never,—never. Follow me in nothing. Teach me your own brave, straight, knightly creeds. Let me see your noble honesty of thought and purpose, and let me steep myself in truth, and have it cleanse me if I can! Ah! once before we go, let me hear you say that you forgive me. Forgive me all you know — forgive me all that is hidden from you."

The remorse with which, in the dawn of that day, she had bidden him flee from her for ever, the abasement that had broken down her dignity, and laid her subject before him, were tenfold intensified now in a humiliation that crushed down like a bent reed the bold imperious spirit that had never quailed before. She seemed broken by an unutterable contrition; stricken before him by the conscious guilt of a criminal before her judge; the prayer for pardon, the thirst for his mercy, seemed to be as intense as if the crime against his life had been woven by her brain, and instigated by her will, as though the hand of the Greek, sleeping unconscious in the hollowed cleft of rock below, had been her tool and servant.

Yet there was not one pause of doubt, one hesitation of dread, in the answer that came to her with a gentleness, grave and infinitely sad.

"Forgive!   That is no word between you and me.
Yet,—if there be anything of pardon needed from my
life to yours in past, or present, or future, I give the
pardon now, once and for ever; you cannot stretch it
farther than my love will yield it."

She heard, and her head sank downward, till her
lips touched his hand in the sign of homage and allegiance that she had refused to the claim of monarchs.
Her eyes were blind with tears, her heart was filled
with a despair bitter as death, with a sweetness sweet
as life; he was at once her slave and her ruler, her
judge and her saviour.

"Ah, Heaven!" she said, in her soul.   "How vainly
I sought for a great nature amidst those who called
themselves the leaders of the earth.   I never found
it until now; and now—how little it knows itself as
great!"

Without a word he loosed her from his arms, as
though by that abstinence from any utterance or caress
of passion to show that no mere passion goaded him to
the forgiveness which a higher and purer tenderness
bestowed, and would so bestow through the uttermost
ordeal, and up to the last hour.   Silently he led the
horses from the place, their hoofs noiselessly sinking
in the rank deep grass, drew the girths closer, and
made the few preparations that were needed for their
night-ride to the sea.

His foe was left in peace; it was a heavier surrender
to her than any that had ever been made, many and
wide and weighty though they were, the sacrifices that
she had wooed, or commanded from those who had
obeyed no law like the bidding of her lips.   His heart
was sick within him.   The old religion of revenge,

which had been sacred to his forefathers in the age
when murderers were proven by bier-right, and the
flaming cross of war was borne alight over moor and
mountain, was in many a moment his religion still; it
was "wild justice" in his eyes, and a justice best meted
out from foe to foe without the judgment of any alien
voice. To turn away and leave his enemy unaroused;
to skulk and flee as though he were the evil-doer; to
let the murderer lie there unawakened, unarraigned,—
a deadlier thing than this she could not have demanded
at his hands.

The sweetness of the day had died with the setting
of the sun, and the darkness of night had fallen on
their lives as on the earth where they dwelt. Silently
they mounted, and passed away; silently they turned
and looked backward with a long and lingering gaze
at the forest roof, which well might prove their last
refuge together, the last shelter in which they should
ever dream of freedom and of a future. Then through
the first shadows of evening, under the deep gloom of
the woods, beside the melancholy moaning of the
hidden river channels, they went onward in their flight
from Church and King, onward to the sea, if they
could ever reach the sweet fresh liberty of its wide
waters.

And as they went—where the leafy depths enclosed, and the forest twilight hid them—the Greek
rose slowly, with the heavy lethargy, and the weakness
of overwrought fatigue still on him, like some fierce
yet timorous panther that has been roused from rest to
a craven dread and a longing for slaughter both in one.
Through his sleep words had come to him, mingling

with his dreams; instincts had stirred in him while yet
the weight of that death-like slumber had laid like lead
on his eyelids; a voice had roused the dormant images
of memory; a sense of some presence, some peril, some
rising of hate and of fear, had come on him ere he had
been sensible; he had shaken the clinging stupor from
him with supreme effort; he had glanced upward through
the boughs of cedar; he had made one eager, springing
movement like a panther, with a panther's lust in his
eyes, and a thousand warring passions at his heart;—
then the craft of his nature, the cowardice of his nation,
conquered the bolder and more ferocious impulse, as
well as the jealous, wayward, tyrannous affection that
still, with all his vice, lived in him; the dread of his
antagonist was blent with the instinct of his blood towards treachery in the place of defiance. He feigned
sleep afresh, lying as though still in the profound peace
of that dreaming rest; lying so with the soft brown
lashes on his cheek, and his head idly thrown back
upon his arm, until the hoofs of the horses had ceased
to crush the cyclamen and hellebore, and the screen of
forest foliage had fallen between him and the man
whom he hated with the reckless bitterness of the injurer
to the injured, the woman whom he loved despite all,
though he adored tyranny and evil, and gold and selfish
gains, and the brutal exercise of a pitiless jealousy, far
more.

Then, as they passed away, he staggered to his
feet, and stood a moment, in the red after-glow that
streamed upon him, erect, quivering, instinct with rage
like some lithe, beautiful, murderous forest beast, the
ruddy light burning in the glow of his eyes, and cast
luridly on the spirited head and perfect form that were

graceful and splendid as the legendary beauty of Arin-
thœus.

"*She* can love?   The world should end to-night!"

CHAPTER IX.

"Athene to a Satyr."

By dawn they had reached the shore, having bent
far southward of where Naples lay, and so round to
the sea.

Here the worn-out horses, fasting and drenched with
steam, and spent with fatigue paused, under the great
shadow of a mighty wall of cliff that rose up from the
breadth of smooth and yellow sand, its sides jagged
and honeycombed, its crest overhung with festoons of
wild vine and crowned with the grey plumes of
olive, the waters idly lapping the amber beach below,
and reaching outward till the dim sea-line and the mist-
laden skies of morning blent in one. Involuntarily
she stretched her hands to it in welcome and in
prayer, as though the Sea-God of her fathers lived
and heard.

"Oh waters! give me your liberty."

They looked so wide, so cool, so deeply still,
stretching out in their measureless freedom to the infinite.

"It is gentler than earth," she muttered. "Men
die hardly on the bitterness of the land—the land
which devours them that she may blossom and laugh
with fruits born of corruption;—but the very death
that the sea gives is dreamy and tranquil. And the
sea will not render its dead, but loves them, and lulls

them, and holds them ever with their stories untold. Where is there any other thing so merciful as that?"

There was the longing of a melancholy, weary to despair, through the poet-like thought of the murmured words; in that moment she would gladly have sought the unbroken rest that could alone be found in the deep sea-bed, beneath those fathomless and changeless waves.

She sank down on a broken pile of rock, with the ribbed sand at her feet and the bulwark of the mighty cliff rising above; her face was colourless, haggard, almost stern, as though there were set on it such hatred of herself that all its youth and brilliancy changed to one bitter heart-sick scorn; her hair was thrust back off her brow; her eyes looked with a tearless, thirsty pain over the waters. There had been silence between them well-nigh through all the hours of that night-ride to the sea; there was silence still; he stood beside her with the darkness of her thoughts flung back on his.

"You are certain?" she said, suddenly, at last.

"Dou you think men forget their murderers?"

She laughed slightly—a laugh that sent a shudder through his blood.

"Well—your murderer was the man that had the hewing and the shaping of my life. Do you wonder now that it was evil?"

"Of yours? Oh God!"

"A fair comrade!—a noble tutor! What think you? A lofty close for my imperial ambitions, is it not? A priest's cell my prison-house, a criminal's flight my safety, a thief and an assassin my associate, my——"

Her teeth closed once more, shutting in the word

that would have escaped them; a shiver of agony shook him as he heard.

"Twice you have checked my vengeance, and bidden me 'spare!'" he muttered. "If these brutes *be* your foes, why call me off their throats?"

"A lion shall not choke snakes."

The brevity gave the deeper meaning to the words.

"Why speak in parables? You must know——"

"That your faith is dying? Well, let it die. It has every right. *I* will not reproach you!"

"It will never die. But—why should you wring my heart to test it?"

"Test it! Ah! do not wrong me like that! Do you think I would cause you an instant's pain that was in my power to spare? Do you think I would spend a woman's miserable chicaneries and heartless vanities on you, or triumph in them at your cost?"

"Answer me," she pursued; her voice had changed to intense appeal, to vivid emotion, and she held his hands close against her heart, looking upward at him with a longing that broke down all her courage and her pride—the longing that he, at least, should know that she was true to him, though she must withhold him from his justice, and deny him all he had a title to hear. "Be my law, my conscience—I have been steeped so long in evil, I have lost all fitness to judge honour or dishonour aright. To tell you all, to lay my life before you as it should be laid, I must break my oath, I must belie my word, I must be false to the chief thing that has ever redeemed my past. Answer me—shall I do it?"

She saw a tremor shake him as a great storm shakes the rooted strength of cedars; his head sank;

a fierce conflict was at war within him. For a while
he hesitated; torn by an anguish of desire to speak
the word that should unloose the bonds of silence
between them.

Then a brave gentleman's inborn instincts conquered him:—

"No," he said simply. "Be true to yourself, and
you will never be false to me. For the rest, you know
me. I can wait."

And she who heard him knew that with that refusal he had put from him what cost him more in the
renunciation than sceptres laid aside have cost to those
who put them by at the dictation of a pure and generous honour beyond all selfish sway, as his was now
beyond it.

"You are great beyond men's nobility," she answered
him. In that momentary weakness she had longed that
he should bid her sacrifice her word and her bond to
him, but he was far higher and dearer in her sight
because he denied that weakness its way; she had much
strength herself, and she loved such strength in men.
"But—but—have you no fear when I tell you that my
life has been tainted by such as he?"

"I have but the fear that, if I look ever on his face
again, I shall turn murderer like him."

A shudder passed over her.

"Nay! why not revenge yourself on me? I was
his associate. How can you know I was not his accomplice?"

"How! Have I not looked into your eyes?"

The infinite trust that the reply breathed was rather
in the tone than in the words.

"Well! What do a woman's eyes ever do but lie?

And yet look, look for ever, if you will, so that you learn from them that my heart is truth, but that my past is—shame!"

He stood beside her, silent; his faith would not leave nor his love forsake her, but the abyss of a heavy guilt yawned between them, the barrier of a pitiless silence severed them.

Yet—passion and faith were strong in him; stronger than wisdom, stronger than vengeance. He stooped and laid his lips upon her brow.

"The shadow of others' shame may darken you; no shame of yours is on you. Whatever you are—be mine!"

The sea stretched outward, league on league of still grey water, with no colour on it in the young hours of the dawn, no life, save the movement here and there of some awakening ocean bird. The cliffs, tawny and water-stained and sun-browned, rose aloft, curving inward, and shaping one of the many indents of the irregular southern coast; mighty shafts of stone that seemed to touch the skies, and were deeply riven here and there in fissures filled with the clinging of the vine. Grand, solitary, wild, there was no human aid, no boat's help to be looked for here.

The sea lay there, but between them and liberty it stretched, an inexorable desert, impassable, and giving no freedom except death.

"Moments are years; we cannot waste them," he muttered, as he looked across the waters, where no sail broke the space, and upward at the rocks which frowned, sterile and lonely, locking in the breadth of ribbed beach-sand. "A fisher-boat, sea-worthy, might save us still. There is a village that should lie not far from this. A cluster of fishing-cabins——"

"Yes, there is one a mile northward of us. A few huts under the cliff, and men who have the sea's strength in them when once they are afloat. Go you to them."

"Go! And leave you?"

"Else we must perish together."

"Better that!"

"No; you shall not die by Bourbon steel for me. I am known well in the country; the story of my arrest must be common to all now. This masque dress, which is all they left me, would draw curiosity at once. You look like a *marinaro;* you can hire the boat unsuspected, you can steer here, and, once here, with our pistols at their foreheads we can make the sailors take what way we will. Go. I shall fire if any danger come. You will hear the shot far in this still air."

"Is there no other way?"

"None. Leave me—there is no fear. And, in truth, I could not move farther yet. I am worn out at last."

She spoke faintly, wearily, and a grey hue stole over all her face, as she leaned her head upon her arm, her eyes lustreless, and with their lids heavily drooped, looking outward at the sea, whose grave she coveted. The fearlessness that had challenged death; the force that had endured any torture rather than purchase peace by the betrayal of comrades; the high and dauntless spirit that had laughed at danger, and loved peril for its very hazard's sake: these, which would never have yielded to any tyranny, or pang, or

jeopardy that could have tried them, were unstrung
and crushed by the horror which had possessed her
from the first moment that she had seen the sleeping
Greek and heard his crime. Humiliation rested on
her; the deadliest suffering such a nature as hers can
ever know—a thing which, until the sun had set in
the past day, had never touched her temper. A shame
that was ineffaceable seemed to her burnt into her life
for ever, and under it a strength which had never
succumbed, a dignity which had never blenched or
quailed before the sternest trials, surrendered at last.
She had had the fortitude of men, the fearlessness of
soldiers, but they seemed, for the hour at least, to die
out in her now.

He looked at her, and he saw that the privations
of her prison, the scant food of many days, the exertion of the long and breathless ride, had told heavily
upon her;—and he who would have coined his very
life to purchase aid for her, could do no more for her
than the flock of sea-gulls that flew past them with the
breaking of the morning.

He struck his heel into the sand with an agony of
powerless grief.

"You will perish here of hunger, of thirst, of sun-
stroke, of misery! I will go. I will bring help, if
there be help on earth."

He went down the low strip of sanded shore, under
the beetling shadow of the cliffs, northward to the
fishing village on the edge of the waters, with low
rounded cabin-roofs that were like clustered brown bee-
hives beneath the giant shadow of the rocks. The wall
of stone screened him from view; the hamlet was a
mile or more along the coast; she was left alone, with

the hound at her feet, the loaded weapon in her hand,
the glistening sea ebbing away into the distance where
her eyes were fixed.

She sat motionless, whilst the noise of his footfall
on the wet sands died gradually away. She listened
to them to their last faint sound.

"Ah! if only for his sake he could pass out from
my life for ever," she murmured. "Either way I must
sin to him;—by forsaking him, or by cleaving to
him. To go to his heart with such dishonour as *that*
untold——"

She could have wished that the stroke of the sun,
rising stormily eastward, could reach and still her life;
that the waves rolling slowly one on another to her
feet could come to her and wash her down into their
darkness. For she felt tainted with an assassin's and
a traitor's guilt of secrecy and shame. She laughed a
little, with the unutterable weariness of futile pain;
with the ironical temper which had so long made
jest of every suffering, that it scarcely now spared her
own.

"I know now what sort of despair fills monasteries
and makes saints," she thought. "How honourable to
Deity, to give him the flotsam and jetsam of a wrecked
existence!"

Twelve hours before she had said, and said truly,
that none of her race ever failed; she had known that
her life had been great in much even whilst blamable
in more; she had spoken of a future, in which much
of dominion, of magnificence, of a pure and noble ambition would still linger;—a future in the glow of
eastern suns, in the lands of her inheritance, in the
exercise of a chieftainship, where boundless evil re-

mained to be conquered, and boundless liberty to be enjoyed; a future in consonance with the hatred of all bondage, and the genius to rule, that were inborn in her. Yet now—now, since she had stooped down and seen the ruddy afterlight upon the face of the slumbering Athenian—an endless night seemed to have fallen on her, and every dream of future and of freedom to be mockery.

Through the silence of the quiet dawn she sat without any movement; the half-dead horses were feebly trying to find food from the salted grasses and drink from the brackish pools; there was no sound, except the monotonous chiming of the Mediterranean at her feet, no refuge in the hard and barren surface of the colossal seawall. She had sent him from her, chiefly for his sake, that he should not wait beside her till he was netted by the Church's webs, or slaughtered by the monarchist's steel, and an unutterable loneliness was about her; there seemed no mercy on the face of the waters, but only a cold and dreary smile. Beyond them lay liberty; but she felt as though even the force to arise and seek it had been killed in her.

Time passed in slow, sickening measure; the sullen light of a tempestuous morning burned higher in the heavens; full day was come; the couchant hound awoke with menace in his eyes; across the sands at her feet a shadow fell: there was no sound, no word, but she felt the presence, as men feel the gliding abhorred presence of a snake, the stealing velvet-footed approach of a tiger, ere they know that either are near. She started, and rose to her feet, and fell slowly backward step by step, till she rested against the wall of cliff, her gaze fastened on Conrad Phaulcon as he

stood, with the crimson sun in his face, and the grey
water lying in a lonely waste behind him.

"Ho, Miladi!" he cried aloud, "others can ride a
wild ride besides your lover and you. I have been on
your track all the night through. Where is he?—
where? Answer me, or——"

She threw up her hands with a gesture, that even
in that moment awed him:

"Never dare breathe his name!—*you*, his robber,
his assassin."

"Robber! Assassin! Strange words to me."

The fire of his wrath was bated for an instant before the resurrection of the crime he had deemed buried
from her reach beneath the solitary shadows of the
Carpathian pine-woods.

"Would that they *were* strange to you! I knew
that coward sin had your hand in it, and you swore by
the only memory you have ever reverenced that you
were innocent. I believed you—I was fool enough for
that!—because, though treachery was your native air,
you still at your worst had never taken perjured oath
by that one name."

She spoke slowly, wearily, with an unutterable reproach and bitterness in the quiet words; under them
he was for the moment cowed; he shook slightly through
all his limbs, and his teeth gnawed the gold curls of
his beard.

"It was to serve what you worship—Liberty!" he
stammered.

"Liberty! No marvel that the peoples are in chains
if the apostles of their freedom think to serve them
thus."

The words echoed over the stillness of the tranquil

seas with a profound eternal pathos; it was the sigh of the Girondists, when through the death-mists of the scaffold they saw the angel of freedom they had dreamed of changed into a vampire of blood.

The man before her, the lover who had left her, were alike forgotten; in that moment her heart was with the nations of the earth, the blind who find but the blind to lead them when they escape the iron heel to track them down; the vast sum of suffering and heart-sick humanity that has no choice betwixt those who leave it to perish in its slough, or beat it forth to rot on battle-fields, and those who fill its parching throat with the fetid water of distorted truths, and fool its patient ignorance with lying grossness, that by it they may force upward into power.

First—beyond all, grief for them was with her; for those innumerable, uncounted, uncompassionated millions who are the prey alike of despot and of demagogue, by each alike condemned to be the long, unnoted, pitilessly-consumed coil of fusê, lit and burnt out, to bear the flame by which ambition may show red against the skies, or to carry incendiarism in a conqueror's van. This reigned with her beyond all things; had so reigned ever, and would reign until her grave; this impersonal love, this infinite pity, for the concrete suffering, the weary destinies of the peoples, on whom "the burden of the unintelligible world" is bound so hardly, so unequally.

Phaulcon laughed out in defiance of the scorn that lashed him like a whip of scorpions.

"Fine acting—you were always a fine actress!— but this could come as nothing new to you, Miladi. You were sure that your friends were in it——"

"God forgive you! I *was* sure until you swore your innocence; and then—though I might have known that truth trying to pass your lips would become false-hood in such tainted passage!—I did you too much honour, and believed you."

No virulence and no invective could have cast on him so much shame as these last words.

He laughed carelessly still; where he felt himself a coward there he became a bravo; with the rankling wound of humiliation came the brutalised instinct to insult.

"Said you believed me rather! The Countess Vas-salis was always famous for her finesses. Beyond a doubt she had the tact to assume a fitting ignorance of anything that might have compromised her."

She looked him in the eyes till his own fell: she deigned no further answer.

"Idalia!"—he began to plead more huskily and hurriedly.

"You have lost all title to call me by that name. Put land and sea between us henceforth for evermore. Never let me look upon your face again—never, never, never!"

Her voice, losing its controlled coldness, broke from her with an irresistible intensity, while as her arm pointed outward to the waters, she banished him from every soil she touched, from every air she breathed. For one moment the force of the magnificent gesture, rather than of the words of banishment, thrilled, awed, and intimidated him; he fell back involuntarily a step or two upon the tawny sands.

"Go, go!" she said, still with that movement of her hands which thrust him from her with such com-

mand as that wherewith the Scandinavian priest thrust
back with his golden crosier the bloodstained King
who came to the altar-steps with murder on his soul.
"Go! Show the only remorse and reparation that you
can still reach, and let my life be free of you for
ever."

Again it had its weight on him, that sentence of
banishment, grandly given, yet withal having in it a
certain aching regret as of one who once had loved
him well, though he had fallen; as of one who owed
him deadliest wrong and abhorred in him deadliest
guilt, yet who, for memories not wholly perished, could
not yield him up unpitied to the dominion of evil, to
the wreck of body and soul. He remembered all that
this woman had endured through him; he remembered
how by him shameful treachery had attainted the glorious
morning of her youth; how by him shadows that could
never wholly pass from her had been flung across the
splendour of her womanhood.

"Stay, hear me a second," he said, with a gentler
accent in the hesitation of the words. "You think I
bear you no tenderness—I do, by Heaven I do, though
often I come so near to hate you. If I had been
at Antina, those brutes should never have touched
you. Ever since I first heard of it, I have been seeking you. And it is in peril of my life I stay an hour
in the kingdom; twofold peril, from the Bourbon's
grip, and from one surer still to know it and to
strike."

"Surer? One does not live."

"Yes, *one* does; one that is ten thousand eyes and
ears and lips incorporate, one that is thrice ten thousand intellects fused together, one that may strike me

down from behind, and throw me like a dead dog into a wayside ditch, only for this, that I disobeyed and stayed in Naples to be near your prison."

She knew that the "many in one" he spoke of, the far-reaching invisible hand, the wide unerring prevision and condign vengeance that he dreaded, were those of the political society to which he had been bound in the early days of his manhood, when fretting poverty had goaded, restless intrigue had allured, and a warped yet at the first not ignoble love of freedom and of country had impelled him to its far-spread nets.

"You say this? So you also said, by all you held most sacred, that you had no share in and no knowledge of this attempted murder?"

She spoke slowly, and with icy chillness that cast back on him a hundred-fold more piercingly than by invective the thousand times of falsehood when he had dealt treacherously by her, and so forfeited all right, all power to force on her that he now uttered truth. The last two words cut asunder, and broke down as though they had never been, the softer better thought, that in the moment previous had made him well-nigh forget all else except the peril of death, or of a life worse than death, to which she, wronged in so much, had but so late escaped by a hair's breadth.

In that instant, whilst she spoke, the fear had passed from him, the knowledge of his power had risen again; jealousy, and avarice, and lust of tyranny were stronger-lived in him than the sting of conscience, than the awakening of shame.

"Wait an instant," he said, sullenly. "There is too close a tie between us for us to part in that fashion."

"To a tie that you have outraged you cannot appeal."

"We are too needful to each other to sever so——"

"I am needful to you, doubtless. But you will never again make of me, or tool, or weapon, or guide, or gold-mine for your evil service."

"Ah! Fine thing a woman's word. But a few days since you told me, with imperial scorn, that you had some reverence for your oath?"

"I had;—how much, let all I have lost, and sinned, and wrecked, and slain for you bear witness."

"And yet!——"

"And yet—here in your hands I break it, and break from it. I am absolved from my vows for ever. *I* swore them to a patriot; you I know not—*you*, a brigand, an assassin!"

"Is an apostate nobler than an assassin, then, that you vaunt your treachery and upbraid mine?"

"Nobler in nothing; but apostacy is your guilt, not mine. To truth, to liberty, to the peoples, I am loyal; you have forsaken these—forsaken! were you ever true to them? did ever you know aught of them?— and leagued yourself with fraud, with avarice, with slaughter."

"Bitter words."

"Bitter? God pardon you!—if you heard but sheer and simple justice of all your guilt to me, would not the blackest words in language fail to yield your due? But—let us part in silence; I cannot give you over to your proper fate, for the sake of the only life we ever cherished in common. Tempt my vengeance no longer; if you be wise, go—go while I can still let you go unharmed."

"I stayed, at peril of life, to succour you if I could—to learn your fate, to find your enemies, and, in reward of that, saw you ten hours ago lavishing love upon your foreign favourite, on his heart, in his arms—*you!*"

"Well?"

She looked him full in the eyes still, with a deep and steady gaze; there was a firm, lowering gloom in her own, like the look which comes into the eyes of one who, brave and resolved, still counts the danger that lies before him, and finding it vast, yet resolves but the more fixedly to go through it.

"You did it maybe to dupe him?" he pursued, with the insolent riot of his silver-toned laughter, the louder because he had no belief in his own translation of her acts. "He had a strong arm to force back your gaol bars, and a wild brain to be lulled with your charming. You played the comedy with many—who so well?—was it but acted once again with him? You have done scores of daintier and more dangerous things, than so easy a victory as blinding and duping this mountain athlete, and you have fooled men for far less stakes than to free yourself from the gripe of our holy Monsignore. Tell me that was your project, and I will pardon it, though you blackened my name so heavily in the little melodrama. Was it? Yes, or no!"

"No!"

The answer was brief and cold; she knew that for it this man was likely enough to fire into her bosom, where he stood before her, the weapon whose muzzle thrust itself out from the folds of his striped canvas shirt.

For once he kept his coolness; she knew him then

to be at his worst; his vehement, eloquent, womanish wrath was never so dangerous as when, contrary to all his temperament, he held it in check and waited, softly, silently, warily.

"No?" he laughed in echo. "What! has Miladi Vassalis gone scatheless in her scorn for all these years to be charmed by a rough-rider's iron sinews and gigantic limbs at last! Bathos!—terrible bathos! And what will you do, madame, with your new lover?—have him killed to keep the secret of your weakness, like that fair frail Jewess of the French Regency of whom we read?"

Under the coarse infamy of the sneer her face never flushed, her eyes never relaxed their steady challenge of him; but a hatred beyond all words gathered darkly in her regard, a scorn beyond all words set on her colourless lips.

"What will you do with him?" he repeated, scoffingly. "How will you square his claims and mine? If you should get your liberty again, my Countess, your favourite courier will slightly embarrass you!"

"You possess no claims."

"Truly? We will see that. But first, what will you do with him?"

"What shall I do? I will tell you. Give him my life, and defy yours."

"Ah! As his mistress or as his wife?"

"His wife."

"Indeed! And make him a chieftain in Roumelia, I suppose?"

"Why not?"

"Why not, truly! He will be admirably fitted to play the mountain king, the barbaric lord; and you—

well, your new fancy may endure six months. I will
give it that lease of life; and then—men easily dis-
appear in those hill fastnesses, where every creature is
your humble vassal!"

Her face flushed with a dark tempestuous shadow
as she heard; she gave one movement, rapid, passionate,
involuntary—it was to raise her pistol for the signal
shot. The gesture was restrained; she looked her antagonist firmly in the eyes.

"Cease this. There are none here to be cheated
with your outrages, and to insult me will bring you no
result. Once for all, hear and understand;—this one
man has become dear to me, and, what is more, is
honoured by me. I shall be true to him, and I shall
defend him—as he has given truth and defence to
me."

The words were very passionless, but they were
inflexible as steel; his face changed lividly as he heard.

"Wait! You know the fate we give deserters?"

"Death? Well, you can slay me if you will. It
will worthily close your course. Be sure of this—you
will not scare me with the threat of it."

"'Threat! Miladi, you will find it more than
threat."

"'Too likely. But I shall be his before it is borne
out."

"What! you love him well enough to risk death
for him—such a death!—by night, by stealth, in your
beauty, in your youth?"

"Else should I love little."

The Greek looked at her in silence for a moment.
He had dealt with her in many moods, but never yet
in one where this emotion ruled her. He had never

known its pulse beat in her; he was stunned and bewildered by his own rage; he could almost have found it in his soul to deal her there and then the fate that she so tranquilly accepted and defied.

"Wait, then," he said, slowly, "You do not fear it for yourself—do you for him?"

She did not answer; he saw a slight shiver pass over her; he had found the one weak link through which to pierce the armour of her proud and resolute strength.

"You do? That is well. Then listen to one warning: the first night this man sleeps in your arms shall be his last. Wed him and kill him, if you like!"

CHAPTER X.

"The Serpent's Voice less subtle."

The fishing hamlet lay under the shadow of a sea-worn, red-brown, sullen cliff, that had the mists of the dawn still on its rugged forehead, and the foam of the uprising tide now angrily splashing its feet; a mighty fortress of rock, that would break from its gloom to a wonderful beauty when the sun should come round to the west, and the glory spread over the waters. There were but four or five cabins, dropped in among the loose piles of stone and the pale plumes of the sand grasses; huts low nestled, and hidden like the nests on northern beaches of the sea-hovering tern. And these few were deserted; the men had been out two days with their boats and their nets, and their womankind were alone left, with children wild-haired and ruddy-cheeked, and with naked limbs of a marvellous mould and grace, who lived all day long waist-deep in water, and slept all night long on a wet sail, and not seldom crushed the seaweed between their bright hard teeth in the sheer desire of famine; and yet who, with all that, might have thanked God, had they known it, that they were born by the water's width and to the water's liberty, instead of in the stifling furnace of cities, where human lives breathe their first and their last, never having known what one breath of ocean wind blows like, or what the limitless delight of a horizon line can mean. They and their mothers said little, comprehended less. The shine of silver made their eyes glisten, but they could give nothing in return for it. Of the boats, there was not one left; not the craziest craft that ever was hauled high upon a beach to be broken up into firewood; nor of the boys did one remain of years enough to handle a rope or hold a tiller.

He stood on the narrow strip of yellow sand, with the ripple of the foam rolling upward and over his feet, and looked over the sweet, fresh, tumultuous vastness of the waters as men, when camels and mules, and even the hardy sons of the soil, have perished one by one in their rear, look over the stretch of the desert where no aid is to be called, no change can come, except the aid and the change of the death that shall leave their flesh to the vulture, their bones to the bleach of the noon.

All he had done had been in vain.

Reaching the sea, they were as far from liberty as when the monastery's doors had closed them in; unless some vessel could be chartered to bear westward before the day should be at its meridian, they must turn back, and share the wolf's lair, the hare's terror, the stag's life of torture, when on every breeze may come the note of chase, when every curling moss and broken leaf may bear a mark to bring the hunters down.

There was not a sail in sight, as far as his eyes could reach over the water line; it might be two or three nights more yet, as the women told him, before the fishing-boats would come in; to leave her for the length of time needful to traverse the coast was impossible; he saw no course but to retrace his steps to her, and leave the choice of their retreat with her.

He stood there some moments, looking westward from the beach, his head sank, his thoughts were very weary; he was condemned to the torture of inaction, the deadliest trial that can be fastened on high courage and on eager energies. He turned swiftly as he heard steps passing along the loose stones that made a sort of stairway from the high ground, down between two steep and leaning sides of rock, and looked up in anxious hope of welcoming some boatman who could help him to a vessel. As he did so, the morning sun, shining from the east, that faced him as he turned, fell full upon his head and throat, and standing thus, catching the brightest glisten of the morning beams, the barcarolo dress served little to disguise him, and through the mist-wreaths that still hovered round all the upper border of the shore, his eyes, ere escape or avoidance was possible, met those of the man above upon the broken tiers of cliff.

They were the keen blue serene eyes of Victor Vane.

For a moment they looked in silence at each other, met thus face to face, in the coolness of the young day, in the solitude of the unfrequented shore. Then, with an easy supple grace, the man, in whom Erceldoune's

instinct felt a foe, swung himself downward from ledge
to ledge, and dropped upon the sands beside him, with
the common courtesies of a carelessly astonished and
complimentary greeting.

"I came to bathe; I am staying for a villeggiatura
not far from this," he said, as his words of welcome
closed.   "You are yachting, I suppose?"

"No."

"No? I thought that fisher-costume was surely a
sailor's dress. May I ask what brings you, then, to
this world-forgotten nook?"

"I came to get a boat, and a boat's crew if I
could."

"Ah! you have lost your way?"

"I know the coast well. I merely need a boat—
of what kind matters little. Can you help me?"

"I grieve to say no. My friends' residence is some
way from here; and, besides, they have not even a
pleasure skiff; they care nothing for the water. But
you would not put out to the open sea in a mere
boat?"

"Why so?"

"Why! Because I fancy no man would who was
not weary of his life—or whose life was not menaced
on the land."

Erceldoune looked up; with a flash of his fiery impatience.

"Explain that phrase."

"Translate it for yourself."

"No I. I am in no mood for enigmas. You had
your meaning; out with it!"

Vane looked him steadily in the face; a serious,
compassionate, candid gaze.

"I am sorry you trust me so little."

Ornamented protests would have forewarned and forearmed his listener, whom the simplicity and manliness of the reply put off his guard; they made the loyal, generous nature that they dealt with repent as of some sin of false suspicion; rebuke itself, as for some ignominy of cowardly injustice. 'Moreover, Ercoldoune saw that he knew much—how much it was best to learn at once, let the learning cost what it should.

"He has eaten at her board; he has enrolled himself her friend; he cannot turn traitor to her; he cannot play false to a woman!" his thoughts ran swiftly, in the tumult of a thousand emotions. It seemed to him so vile a thing, that to suspect even his rival of it looked base to him.

"Let us waste no words," he said, rapidly, while he stood facing the new-comer with the challenge of his gallant regard testing the truth of that glance which met them. "Time is life to me, and more than life. You guess rightly so far. Answer me two things. What do you know?—and why should you be trusted?"

"The latter question, I imagine, one gentleman should scarcely put to another!"

"That may be. I am in no temper for these subtleties. I know nothing of you except through rumour. Such rumour would not incline me to place confidence in you. You used strange language: you seem aware of my present peril. Simply, say what it is you know."

The other, with a dignity that had in it the compassionate forbearance of one who respects and pities another whose insolence he can afford to pass over and

extenuate, answered him, without hesitation, in a grave
and regretful accent.

"Well,—I forgive your inuendo on myself, since
the extremity of your peril may serve to excuse it,
and I believe that this peril has fallen on you through
a rashly noble and generous action. We have met
here singularly enough. I do not know—positively
—anything of your actions or position; but I should
be half a fool did I not divine much of both. Briefly,
we are both acquainted with a fair revolutionist, who
has been made a prisoner of the royal executive. I
heard, late last night, that she had been rescued from
her captivity—rescued by a man in a fisher dress,
who displayed the most reckless chivalry in her defence, and even implicated himself so deeply as to use
violence to Giulio Villaflor, whereby Monsignore lies
now in danger at his monastery of Taverna. I heard
this; such news soon spreads, specially to Court and
Church; and I heard also that both soldiers and sbirri
are on the track of the fugitives, who are known to
have made their way seaward. Now can you wonder
that it needs no great exercise of intelligence to recognise in you the *barcarolo* who despoiled Church and
State of their captive, and to conclude that the vessel
you stand in need of is to be employed in the service
of Miladi Idalia, for whom, living or dead, both
Church and State would give as weighty a reward as
the full coffers of the one and the lean treasures of the
other could afford to yield? Scant penetration is re-
quisite for such a discovery; every sailor on the coast
will make it with me in a few hours' time. It is not
a little thing to free a political prisoner, and to leave
a mighty prelate half dead among his own monks."

He spoke perfectly quietly, his eyes, with an un-
usual melancholy, looking straight and calm into the
eyes of the man before him—eyes that said without
words, "You see, she and you are in my power. One
word from me, and both are lost!"

Erceldoune gazed at him, answering nothing; his
chest and sides heaved like those of some magnificent
animal caught in the toils of the trapper. He cared
nothing for his own life; he would have sold it dearly,
content enough, if he died worthily; but she—for her
he had no strength; for her he had no courage; for
her he could sue what he would never for himself
have sought; for her the grave was horrible to him.

To parry facts with lies, to turn aside discovery
with subtle feints, was not in him; to deny that which
he knew to be a truth never even passed his thoughts.
This was another calamity, another danger, the darkest,
perhaps, that could have come on them; but his instinct
was to brave and meet it, not to slink from it under a
poltroon's mask of falsehood. He went with a single
step close up to his companion's side, and stood above
him.

"Grant your conclusions right—what then?"

"That is rather for you to answer. Your future
is a very hazardous one."

"I did not speak of my future, but of your course.
What will it be?"

"Do you insinuate that I should betray you?"

"I do not insinuate; I ask. If the world may be
believed, you have not been always noted for your
fealty."

"Coarse language, and not over-wise——"

"I cannot stop to refine, nor yet, perhaps, to

reason. Tell me how I am to deal with you. As friend or foe?"

"Sir, that is scarcely the way to learn. Diplomacy would not dictate such rough-and-ready questions."

"Possibly. But I am no diplomatist."

"I imagine not. No one would suspect you of it."

"Spare your satire. Give me a plain answer."

"Not a popular thing, commonly."

Erceldoune shook with rage. This play of words was to him in his extremity as the irritation of the whip's light lash is to the caged tiger in' its wrath. He flung himself away with an unconscious violence.

"Do your worst, if you choose to do it. Go and turn traitor against the woman at whose table you sat, and under whose roof you were welcome. Adventurers fitly end in renegades."

"Wait. You mistake."

Erceldoune paused.

"Show me my error, and I will confess it."

Vane smiled a little, in compassion. This nature, so warm, so bold, so free from every suspicion, so willing to avoid every injustice, seemed to him so pitiable in its simplicity; its naked strength, that could so easily be pierced; its unselfish impulses, that could so easily be duped; its creed of truth, that was followed so blindly and so recklessly!

"You wrong me," he said, with that tranquil dignity which had again replaced the ironic frivolity of his usual manner—"wrong me greatly. Think but a moment, and you will yourself see how. The cause for which Madame de Vassalis has been arraigned is mine; would it be likely that I should find favour with

Court or Church, even were I base enough to seek it?
She is the life, the soul, the inspiration, often the
treasury, of our projects, the Manon Roland of our
latter-day Girondists; is it not palpable that what
strikes at her must strike at us? Besides, leaving
every such reason aside, can you believe that, as a
guest, I should harm my hostess; as a man, betray a
woman? Rather do me some measure of justice. Believe, at least, that I can have some admiration, some
sympathy for your magnificent daring; quixotic I may
deem it, but reverence it I must."

Erceldoune heard him, swayed against his judgment, influenced against his instincts. The tone of the
appeal touched that temper of trust and of liberality
always dominant in him; he hated this man, but to let
his hate prejudice him to injustice seemed very vile in
his sight; he thought that he owed a wide measure of
justice, a more limitless extension of tolerance, to an
enemy than a friend; where his impulses set him
against, there he felt that his honour should more
closely strive for fairness to, a foe. A code that had
in its results, perhaps, a folly unutterable, yet had in
its root a magnanimity scarce less great, and such as
men would do well to strive after in giving judgment.

"Trusted, even a scoundrel will quit his baseness.
And, if he have ever loved her, he can hardly be a
traitor to her," his thoughts ran as he paused there,
and heard the measured sweetness of his rival's voice.
And on those thoughts he spoke, making the error that
costs so many dear—the error of gauging another
character by the measure of his own.

"If I wronged you, I ask your pardon. Your jests
fell sharply on a heart so sore as mine. You have our

lives in your power; for her sake, hold them sacredly.
All the help you can give us is silence. I thank you
for your promise of that. Farewell! And forget my
words if they did you an injury. They were spoken
in passion and haste."

. For the moment the words touched his hearer—
awoke something of shame, something of admiration,
something of compassion, that had no scorn in it, but
a dim instinct of honour for this noble madness that
believed in him, for this self-rebuke that was spoken
so generously, content to take blame rather than to
hold to an unjustified suspicion. All the cruelty of
jealousy, all the pitilessness of hatred, all the unmerciful heartlessness of craft, were in him against the man
whom he instinctively knew that the woman he coveted
loved. Yet they were for an instant stilled under the
vague emotion that woke in him—that emotion of involuntary homage which even the shallowest and the
basest natures will at times yield reluctantly to the
greatness of a brave sincerity.

But it was very fleeting with him; too fleeting to
change the hard set purpose that had possessed him
from the moment when his knowledge of his rival's
temper had made him at once divine who had been the
deliverer of their mistress, and had sent him seaward
to trust to hazard for the accident that should bring
him across the fugitive's path.

He stretched his hand out with frank grace.

"That was very nobly said. We may surely be
friends?"

Erceldoune did not take his hand.

"Pardon me—my friendships are few, and I add
16*

to them rarely. Aid *her*, and no friend shall be so close to me as you."

"You speak strongly. Is the Countess Vassalis so dear to you, then?"

"Judge by the risk I have run for her."

"True! You are not the first——"

"The first for what?"

"Well—the first who thought his life well lost for her. And—forgive me the question, I have known her so long—what does she promise you for it?"

"I fail to apprehend you."

"You do? I mean, what reward does that fairest and most fatal of sorceresses promise you if ever you escape the dangers you have incurred for the sake of her eloquent eyes?"

"Her insults are mine. By what right do you use such a tone?"

"By what right do you constitute yourself her champion? It will be a thankless office!"

"By the right of a man to defend his wife's honour."

In the deep shadow of the overhanging cliff he did not see the ashen colour to which the fairness of his listener's face faded; in the tumult of his own thoughts and passions he did not hear the quick, sharp catch of his companion's breath. It was soon suppressed in a careless, soft, ironic laugh.

"Ah! Miladi must think her jeopardy very imminent. She never proffered so heavy a bribe before."

Erceldoune's hands fell on his shoulders, swaying him heavily to and fro.

"What do you dare to mean by that!"

"Simply what I say."

"Why? Am I so loathsome?"

"Certainly not. You are a magnificent man; the very man for a lover. But marriage——"

"Finish your sentence. Marriage——"

"May be a word on her lips, but will never be a chain upon her liberties."

"You dare to mean——"

"Release me, and I will tell you what I mean. I do not speak for any threats of force."

Erceldoune slowly let go his hold, and stood before him with the morning sun-gleam on his face that was stormily flushed. His rival's eyes met his serenely; in the calm transparent depths there was an unspoken pity that made his listener's blood glow like lava.

"In a word—I mean this. She has bought you with syren words; do you dream how many she has bought likewise before you, and—destroyed?"

"I know that no man living shall insult her name to me unpunished."

"Ah! you will stop my lips with a blow? Honourable women do not need such tragical defence. Let me ask you one thing only."

"Ask it."

"Who fired at you in the Carpathians?"

In the warm glow of the summer dawn Erceldoune's limbs grew chilly with a sudden sickly cold. He did not answer. He divined the drift of the inquiry.

"You do not know! You should do so. Did you ever ask this woman who is to be your wife?"

His chest heaved heavily with hard-drawn breaths; his memories were with the evening just passed by, when the sunset had shed its ruddy hues on the face

of the slumbering Greek, and she had bade him spare
that worthless life with a passionate force of supplication to which she had never stooped when her own
existence had been in jeopardy. · But he was too loyal
to her for his answer not to rise hot and instant to his
lips.

"Ask her? Would I do her so much outrage?"

"Yet no one could tell you so well."

"What! you are vile enough to say——"

"The villany is not mine! I say that Idalia Vassalis can tell you better who is the man that sought to
take your life than can any one else in Europe."

Erceldoune heard in silence; he felt giddy, blind,
heart-sick; his knowledge of her association with his
enemy was lying like a dead weight on the indignant
scorn with which he would, without it, have flung back
the insult offered her; the remembrance was upon him
of her intercession that had screened the criminal from
justice, of her conjuration that had interposed between
the guilty and his retribution, of the mingling of shame
and of terror that had broken and bent her haughty
nature like a reed.

"You lie," he said, savagely, seeking only to defend
her at all hazards. "She never knew;—he is her foe
not less than mine."

"Ah! she has spoken of him then!"

"What if she have?"

"Nothing. She said he was her foe, did she? What
other things did she say of him?"

Erceldoune's hand seized him by the linen of his
vest, and shook him as a strong grasp will shake the
slender stem of a larch-tree.

"You will make a brute of me! You have some

hellish meaning hidden—speak it out, if you have a man's heart in you. What would you dare bring against her?"

Vane freed himself with difficulty, and moved slightly aside; but there was no anger in the serenity of his voice, only some pity and much patience.

"I have nothing hidden; if you hear me, you will know as much as I know. I see your error; many have made it. You have thought in such divinity of form divinity of soul must dwell. Scores have made your mistake, and died for it—as you may before the game is out. Miladi has had many lovers, and—dead men tell no tales."

He paused; his rival's hand was on his mouth, and the steel tube of a pistol was pressed against his forehead.

"Another syllable like that, and, by Heaven! I will shoot you with the lie on your lips."

Courage had never been lacking in him; his eyes looked up none the less tranquilly into the dark, flushed, haggard face above him, though the cold ring of the weapon pressed its mark on his skin.

"You can, if you choose. I am unarmed. You will oblige your mistress too. I know many of her secrets."

Erceldoune's arm fell to his side; he shivered through all his frame; he could not use violence to a man without the power to return it; he could not force to silence words which, if he refused to hear them, he would seem to know were true in all their shame. He dropt the pistol down on the sands between them, and crossed his arms on his chest.

"Say your worst. Our reckoning shall come later."

"Well, my worst is—the truth. You love this woman; but you are not in her confidence; you never will be."

He saw a quiver of pain break the wrath on his listener's face, and he saw that the bolt had struck home.

"You believe everything she tells you? I never found the man who did not. I doubt if a man can look long at her, and see clearly, unless he have known her well, and come forewarned to her—as I came. Well, you have thought her a mistress for 'Shakspeare's self;' you have seen her in great dangers; you have imagined her foully wronged; you have cast away all your heart on her, and now are casting your life away after it. And you do all this without ever having asked yourself and the world what a woman must be who, titled, is yet out of society; who, young, yet recklessly defies all custom; who, rich, can summon round her none but men, and those men adventurers or conspirators; who shelters your assassin in her Turkish gardens, yet affects all ignorance of his identity or vicinage; and who, driven at last to speak of him, tells you he is her foe, yet omits altogether to explain why, if so, she has so long shielded him from your discovery and the law's justice. You love, and therefore you are blind. Yet is it possible that even that blindness can be so utterly dark that you have never remembered all these things?"

The black blood gathered in his listener's face; he kept his passions down, because, for her sake, he held it best to hear all her calumniator would bring against her; but they well-nigh mastered him, rising the darker and the stronger for the keen pang of truth that every shaft of the abhorred words stung him with—truth that she had herself placed it beyond his power to refute.

"Go on," he said, simply. "You called yourself her friend, 1 think?"

The rebuke was bitter, yet it did not move the man it lashed.

"Scarcely so much," he returned, quietly. "Her acquaintance—indeed, her associate in not a few political matters—but scarcely her friend. Miladi's friendships are too perilous. Look you; I had a friend once, an Austrian, though I bear Austria no love. We had been lads together in Venetia, and the war-feuds failed to divide us. I think he was the brightest and the bravest nature I have ever known. Well, in an evil hour he fell, as you have done, under the eyes of Idalia. He had a military secret in his keeping; a secret, granted, that was of import to Italy, so perhaps you will deem what she did was justified for Italy's sake. I might have done so, had I not known him from his boyhood; I might have done;—who touches politics fast grows a knave. Well, she sunned him in her smiles, till sense and judgment both were gone —as yours are gone. Then, while she promised him her beauty as its price, she stole his secret from him —bought it with those caresses you believe are only yours—and, when his honour was yielded up to her, turned him adrift with a laugh at his weakness. Ah! that is Miladi's way! So—I saw him shot one sunny summer dawn; with the balls in his throat, fired by a volley of his own Cuirassiers. Politically, we owed her much; personally, I never in my soul could trust the woman who betrayed Hugo."

Ercaldoune shook through all his limbs; the spasm not alone of rage but of a more cruel emotion. The tale had too close a likeness with her own self-accusing confession, her own keenness of remorse, not to bear a burden of possibility with it—a hideous surface of truth which made it impossible it should be cast away as calumny. Yet through the dizzy misery that came upon him he grasped one thought still foremost of all —to defend her.

"Is that all you stayed me to tell?" he asked. "It was not worth your while. I have no heed for libels."

"It is not all. I know well that my words are wasted, and that you think me a slanderer for them: that is a matter of course. Hugo thought me the same when I told him what the tenderness of his imperial mistress would prove worth. I will not strain your patience longer; let us keep close to one fact—the attempt upon your life. You deny the association of Idalia Vassalis with that crime?"

"I deny it—utterly."

His voice had a harsh vibration in it like the tone of one who speaks under unbearable physical suffering. He denied it in her name; but whilst he did so there ate like fire into him the remembrance of that horror, that remorse, that passion, with which she had looked upon the Greek, and held him from his vengeance. With his last breath he would have declared her guiltless; with his last thought held her so; yet the shadow of guilt fell on her, and he could not drive from her the taint and the tarnish of its reproach.

"You do? She is indebted for your chivalry," re-sumed the slow, sweet voice of his companion. "I see how little you must ever have heard of the finest mistress of intrigues that Europe holds, to yield it so unhesitatingly. Now bear with me a moment while I ask you why you are so certain that she had no share in the attack made on you?"

"Ask yourself. You know her."

"And you mean that none who do can doubt her being the proudest and the purest, as well as the fairest among women? Ah! but then I have passed by that stage; *I* knew her by repute long before I ever saw her face. Your reasons for thinking her both innocent and ignorant of your attempted assassination are these: that she was on the spot at the time you were shot down; that she saved your life, and concealed the action even from yourself, allowing it to be believed that Moldavian herdsmen rescued you; that you chased the leader of the band as far as the gardens of her villa at Constantinople, and there lost sight of him, though the walls of the gardens were so disposed that he could only have been concealed within them, if not in the house itself; that she invited you to spend many hours alone with her in her Eastern hermitage, and so spent them that she found little difficulty in making you believe her all she would; that she then sought to throw you off by leaving you abruptly without any clue to her movements; and that when you persisted, against her wish, in seeking her, you found her, first the associate, and a little later the fellow-prisoner, with the men of that very party of extreme liberalists to whom you have always attributed the murderous onslaught made on you. These are your reasons for holding her innocent of all treason to you; they would not be very weighty evidences in law and in logic."

As the chain of circumstances uncoiled link by link in the terse, unadorned words, it seemed to tighten in bands of iron about the heart of the man who trusted not less than he loved her. His face changed terribly as all the force of meaning and of circumstance arrayed itself against her, and the vague doubts, that he had strangled in their birth as blasphemies against her, stood out in unveiled language. A dogged, savage, sullen darkness lowered on his features; it had never been on them before then; it was a ferocity wholly akin to his nature, hardened and embittered by the knowledge of his own powerlessness to repel or to refute the evidence arraigned. They were but facts which were quoted—facts not even distorted in the telling; the inference drawn from them was the inevitable one, however his loyalty to her disowned it. He felt driven to bay; he was fettered to inaction by the knowledge that on him alone her safety hung; he was weighted to silence by the memories which thronged on him of her own acts and words, of that poignant remorse which had sunk so deeply into her nature, of that self-condemnation which had so unsparingly condemned her. Yet amidst all he never hesitated in her defence, and his eyes fastened on her accuser with a steady unyielding gaze.

"I am no casuist and no rhetorican; you are both. Once for all—no more words. If you have been her friend, you are a traitor; if you have been her foe, you are a slanderer. Either way, one word more, and I will choke you like a dog."

"An unworthy and a coarse threat. What falsehood have I told you yet? I named but facts."

"Your outline might be fact. It was your colour
was the lie."

"I think not. I can prove to you that your mistress was in the secret of your assassins."

"And your motive in that?"

The lion-like eyes of Erceldoune literally blazed
their fire into those that met them with unchanged
serenity. There were volumes in the three words; all
of distrust, disbelief, hatred, and scorn that his heart
held for the one who had turned counsellor to him.
Their sting pierced deep; but the wound of it was
covered.

"My motive is this. A party with which I was to
a great extent associated, yet from whose measures I
very often dissented, implicated me by their extreme
opinions in many courses that I utterly disapproved,
and implicated my name still oftener unknown to me.
I am entirely against all violence and all fraud—not
from virtue—I do not affect virtue—but from common
sense. Politically, much is permissible——"

"I am not inclined to hear your creed. I make
no doubt that it is an elastic one! Your motive?"

"You pass it in your haste. I endeavour to explain it. I became entangled in earliest youth with
men whose association has been the greatest injury
of my career. I have never been able wholly to free
myself from their influence, but I have long ceased to
countenance their more unscrupulous intrigues — not
from virtue, I distinctly say, from policy. It is a lack
of sagacity that produces all crimes; nothing else; ex-

cept an excess of animalism, which produces the same results, because it amounts to the same thing."

"Spare your ethics! Your motive?"

"Springs from the inability of my late associates to discern the kinship of crime and foolishness. When I first heard of your robbery, I had my suspicions; I was baffled in my inquiries; I believed that men with whom my name was connected were concerned in it, but they feared that I should learn their complicity, and for some time succeeded in concealing it. Recently —indeed, the day before the affair of Antina—I found my suspicions right. I am ashamed to say that I have traced that melodramatic villany to those who call themselves of my party, although I have fully and finally broken off all collusion with them. In a word, I have felt disgraced that men with whom I have been allied should have been capable of such an outrage, and so much reparation as can lie in the acknowledgment is of course your immediate due. I care little how you revenge yourself, so that your vengeance may be the executor of mine for the deception passed on me. Moreover, in learning the truth of the crime you suffered from, I learnt what you have a right to know, since you believe the Countess Vassalis worthy the surrender of your own life, which is probably the cost you will pay sooner or later for your loyal efforts to save her."

Erceldoune breathed fast and heavily; a sickening sense of mystery, of treachery, of evil, of half-truths told him only that by them he might be led deeper into error, was upon him.

"Had I twenty lives, she commands them," he said briefly. "Say out your meaning—honestly, if you can."

"Very simply, then;—the woman to whom you would give a score of lives, if you had them, has from first to last sheltered your assassin from you, and has counterfeited tenderness for you that she might gain an influence strong enough to enable her to turn aside your vengeance from the only man Idalia Vassalis ever loved."

The words were cold, clear, incisive, calm with the tranquillity of unwarped truth. Under them he staggered slightly, like one who reels under a deep knife-thrust; his hands fell once more on his torturer's shoulders, swaying him dizzily to and fro.

"Own that you lie, or by——"

The closing oath rattled hard in his throat; in the moment he could have choked her traducer dead with no more thought, no more remorse, than men strangle the adder that has destroyed the life they treasure closest.

Vane, deficient neither in courage nor in supple strength, shook himself loose with a rapid movement, and lifting the pistol from the sands, held it out with a grave, graceful gesture, as though the weapon were a branch of palm.

"Take it back, and lay me dead with it, if you find that I tell you untruth."

"*If!*"

"Yes—'if.' I am no slanderer weaving a legend; no gossiper trafficking in cobwebs. I tell you a hard, unglazed, pitiless fact; there are many such in the history of the woman you imagine has so stainless, so martyred, so royal a soul! Take back your weapon, and use it if I play you false. You are longing to kill me now—I see that in your look; but you are a

lion, not a fox, and so you will not kill in the dark.
Make it day about you, broad noonday, by which you
can read the depths of your mistress's heart, and then
—if she prove guiltless and I a liar—then compensate
yourself as you will."

Erceldoune answered nothing. A dusky reddened
light was glowing in the darkness of his eyes, the
light that glows in a dog's when the longing to seize
and rend is rousing in it; his blood felt like fire; the
dawn seemed to grow like night; the corrosion of a
jealous hate was in him, and 'in its evil all other memories were drowned, all desires quenched, all loyalty
loosened.

The other touched him as he turned and strode
over the wet stone-strewn beach.

"Wait. Where do you go?"

"I go to 'make it daylight,' as you say—daylight
strong enough to unbare your villany."

"But first you must hear——"

"I have heard too much."

"Stop an instant. Remember, I have known the
story of Idalia as you will never know it."

"The more you know, the more honour should
bind you into silence."

"Madman! When I tell you——"

"Mad I may be. Rather that than a traitor."

"It is a traitress of whom we speak."

Erceldoune's eyes flashed a strange glance into
his; it was scorching as fire, yet it had in it a terrible
appeal.

"Take care what you do. You will *make* me kill you."

"No. But I will make you prove my words truth
or slander."

"I go to do it."

"You think you do; you do not. You go to hear
a few soft words from lips that have duped the subtlest
intriguers in Europe, and to believe every phrase that
they breathe with a kiss upon yours, as though it were
witnessed by angels! I tell you that my honour shall
not rest upon so wayward and so frail a thing as her
caprice of invention."

"And *I* tell you that *her* honour shall not rest upon
the tongues of traitors. You have dared to say she
shielded my assassin——"

"I say more;—I say she loved him. No! Take
your hand off; you can seek my life later on; at
present you must save your own, if you do not want
a Bourbon bullet through your lungs for this woman
who has fooled you, as she fools us all. There is one
man, one only, that your mistress ever loved. She has
wearied of him now, found him a thorn in her side,
learned to hate him as such women can hate, drawn
all the fragrance from her rose, and thrown the old
withered leaves away—only the leaves are poisoned,
and they cling, they cling! One man she loved, and
she lavished her gold on him, and she reared her
ambitions for him, and she was half his slave and half
his sovereign, while she was for all the world beside
that beautiful, cruel, wanton, pitiless, divine, and
devilish sorceress that we know. She has had many
lovers, but she duped them all. This man she never
duped. A panther, with a velvet eye and a glorious
beauty; a sun-god, with the soul of a fox and the
heart of a carrion-crow — nothing more. But who
shall measure the passionate fancies of a woman?—
and such a woman? Well, she loved him; and he was

your assassin.   No way so sure to shield him, as to
bring you under her dominance! It may be, it is true,
that whilst fooling you for his sake, you dethroned
him, and she grew in earnest, and it is he who is now
to be thrown *ad leones*.   It may be; Miladi has had
many such caprices! That you may know I say truth,
and not falsehood, go and put but two questions to
her.   Ask her first, who the man is who left you for
dead in the mountains.   Ask her last, what the tie is
that binds her to the companion of her life, Conrad
Phaulcon."

Erceldoune had listened, without a word, without
a breath, his face with that tempestuous darkness
lowered on it, and a great horror, a great misery
gazing vacantly out from his dilated eyes.   Yet the
loyalty and the faith in him were stronger than all
tests that wrung them; he struggled to keep his hold
upon them, and to keep them pure, unsoiled, unswerv-
ing, as men may strain to guard their honour unwarped, when all the dizzy world about them reeks
with infamy, and presses them on to crime.

"I *will* ask her," he said, hoarsely, while his lips
were white and dry as dust. "Not to prove her purity,
but to prove your shame."

Then, without another syllable, he turned and set
his face southward, and went by great swift steps, that
sank into the sand, backward to where he had left her
—backward, with the Sicilian sea lying silent and
untroubled by his course, and the sun rising higher
from over the red wall of rock. Belief in what he had
heard there was none, even yet, in his heart; off the
brave allegiance of his rash nobility the evil fell,
finding no grappling-place, no resting-lair; but on him

a heavy, breathless, deadly oppression lay, and the first fear that his bold life had ever known ran like a current of ice through all his veins. The poison of doubt had been breathed on him, and its plague spot widened and deepened, let him rend the canker out as he would.

Once he stretched out his arms to the vacant air as he went on in his loneliness, as though he saw her beauty, and drew it to him, though death should come with it.

"Oh, my love, my love!" he muttered unconsciously, in the longing of his soul. "What matter what you be, so you are *mine!*"

It was in the blindness of the senses that he spoke the mere idolatrous desire for the loveliness that to him had no likeness upon earth; the cruel, intoxicated, fiery riot of the "love, lithe and fierce" that counts no cost to itself or to its prey, and that would plunge into an eternity of pain to purchase one short hour of its joy. A moment, and the nobler emotion in him rose; the perfect faith, without which his one idolatry would be but brutalised abandonment, rebuked him; his head sank, his eyes saw the grey, glooming sea, through a hot rush of tears.

"God forgive me so much sin to her as lay in the mere thought!" he murmured as he went; to think that the lips which had lain on his had ever breathed the kisses which betray, to think that the heart which had beaten upon his had ever throbbed to the warmth of guilty pleasure, seemed to him a blasphemy against her that was sin itself. For, even though those lips should be his, even though that heart should beat for him, if there were past treachery or present infidelity

in her life, she would be dead to him—dead, more
cruelly than though the steel had pierced the fairness
of her breast, and the golden trail of her hair been
drawn through the trampled dust of blood-stained
streets.

If truth abode not with her, and the fealty of
honour, she was dead to him.

"If her eyes shrink from mine, let the seas cover
me!" he prayed in his soul; and the length of the
shore seemed endless to him, and the tawny stretch of
the beach to be the waste of a desert, and the surf, as
it flowed up and broke at his feet, to force his steps
backward and backward, and to bind his limbs as with
lead.

For many moments the man who had tortured him
stood motionless, following with his gaze the retreating
shadow. The grave patience, the gentle tranquillity,
the subdued regret his features had worn throughout
their interview, passed away; a thousand emotions, a
thousand shades of thought, of feeling, and of suffering,
swept over them; alone there, with no living thing near
him save the white gulls resting on the curl of the
waves, he had no need to wear a mask, and he endured
as sharp a misery as any he had dealt.

The deadliest pang in it was shame; the carking,
jealous, bitter shame that where he had failed another
should have won; the knowledge that the love borne
her by the man who had left him was to the love that
he himself had borne as the purity and value of purged
gold against a pile of tinsel. It stilled in something
the tortures of jealousy, it sated in something the thirst
of hatred, to cast—were it only in thought—irony

and invective, and scornful calumny upon his rival; it was natural to him to despise with all the contempt of his fine and subtle intelligence a character that its own frankness and loyalty and high courage left naked to all poisoned shafts, and that was so rashly liberal in faith, so unwisely incapable of falsehood, so blindly and wildly careless to how it wrought its own weal and woe. Yet the most carking wound of all that now ached in him was the latent sense of *superiority* in the one who had supplanted him, who had succeeded where he had been vanquished, and whom he had regarded, with the cold disdain of a flippant wit, as holding all his worth and merit in an athlete's mere physical perfection of thews and sinews. Steeled against all such emotion as he was, the greatness and the nobleness of Erceldoune's faith forced themselves on him; they wrung a reverence out of him despite himself, and they dealt him a mortal pain; pain that was in one sense vanity-moved, since it would no longer leave him the one solace of scorn for his rival, but a pain that sprang from, and that moved, a deeper, better thing,—a recognition, tardy and unwilling though it was, of some greatness he had missed in missing truth; some base and guilty cowardice that he had stooped to when once truth had passed from off his lips, banished with a scoff as only fit for fools.

Beyond jealousy, beyond hatred, beyond every other feeling in him as he stood looking southward at the great shaft of russet stone that screened the pathway of his rival from his sight, there was on him then an intense humiliation. Beside the sincerity, the fealty, the self-surrender, the brave patience of a generous trust, his own subtleties looked so unworthy, his own fine craft so poor; another could render her a love that deemed life itself well lost for her, and he—he was her traitor!

There was enough of honour and enough of tenderness in him for the contrast to strike into him, hard, sharp, swift as steel. This man whom he had contemned with all the mockery of his brilliant mind had grown great in his sight simply through the ennobling influence of a mighty passion and a heroic faith. He still cursed these with his lips as insanity, as idiocy, but in his heart he knew their greatness—a greatness that he had by his own choice, his own act, put far from him for ever.

Away in the world again he would again cleave to his old creeds, and deem this moment womanish weakness; but here in the loneliness of the morning, under the sting of an intolerable torment, the man he hated was great in his sight, and he himself was base exceedingly. Where he stood, with no eyes on him that could read his shame, a red flush slowly stole over the wanness of his face; none living could have brought it there, but the scourge of his own thoughts did.

For though he had fallen willingly, the fall seemed to him hideously vile; as in the grey, cold, unpitying light of a dawn that brings him no slumber, the sins and the burdens that a man counts recklessly, and bears lightly, in the crowds of the daytime and the dissipations of the night, stand out in their true colour, and grow unendurable in his sight and his memory.

But the better instinct too soon perished; there was passion in him, and passion choked conscience; he could not have told whether he most loved or most hated this woman, but whichever emotion swayed him

furthest, the jealousy that he had so often laughed at
as a barbarism of a bygone age was born of both, and
in its fire quenched all other things. He felt for her
that covetous, sensual, pitiless growth of mingled envy,
admiration, and ambition, which, long after all tenderness has perished out of it, will retain all its imperious
egotism, and all its thirst for sweeping destruction of
everything preferred before it. An acrid bitterness
against her for her pride, her power, her keen wit, and
her fearless intellect, had been blent with the earliest
hours of his subjugation to her; and this served now
to strengthen tenfold the fierce, mute, aching impatience
with which he now mused on the possibility that this
woman, so cold, so merciless, so full of mockery for
him, had ever stooped to the weakness she had often
played with, and so often ridiculed.

"Is it possible! Is it possible!" he muttered, while
his delicate lips shook and worked in the anguish which,
in a youth, would have been spent in tears. "She—
so victorious, so ironic, so chill, so world-worn, love for
sake of a wanderer's eagle glances, a rough-rider's lion-
graces! She!—a woman who could fill a throne, and
rule it single-handed. Pshaw! she is a voluptuary, she
is a coquette, she has her caprices—Miladi! And he
is handsome as a gladiator. She loves him—oh yes
—she loves him for six months, six weeks, six days.
And what price will he pay for the paradise?"

The venomous words were murmured to the solitary
shore; even thus, and alone, it was a cruel solace to
him to taunt her with those sneers, to soil what he had
lost for ever, to libel what he envied. It could not
harm her thus to slander her, where none made answer,
but he felt a relief in it, a joy kindred to that with

which he had sold her into the hands of Giulio
Villaflor.

Moreover, he believed what he said; partially because his suffering made him cling to whatsoever could
lessen it; partially because the character of Idalia had
escaped him in many of its hues, keen and varied as
were the worldly experiences by whose light he had
first set himself to read it. He had known of her through
a thousand tongues ere ever he had looked upon her
face; the poison-mists breathed from their distortions
had never wholly faded from before her in his sight.
Such a woman needs a mind singularly truthful and
singularly liberal to understand her aright. Truth he
had not in him, and to all talent save his own he was
illiberal; thus he had failed in following the complex
meanings of her life and of her thoughts. He had
uttered but what he held himself when he had said that

> beautiful she is,
> The serpent's voice less subtle than her kiss,
> The snake but vanquished dust; and who will draw
> Another host from heaven to break heaven's law.

But he had withheld what was not less true, that it
was because she had this sin of merciless destruction in
her, this serpent skill of tempting, this guilty power
over the fates and souls of men, that he had first been
fascinated to her dominion, and first seen in her a
mistress by whom and with whom he could reach all to
which his restless and insatiable ambition aspired, and
aspired in vain.

"Will he believe?" he wondered, as his eyes vacantly
rested on the sands were the footprints of his rival had
sunk. "Not he. What man would believe the witnessing
voices of the whole world if *she* once whispered them
false? And she pays him, too, with love-words, with

the sweetness of her lips, with the touch of hair on his cheek;—ah, God!"

He could have thrown himself on the sands and bidden the sea surge up and cover him, when he thought of that caress which already had been the reward of the man who had succoured her. And he —he who betrayed her, what had he won by the treachery?

"Revenge at least," he thought; and as he thought so his head sank, his limbs grew rigid, his chest rose and fell with a single voiceless sob. He only remembered that revenge was valueless, since revenge could not bring him the lips that he longed for, the beauty that he desired as the ice-bound earth desires summer.

Valueless?—yet not so. It could not give her to him, but it could withhold her from any other.

A young, shy, gentle, little sea-bird, whose wings as yet could scarcely bear it, rose at his feet as he mused, and fluttered a hand's breadth, and then trembled and fell, panting and glancing up with its bright, dove-like, brown eye. He took it savagely and wrung the slender snowy throat, and flung it out on to the crest of a breaker—dead. He had never before been cruel to birds or beasts; such fierce and wanton slaughter was not natural to him, but in this moment it had a horrible pleasure in its brutality. He had subdued all his impulses of hate so long, it sated them, if ever so slightly, to wreak them on that innocent thing. He had seen the dying eyes glaze and fill with misty fear with a gladness he would have believed impossible; he wanted to see hers fade out thus; to stand by and see them fade with just that look of terror and of helplessness;

—eyes that had given such smiling scorn to him, such passionate eloquence to others. He watched the tumbled heap of white ruffled plumage washed in and out by the wind-moved caprices of the "tideless sea."

"I can destroy her as easily as I killed that bird," he thought, and the worst instincts of his nature had their sway once more, as his mouth laughed with his slight, soft smile. "Barbaric! Terribly barbaric!" he murmured. "And I was so wise in my diplomacy with him; I told him only truth. · Talleyrand is right. Truth is so safe and so sure!"

Then leaving the dead curlew floating on the water's play he went whither he came.

"Monsignore will rally enough to sign an order," he mused. "A half-score soldiers, and they will be netted. Miladi's passion will not be smooth in its course!"

CHAPTER XI.

"Shall evil be thy Good?"

WHERE the Greek faced her on the sea-shore there was a long silence between them—a silence breathless and pregnant, like that which precedes the first low muttering of a storm, the first dropping shots of a battle. Many times their strength had come in conflict, and many times the variable, unstable, serpentine will of the man had been crushed under the straight, scornful, fearless will of the woman. Now, for the first time, he had his vengeance, and she could not strike back on him, because for the first time he had found weakness in her, and could reach her through the life of another.

He laughed aloud in his victory.

"Choose, Miladi! Your favourite Maxims say, after the first passion all women love the love, not the lover. If you indulge the first you will slay the last. Choose!"

For all answer she swept with a sudden movement so close to him, that he fell back with the coward's instinct of physical fear.

"You have been often bought *for* murder. What price will buy you *from* it?"

The words left her lips with a scorn that burnt like flame, with a bitterness that cut like steel. Neither touched him; he laughed again in the content of his triumph.

"What price, my Countess? None!"

"You want gold—you love gold. You would sell your soul for gold. You shall have it."

The dread upon her made her voice deep and hushed, like the stealing of an autumn storm-wind through forests; the scorn within her made her face flush, and darken, and quiver, as though the flicker of a torch played on it. Neither moved him to shame.

"Oh yes," he said, with a slow smile—"gold, gold, gold. Of course you would give me that. As much as you would throw away on a banquet, or a diamond, or a web of lace, should come to *me*, if I would stay aloof and hold my peace, and let the Border Eagle build his eyrie on the Roumelian hills, and Miladi pleasure her new passion among her rose-gardens. Oh yes! gold—as much gold as you have twisted in your hair for a mask ball might be mine, of course; and he —he should succeed to Julian's dominion and Julian's domain; he should have all that wood and water, and

palace and mountain, that I have been banned out of
so long; he should be chief there, and lord, and his
sons, maybe, have the heirship of the Vassalis line! A
charming cast for us both! With all gratitude for my
share, and your will to allot it me, I must decline such
a distribution betwixt your lover and me. Gold, gold!
No, Miladi, gold will not strike the balance between
us now."

She listened in silence; only that passionate shadowy
quiver, as of the light of a flame, on her face giving
sign or response to him. Her lips were close pressed
together, and scarce seemed to move as the words came
through them, hard, like the dropping of stones on a
stone.

"Your sin is envy? Well, it is only another added
to a long list. Mere gold will not buy you. What
will?"

"Nothing."

"You are so incorruptible!"

"Yes, here."

"Through envy, avarice, and hate!"

"Through three common movers of mankind, if so."

"You own them yours? Then listen here. I speak
nothing of your guilt to me—nothing of your crime
against him. I will deal with you as though none of
all that measureless iniquity were on you. Conscience
you have not; shame you do not know. I appeal to
neither. I will treat with your avarice alone. You
love self-indulgence, luxury, vice, mirth, indolence,
splendour; you have coveted my heritage from the Vassalis, you have been thirsty for my riches; you have
wanted all that Eastern pomp and princely fief, you
have hungered for Count Julian's possessions, you have

hated me for many things, yet for none so much as for the inheritance of that great wealth; that you used it, and wasted it, and were welcomed to it long as though it were your own, mattered nothing. It was mine, and not yours; you never forgave the difference. Well, hear me now.   All that shall *be* yours—all—all—to the last stone of the jewels, to the lowest chamber of the palace, to the poorest fig-tree on the hills, to the farthest landmark on the plains. You shall have all, and reign there as you will."

An intense eagerness thrilled through her voice, the wavering light upon her face grew hotter and darker, the chained bitterness and fierceness in her gave but the subtler inflection to the eloquence and the command that ran as of old through all her words; for the moment, she dazzled and swayed and staggered him.

"All!" he echoed.   "*I!*"

"Yes—all! Every coin, every rood, every bead of gold in that treasure-house of splendid waste: I will make all yours—all that the Vassalis over owned.   I will not keep a pearl from the jewels, or a date from the palms.   All shall be yours—all the things of your desire."

"And you?"

"I—I shall be beggared."

Yet while she spoke, over her face swept one swift gleam, like the glow of an Eastern sun.

He gazed at her like one blinded.

"And for all this what will you ask of me?"

"Of you I shall purchase—my freedom and his life."

His mouth quivered with rage as he laughed aloud once more.

"So-so! Ah, the wildness of woman's passions! You would buy your lover at *that* cost? Oh, fool! you who once were subtle and wise as the serpent!"

Her teeth set tight, but she kept down her wrath.

"Profit by my folly," she said, briefly. "Take all I have—leave me only him."

The first words were stern; over the three last her voice unconsciously softened with an infinite pathos and yearning.

That involuntary thrill of longing tenderness steeled him in an instant to the first eager impulse of acceptance, prompted by his lust for wealth and ease and power, and all the half-barbaric voluptuous royalties of the Roumelian palace, that had seethed in him for so long. Other evil instincts were more potent still than avarice. He smiled—a slow and cruel smile.

"Magnificent ransom for a landless courier. But at what price will not your sex gratify its caprices—especially the caprice of the passions? For myself, the bribe is high; but I decline it."

The blood faded from her face, even from her lips; a grey, heavy shadow, as of desperation, fell over her, that seemed to drain the very colour from her eyes and from her form, and leave her, white and chill there, as a statue.

"What will you gain?"—she spoke with a hard, brief, stony tranquillity.

"Why—a romantic thing to be sure, and an unremunerative; yet the sweetest thing, as men find, that the world holds—vengeance."

"Neither he nor I have wronged you."

"Maybe. But both have galled me; both——"

"Been wronged by you. True. I forgot the reason of your hate."

His face flushed darkly.

"I do not bear *you* hate. I tried to free you. But I swear this man shall not wed with you, and live."

"And why? Have you not done us injury enough? You poisoned my life with infamy, and would have taken his in a thief's slaughter. Can you not let us be? Can you not sell yourself for pity's sake, as you have so often sold yourself for shameful things? Take my bribe. Impoverish me as you will; enjoy all I have to give; seize all you have ever coveted; bind it fast to you on what terms you choose; make me poor as the poorest that ever asked my charity; only leave me this one thing, his life."

She spoke still with the same strange enforced serenity, but beneath it there ran an intense melancholy, an intense yearning; they could not move, but steeled him in, his purpose.

"The thing I will *not* leave you," he said, savagely. "Ah! I know how men go mad for that beauty of yours; he would hold himself rich as emperors were that his own, though you had no other gold than just what gleams in the coil of your hair. I know, I know! And so you can love at last, my queen!—all that ransom for one wild mountaineer! But you shall only ransom him one way, Miladi; only by—forsaking him."

"I will never forsake him."

"So! Then his wedding-night will be his last."

Her hand worked with a fierce, rapid, clenching movement on the butt of the pistol.

"Wait," she said, slowly, while each word fell on the silence like the falling of the great slow drops of a storm. "You threaten him? One word from me, and he will give you over to justice for your crime to him. One shot this moment from me, and he will be here to take his vengeance."

He shrank slightly, for cowardice was ingrained in him; but he knew how to deal with the brave and generous nature of the woman whom he tortured. He looked her full in the eyes.

"True. You might send me to the galleys. But you will not."

Her lips parted, her breast heaved, a great shudder shook her. She answered nothing.

"You can summon your lover," he pursued, after a pause. "You can tell him of my 'crime,' and—also of my tie to you. You can see us fall on each other, and fight as tigers fight. You can wed him in peace if he kill me; as most likely he will, since he is so far the stronger. You can do this. But you will not."

"I *cannot!* You know it."

He laughed slightly.

"No. I did not know it. Women soon vanquish scruples and tread out memories to gratify a passion. Well, since you hesitate so far, perhaps you will hesitate yet farther. You will not break your oath by betraying me; will you betray this one man whom you say you 'honour,' by linking him, in his good faith and his ignorance, with *us?*"

She gave a sharp, quick breath, as though a blow were struck her.

"God forbid! I have said, all bonds between me
and the past are severed for ever."

"I see! You will lock the book, and throw it aside,
and your blind worshipper will credit you on your telling that the pages were all pure blanks! And yet—
I thought you said you 'honoured' him?"

All the haughty, fiery blood in her flushed to life
under the subtle sneer.

"I do so; from my soul. Let his name be. It has
no place on your lips—yours—that gave the word
to murder him."

"Fine phrases! And yet you will deceive him?"

"I!"

"Yes, you, Miladi. You will not betray me to him
—you cannot. So—telling him nothing—you will
leave him ignorant. And one fine day, were I to let
you run your passion's course, he would learn the
truth, and find his sovereign, his idol, his mistress, his
wife, my——"

"Wait! You have said enough!"

"No. I say more. Forsake him, and he is safe
from me. Give yourself to him, and I will add him
his marriage gift—death. Just such a death as he
would have dealt me on the Bosphorus shore. I can
see the gleam of his steel, and the thirst of his eyes,
now!"

"If he had killed you, what would he have done
more than justice?"

"At least he would have rendered you inestimable
service, Miladi!"

She stopped him with an irrepressible gesture.

"Hush, hush! Such words between *us!*"

"Well! We are enemies; bitter ones enough."

"Yes; enemies as the wronged and the wrong-doer ever are. But your life is sacred to me; how can you curse mine?"

"Mine sacred to you? Is it so, Idalia? Then—being so, you will not betray me to your lover?"

She turned on him a look that had a weariness, a scorn, an agony, a pity unutterable.

"No! I must bear the burthen of your guilt."

"But you will betray him by leaving him in ignorance of whom he loves—of whom he weds?"

"Though he knew, *he* would find mercy and greatness enough to pardon."

She spoke not to him, but to the memories that rose before her—memories that filled her heart with their bitterness and their sweetness—memories of the exhaustless faith and patience and forgiveness of the man she was bidden to abandon.

"Truly! Then what think you, Miladi? Is it a noble return to cheat him as you meditate? Is it a fine thing to recognise this limitless tenderness borne you, only to dupe it through its own sublime insanity? You have fooled such idolaters scores of times, I know, only—here I think you said you 'honoured' him? Which makes a difference; or might make it."

She knew well how wide the difference was—wide as between innocence and guilt.

She answered nothing; only in the brooding horror of the deep dilated eyes was there reply; they spoke more than any language of the lips.

The Greek laughed softly.

"His bridal-conch made in the nest of his 'assassins!' His stainless and glorified mistress proved the masker

of the Silver Ivy! Madame, I think I might let his
passion run untroubled, and leave my vengeance to
the future—some future when he should reach the
truth from some chance word, from some side-wind,
and hear the secret that a woman who 'honoured' him
never had told all through the days and nights she
lived in his sight and slept upon his heart; hear it
when he was bound to her beyond escape, and could
gain no freedom through knowing her traitress to him
as to all others. Ah! I am not so certain that I will
not let you wed him. It will be a surer stab to him
than comes from steel—that one truth learned *too
late*."

There was a long silence.

She shuddered from head to foot, as though the
scorch of a red-hot brand passed over and marked her;
then an intense stillness fell upon her—a stillness in
which all life seemed frozen in her, and every breath
to cease. He waited, mute and patient now.

At last she raised her head, and turned it full upon
him. As the reddened glow of sunrise flickered on it,
it was dark, and cold, and resolute, with an exceeding
strength and an absolute despair.

"For once you have shown me duty, and saved
me from a crime. My hand shall not touch his
again."

"Because you will not——"

"Because your guilt is on me."

"And yet you were willing to lose all your riches,
and your power, and your victories, and your pleasures,
for this one man?"

"I am so willing."

"Then it is——"

That you have shown me what would be my sin to him. You cannot be betrayed. He shall not be."

"You mean——"

She turned on him ere he could speak with the swift, lithe, terrible grace of a stag hunted and hounded into a fierceness born of sheer torture, and wholly alien to its nature.

"Silence! or I shall forget what you are, and let him take his vengeance on you. Can you not be content? You led me into cruelty and error a thousand times under the masking of fair colours and of fearless aims; you now show me, in the one redemption of my life—the one purer, better, higher thing!—only an added guilt, a fresh dishonour. I lose *all* through you. Are you not content?"

The vivid passion, the agonised irony, died suddenly, as a flame drops to the ground; her head fell, her limbs sank wearily on the broken rocks, a dull apathy returned on her, in which she lost all memory, even of his presence. He looked at her, hushed, awed, moved to something that was almost dread of his own work, intimidated by the suddenness and the completeness of his own victory; he waited, hesitating, and as one afraid, some moments; she gave no sign that she even remembered he was near; every second wasted might cost them both the loss of liberty, if not of life; but he lacked the boldness that could have pressed on her then the question of mere bodily danger, the mere physical perils from the cell and the rods of her persecutors.

There was that in her attitude, as she sat, with the loosened weight of her hair sweeping down into the salt pools of the beach, and an icy calm on the colour-less immutability of her features, that subdued and shamed him.

Some sense of reluctant reverential fear was always on him for the woman whom, nevertheless, he had goaded and trepanned, and injured, through the length of many years. Some touch of love for her ever lingered in him.

He paused a while, at some distance from her. She never noted him; her eyes, without sight in them, gazed at the dusky changing mass of water that here and there beneath the spell of waking light broke into melting lustrous hues, like the gleam of colours on a southern bird's bright throat.

He drew closer at last, with hesitation.

"You will come with me, then?"

She gave no sign even that she heard the words.

"I am not alone," he pursued. Lousada, Veni, and the boy Berto sought you. I fell in with them as I neared here; they are fugitives, and proscribed them-selves; they lie hid by day in an old sea-den of Veni's; they look to get away by the coast in a night or so; they would give their bodies to shot and sabre to save your hand from a rough touch. Will you come to them?"

He could not tell whether she heeded him; he saw her face in profile; it was still, cold, passionless, stern with a mute intolerable suffering, like some Greek head, in stone, of Destiny.

He spoke afresh, rather to break that death-like silence, than for the sake of what he uttered.

"Veni's sea-nest is safe—safe, at least, for a little while; it lies yonder, through there, where a passage-

way pierces the rocks. All that acanthus hides the
entrance. It has sheltered many before; Fiesoli lay
there once, in the first days of his proscription. Lousada doubts little that he can get a brig from Salerno,
and steal away off westward three nights hence. It is
the best chance. You will come?"

At last she lifted her head, and looked at him.

"But for Giulio Villaflor I would go—far sooner
—back to the dungeon of Taverna."

His face baled; he knew her meaning—knew the
unspeakable loathing and scorn of himself that made
the severities of captivity and wretchedness look fairer
in her sight than every recovered freedom shared with
his companionship.

"There is no other alternative," he said, sullenly.
"You will come?"

"I will come."

He was once more victorious; and once more with
victory stole over him a strange chill dread, as he who
has brought down and netted the lioness of the plains
will feel something of awe, something of fear, when in
his toils lies the daughter, the mate, the mother of free-
born kings of untrodden soil—when beneath the rain
of his blows, and from out the meshes of his trap, the
great fearless luminous leonine eyes look at him, suffering but unquailing.

"Why do you wait, then?" he asked.

"I wait—for him."

"So! You will, after all, be false to one of us.
Which?"

"Neither."

"What gage have I of that?"

"That I have said it."

He was silent a moment; he scarcely dared dispute that single bond, her word. Traitor himself to her, he knew that his treachery would never be repaid him by its own coin.

"You wait for him?" he said. "Then so also do I."

"Are you weary of the shame of your life that you seek to lose it?"

"No. But he shall take it rather than I will leave you here."

Through the calm upon her face, the calm of martyrdom, of despair, he saw the conflict of many passions, of infinite misery.

"Will you choose for us to meet?"

Where the forehead rested on her hands that were thrust among the masses of her hair, the great dews started as they had never done when the scourge was lifted at Taverna.

"We shall not part alive," he pursued. "Perhaps you count on that? Your lover is the younger and the stronger; there are few men he would not worst. You rode all day through the heat and press of a battle under Verona once, I remember; maybe you wish to see a life-and-death combat."

She answered nothing; a shiver as of intense cold ran through her.

"You can enjoy your new passion, true, if he kill me;—a dead body flung with a kick into that surf, the waves to wash it seaward, none on earth to care enough for me to ask where I have drifted,—it would be easy work. Is that the reason why you 'wait?'"

"Heaven! how can you link such guilt with me, even in thought?"

"Why not? That will *be* the end if we meet in

your sight to-day, unless, indeed, fate turns the other
way, and your lover falls through me. Sit there, Miladi, and watch the struggle; you will never have seen
two harder foes. Turn your thumb downward, like
those dainty, haughty Roman dames you copy in philosophies and seductions; turn it down for the slaughter-
signal, if you see me at his mercy. How free you will
be then! But—listen just a little—if he press me too
close, we of the south and east have not the northern
scorn of a timely thrust, and it will be but in self-
defence!"

As he spoke, he drew gently half out of its sheath
the blade of a delicate knife that was thrust in his
waistband, and let the beams of the sunrise play
brightly on the narrow shining steel.

The glitter flashed close beside her. It sent fire
and life like an electric shock through all the icy stillness of her limbs; she rose with a convulsive force; her
eyes had the gleam of an opium-drinker's in them, her
voice had scarcely a likeness of itself.

"I come, I come; do what you will with me, so
that his life escapes you!"

CHAPTER XII.

"Is there no Place for Repentance, none for Pardon left?"

HE let the blade slide back into its case.

"That is well," he said, simply, while the radiance
of his conquest played all over his arched lips and his
fair brow; then, without other words, he took his way
across the stretch of sands, and many yards onward
swept back a deep screen of ivy and acanthus that
closed the mouth of a fissure in the rocks, and veiled

it so darkly that no sign of the break in the great mass
of stone was seen. He signed to her to enter: she
obeyed him; having once made her election, it was not
in her afterwards to pause, to waver, to retract; having
submitted herself to his power for another's sake, she
ceased to protest against that power's use. The screen
of matted foliage fell behind her, shutting out the day;
before her stretched the gloom of a long narrow arch-
ing passage-way, hollowed through the thickness of the
cliff, half sea-wrought and half pierced by men. She
had come thither once in bygone years when the great
pleader, Fiesoli, had hidden there, proscribed for too
fearless a defence of a political prisoner; she passed
straight onward now through the thick darkness, her
hand on her hound's mane to still his longing rage,
her tyrant following in her steps, flushed with the wine
of success, yet silenced by a vague and restless dis-
quietude.

The length of the cavern wound like a tangled
skein through the depth of stone, no light breaking
through it, and the air was chill, and close, and dank,
like the air of a tomb; it was cramped and tortuous,
and the hard jagged surface of the rock bruised her as
she went. Once he stretched out his hand to guide her;
she shook it off as though it stung her, and passed on
alone, more rapidly, and full as calmly as though she
swept down some sun-lighted terrace amongst the roses
of a golden summer-time.

"She will never *fear!*" he thought; and to the
heart of the man that unconquerable courage of a woman brought a sullen impatient wondering veneration.
He was a coward—a coward at the mere gleam of
steel, at the mere common, vulgar terrors of physical

peril; but in her he had never known one pulse of fear. There was a pang of wistful, painful envy in his thoughts for that one greatness which nature gave to her and had denied to him.

At the far end of the vault a fitful ruddy light was gleaming; it came from a fire made of brushwood and the boughs of the maritime pine. Where the fire burned the passage opened out into a wider vault, divided into two or three arched chambers—natural caverns widened and heightened by art, and roughly made, by benches, and skins, and stands of arms,· and beds of osiers covered with soldiers' rugs, into a camp-semblance of habitation. A rude place, yet not comfortless, and with a wild beauty of its own, as the flame flashed on the many colours of the riven stone, and the stalactites that hung above broke in the glow into a diamond brilliance. A place that had been once the subterranean way of a great castle, which had long crumbled down to dust upon the cliffs above; then the nest of roving pirates; lastly, the refuge of proscribed revolutionists, of men who suffered for liberty of speech, and were content to perish under the deathly chillness of their country's deepest night, so that through them the dawn might break for others later on. The sea-den was still as a grave, and well-nigh as lonely: only by the pine-logs sat a boy of sixteen or so, with his fair curls turning to a red gold in their dancing flames, and his Rafaelle-like face drooped, pale and weary, over them.

It was the lad Berto; left sentinel whilst his comrades spent the daybreak seeking a vessel down the shore. He was but a child; yet he had long put away childish things; when he had owned but four years he had seen two of his brethren fall side by side at the

butchery of the Villa Carsini, on that awful day of
June, and ere then had been borne in infancy, in a
mountain flight in his mother's arms, and had kept as
his first memory of life the echo of his own vain cries
when her heart grew still under his eager caress, and
there flowed from her breast a deep stream like the
purple flood that wells forth when the grapes are
pressed—for the Papal troops had shot down like a ·
chamois the woman who dared to love, and follow, and
bear sons to a republican rebel.

He started, and rose with a sentinel's challenge;
then, as he saw who came, bowed low; the weary
sternness of his fair countenance never changed in
boyish sport, or youthful laughter, or under the light
of a girl's shy eyes; wrong had been stamped on him
too early, and, if in his future, the purity and greatness of high aims should be marred in him by an un-
changeable unrelenting chillness, like the chillness of
St. Just, the evil would lie with the tyranny which
had made the warmth of his rosy mouth die out on the
ice of his mother's bosom.

Idalia moved forward to within the circle of the
watch-fire, lighted as the sole means they had to illumine the gloom; there was a deadly calmness in the
mechanical actions that sent a thrill through the child
Berto as he watched her where she sank down on the
log, covered with a shaggy ox-hide, that he had vacated.
She seemed unconscious of his presence; and he knew
that more than mere physical peril, which he had many
a time seen her meet so carelessly, was upon her now.

Phaulcon touched him. "I will look to the fire,
Berto; go and sleep. You need it."

"Her Excellency permits?" asked the boy.

He spoke hesitatingly, reverentially. Beside the flower-hung waters of Verona he had known this woman, now a homeless fugitive, ride through the heat of conflict and dismount, and gather the spent balls under a raking enfilade, and heap them in her skirts, and mount him on her charger to bear them to the revolutionary soldiers, whilst she stayed on at her dangerous gleaning.

She looked at him pityingly, but there was that in the look which Berto had never seen but once—once, when a woman of the Northern Isles had toiled wearily, begging her way, into Rome, to look on her son's face, and had reached in time to see the last earth thrown upon his coffin, whilst in the fair spring morning the French drums rolled a cruel music through the violet odours of the burial-place, and over the majesty and the shame of the great prostituted city.

"Yes, go," she said, briefly; "you need rest. I will take your watch."

She drew his rifle to her, and leaned her hands upon its mouth.

The boy went, obedient; in one of the inner hollows that served as bed-chambers his couch of grass was spread; he had not lain down for three nights, and sleep sealed his eyes as soon as their lids were closed. Across the flame of the pine-logs the Greek watched her, irresolute; embarrassed by his own success. It was dark as midnight in the heart of the pierced seawall; the play of the rising and falling flames fell irregularly on the gloom: she sat motionless, as she had sat upon the shore, her clasped hands resting on the slanted rifle, the tawny splendour of the fire cast on the splendour of her face.

She thought no more of him; she thought alone of the man who would return to find her lost once more—the man she must forsake or must betray; whose body she must give to slaughter, or whose soul she must slay by abandonment. She looked down into the fantastic flicker of the resinous boughs as she had looked down into the ripple of the waters; and, as he watched her, the same shame which had moved him for his sins to her, when he heard of her as within the power of Giulio Villaflor, stirred in her companion: it ever slumbered in him; at times it woke and stung him, yet it never stayed him from his sacrifice of her to the needs of his own craft, the lusts of his own avarice. To serve himself, he had warped and misled the idealic ambitions, the fearless genius, the poet's faith, the hero's visions, that he had found in her in her earliest youth; to serve himself, he had taught the keenness of her intellect intrigue, fanned her worship of freedom into recklessness, snared her to evil through the noblest passions that beat in her, taught her to hold her beauty as a mask, a weapon, a lure, a purchase-coin; to serve himself, he had roused her bravery into defiance, her pride into unmerciful scorn, her wit into sceptic cruelty, and—when these were done—had gone further, and soiled the fairness of her life with the dusky imperishable stain of lip-rumoured dishonour, and let the stain rest so that the world saw it as a reality; whilst she, knowing it false as foul, became too proud, too careless, and too callous to appeal against a world so credulous of evil, so incredulous of good, but took up in the haughty courage of an outraged dignity the outlawry which injustice contumeliously cast to her, and lived and fought, enjoyed and suffered, in grand contempt of all opinion, accepting as her sentence the *yo contra todos, y todos contra yo*, until such isolation and such contest became to her things of preference and triumph. He knew that he had done this guilt against her—partly in the cruelty of egotism that profited through her injury, partly in the blindness of partisanship that thought all means justified to secure its end, chiefly, beyond all, in a rankling jealousy of those possessions and that inheritance which had made her so rich in power and in gold, whilst he was penniless and an adventurer; jealousy that the lavishness of her gift, the generosity of her thought, never tempered, but inflamed. He knew that he had done this, and that of his own act he had turned the tenderness of her heart towards him into abhorrence, had changed the faith she had once borne him into the hatred of a proud woman for her oppressor, of a fearless temper for a coward, of a slandered honour for its traitor and its traducer. He knew that long before, in those bygone years when he had crowned her young head with the wild laurel-leaves of Livadia, and wooed her with subtle words to the Delphian laurels of a perilous strife and a perilous fame, the Greek child had fastened her deep eyes on him as though he were a god, and believed in him as though the voice of Delphos spoke in his; and he knew that of his own act he had made the woman on whom he looked now, in the dusky ruby heat of the uncertain flame, scorn him with all the force of her imperious intellect, and alone withhold her lips from curses on him as the ruin of her life, because memories that he had outraged had still their sanctity for her—because to the oaths that he had broken she yet had remained faithful.

It had been wanton destruction he had wrought,

it was irrevocable loss he had sustained; some sense of all he had forfeited and killed when he had become her worst traitor, and had made the eyes that once sought his in love cast on him their righteous scorn, smote him heavily and restlessly now, as they sat, with the burning of the watch-fire between them, alone in the cavernous gloom. In the whiteness and the immutability of her face there was a grandeur that awed him; despite the weariness and alteration of fatigue, of fasting, of endurance, it was the stern, noble, disdainful beauty of the Vassalis race that he hated, Greek in its type, Eastern in its calm. He thought of the great palace of the Vassalis stronghold, far eastward, crowning its mighty throne of cedar-covered hills, with the treasures of ages in its innumerable chambers, and its sun-lightened plains rich in vine and olive and date, and watered by a thousand winding streams deep and cool under lentiscus shadows; all that her great race had owned, and over which she had rule.

"If that had been mine—not hers—I would never have harmed her," he thought. "Wealth is the devil of the world."

The intense silence, the night-like darkness on which the white smoke floated mistily with an aromatic scent, were horribly oppressive to him; he had the nervous susceptibilities of a vivacious and womanish nature. He addressed her; she did not reply. He set food and wine beside her; she did not note them: she sat immovable; the intense strain on all physical and mental power brought its reaction; a dull stupor like that of opiates steeped her limbs, her sight, her brain, in its lifeless apathy.

He looked at her till he grew sick with the heat of the flames, with the blackness of the shadows, with

the spice of the pine perfume, with dead memories that
would come to him do what he would. He rose impetuously; he had been on foot or in saddle many days
and nights, eating scantily, sleeping still less; all his
frame was aching, and his eyeballs were scorched with
want of rest.

"You will not leave here?" he asked her, half im-
periously, half hesitatingly, since, though he commanded,
he yet feared her.

"No."

"You give me your word?"

"Yes."

"Then I will go seek for Veni. He should be here
ere now."

"Go."

The monosyllables were cold, impassive, unwaver-
ing; to her he could be now and hereafter but an assassin, whose crime had been frustrated by hazard,
yet could be none the less vile because in its issue
foiled. She obeyed him lest a worse thing should come
unto the man he had already wronged, but she submitted herself to him in nought else.

He knew that, her promise given, twenty avenues
of escape might open to her, and she would still profit
by none; he had known her keep her word and redeem
her bond at risk and cost that might well have extenu-
ated her abandonment of both. He turned quickly from
the watchfire, and went down into the shadow of the
farther recesses, whence a steep cramped stairway, cut
upwards through the rock, led, like the shaft of a mine,
into the lowest chambers of the building high above on
the crest of the cliff; the bell-tower of the fallen castle,
bare and crumbling to ruin, deserted, except when, as

now, some fugitive who knew its secrets sought its subterranean shelter. The stair was perpendicular and difficult of ascent; he thrust himself slowly up it and into the dull twilight, that by contrast looked clear as noon, of the basement square of the campanile. He had no fear that she would fail her promise, but he had fear—a certain superstitious fear—of that grave, colourless, magnificent face bent above the pine glow; he could not stay longer under the scourge of her un-uttered scorn, under the mute reproach that her mere life was to him. He would not unchain her to free-dom, but he feared her. He breathed more freely when he left the darkness of the cavern for the upper earth; he was fevered and fatigued, and timorous of the danger round them as any long-chased stag; and he cast himself down to rest a while on the thick soft lichens covering the tower stones, close beside the mouth of the shaft, up which every faintest sound from the hollow den below came to him as distinct upon the rarefied air as up the passage of an auricular tube.

Alone, by the blazing tumbled heap of pine wood, her attitude never changed; the light played on the metal of the rifle, in the red-brown of the hound's eyes, on the scarlet and the gold of her soiled and torn masque dress; beyond, on every side, stretched the dense Rembrandt shade of the vault; her eyes never stirred from the one spot in the embers, which they looked at without knowing what they saw.

"It is but just," she thought, with that stern, un-sparing, self-judgment which was strong in her, as her disdain was strong for the judgments of the world. "I never paused for any destruction; it is but just that I must destroy the only life I prize."

And as she thought her eyes filled with a great misery; justice on herself it might be, but how unjust upon the guiltless!—upon this man who spent his heart, his honour, his very existence on her, only by her to be betrayed or be forsaken.

Through all the varied dangers of her past, her courage, her genius, her instinct, her prowess had borne her out, even when at loss and with sacrifice, unscathed and unconquered; here at last no one of these availed her, but she was bound, powerless and paralysed, under the net of circumstance. Before this she had never been vanquished; now she was chained down beyond escape beneath the weight of an intolerable oppression.

The pine-embers' glowing crimson on the grey ash dust seemed to stand out like letters of flame—writing of fire that glowed around upon the blackness of the shadows, and seemed as though 'it repeated in a thousand shapes the words that had fettered all her life. Words uttered so long ago under the great dim oak glades of Greece, while the stars burned down through the solemn woods, and the moan of classic waters stole through the stillness of the night. Words that she had thought bound her by holy withes to noble thoughts, to sacred aims, to patriot souls, to the ransom of the nations, to the armies of the truth. Words pledged with a child's faith, with a poet's enthusiasm, with a visionary's hope, with the all-belief of youth, and with the glow of ambitions too high for earth, too proud for heaven. Words dictated by lips that she had trusted then as though an angel's bidding spoke by them. Words that whilst she thought they but allied her to those who suffered the martyrdom of liberators, who fought for the freedom of speech, and creed, and act, and who were banded together for the deliverance of enchained peoples, fettered her, she knew too late, into the power of one man, into the obedience of evil.

She had taken her oath to Conrad Phaulcon and to his cause, whilst in the splendour of her dreams and the ignorance of her gracious youth she had held the one a stainless patriot, the other a glorified martyrdom; she had been trepanned through the truest beauty of her nature, blinded through the purest desires of her heart. The patriot was a knave, but the more perilous because also a coward; the cause was a lie, but the more perilous because it stole, and draped itself in, the toga of Gracchus, the garb of an eternal truth.

Slowly she had awakened to the sure agony through which all youth passes — the agony of disillusion. Slowly she had awakened to the knowledge that in giving herself to the service of liberty she had delivered herself into an unalterable thraldom; that the guide whom she had followed as she deemed to the fruition of idealised ambitions, and the attainment of a spotless fame, was but a false prophet with a tarnished glory only in his gift, was but an outlawed and necessitous Camorrist, who saw in her beauty, and her talent, and her wide wealth from the vast Eastern fief, so many means whereby to enrich himself and to ensnare all others. And when she had learned it, and felt its bitter falsehood eat into her very soul, he, lest she should break from him, had cast subtilely about her that poisonous film of imputed dishonour which, once breathed, never passes; he had done it ruthlessly,

19*

or rather, let others do it and never said them nay, which served as well. She had been sacrificed, true, but that had been of little account to him, since through it the gold, and the harvests, and the luxury of the Roumelian possessions were shared by him; his name alone, spoken with hers, had cast shadow enough to darken it. Then, when that last evil had been done against her, she had grown hardened to this world, which so easily believed against her; she had grown callous to this outlawry, which was pronounced against her through the errors of another. She was wronged; she did not stoop to appeal or to protest; the bravery of her nature was steeled into defiance, the independence of her life accepted willingly an isolation which yet was a sovereignty; she had a wide vengeance in her power, and she took it—with too little mercy.

Those memories thronged on her as they had thronged on her foe in the loneliness of the sea-vault, whilst that vow of implicit obedience to his will, of unvarying association with his schemes, of eternal silence on his tie to her, and of eternal devotion to the interests of his order, which had many a time aroused in her such passionate and contemptuous rebellion even whilst she repaid his betrayal by fidelity, now seemed to stand out before her in the fantastic lines of the hot embers.

That oath had coiled about her many a time, had stifled, and bruised, and worn, and stung her beneath all the pleasures of her abundant life, had made her the compelled accomplice of harm she strove to avert, had poisoned those enterprises and those perils which were to her the sweetest savour of her years, had bound her down into an abhorred fealty to a dastard, and had driven her to loathe the sight of those fair hills and stately palaces whose heritage had rendered her the envy of her tyrant. Now it wound round another life than hers. She would have accepted as retributive justice all that could have befallen herself, but here she could not suffer alone.

"How can I save him? How can I save him?" she thought unceasingly; save him, not alone from bodily peril and the fruit of his own noble rashness, but from the curse of the love he bore her.

All she could do for him, was to save his mortal life; all she could be faithful to him in, was to withhold from betraying him.

Time passed; she sat still there, her hands clasped round the rifle, her head drooped on its mouth, the flames now dying low to darkness, and now upleaping towards the black roof of the quarried rock. Motionless, with the tawny lustre of the fire on her, she looked like a statue of bronze, the outline of that attitude of frozen vitality, of mute despair, thrown out distinct in the ruddy light against the darkness of the cavern around. A deadening insensibility stole on her; she thought, and thought, and thought, till thought grew an unmeaning chaos; the lengthened want of sleep brought on her the numbness of death by snowdrift; she heard nothing, saw nothing, knew nothing, till a hand touched her, and a voice was in her ear.

"Oh, heaven! what horror you gave me! I traced your footsteps on the sands down to the mouth of this den, or else——"

The words died on Erceldoune's lips, arrested there by the look he saw upon her face as it was raised and turned to him. In a breathless, pitiless silence they looked upon each other, her head turned back over her shoulder in an intensity of terror that looked the terror of an infinite guilt, her whole frame shuddering from him, her haughty beauty changed into a shamed and shrinking thing of fear. He, who had prayed that the seas might cover him if once her eyes fell beneath his own, read worse than his death-sentence in that look. His arms, that had been stretched to her, sank; out of his gaze, that had sought hers in such eager wonder, all the light died; over his face passed the stern, cold, dark shadow of doubt.

"You fear me—*you!*"

The words were few, but they bore to her ear a reproach beyond all others—a reproach too noble in its rebuke to quote the thousand claims upon her trust and honour that his acts had gained. They recalled her to herself—to the one memory left her—that he must be saved. Her head fell—she had not strength to look on him—and she put him backward from her with a piteous gesture.

"I fear *for* you. Go—go—go! This place is death."

"Your place is mine. Why are you here?"

She answered nothing; she cowered there in the play of the fire's glow, whilst ever and again her glance sought the gloom of the cavern's recesses, as a hunted stag's seeks the haunts of the forest whence his hunters may spring. She had said that she would keep truth both to her tyrant and to her saviour; she had said that she would never again touch with hers the hand of the man whom her caress would betray; she had no intent but to be faithful to both bonds. But she had not looked for the ordeal of the actual presence, of the visible torture, of him whom she had consented to forsake; she had no courage to face these; she had taken no thought of how to bid him know their divorce was absolute and eternal. She was usurped by the one knowledge of the jeopardy his life was in whilst near him was the criminal who before had sought it—the criminal she had sworn to screen.

His eyes softened with an infinite yearning as he saw her; it was not in him to harbour doubt whilst pity could be needed; his nature was long-suffering and blindly generous; he only remembered that this anguish was for his sake, and was beyond his aid. He forgot all else, with that noble oblivion of a mind that takes no thought for itself. He stooped and strove to lift her up to his embrace.

"Why have you left me? What is it on you? If danger, I share it; if evil, I pardon it."

She drew herself back before his arms could raise her, and let her head sink lower and lower until her forehead touched his feet;—that dauntless brow that had never bent to monarchs or to prelates, nor drooped beneath threat or before peril.

"As you have loved me, loathe me. Go!"

Leaning over her, he heard the faintly whispered words; he started with a shiver that ran through all his limbs; the memory of the guilt imputed to her rolled back on him, like a great sudden wave of recollection, that broke down beneath it every other thought. "It is a traitress of whom we speak," it had been said to him; it looked the remorse of a traitress that abased her at his feet.

He stood above her, not raising her, not touching

her, the unspeakable love and compassion in him
straining to contest the doubt that froze his blood, the
doubt that still seemed to his loyalty of soul so vile a
crime against her. He was silent many moments,
while the heavy throbs of his heart beat audibly on
the stillness; cast there before him in the hot half-
light, all her beauty of form tempted him with re-
morseless temptation. So that she were his, what
matter what else she should be, guilty or guiltless, dishonoured or honoured, with death or with peace in her
kiss, with cruelty or with mercy on her lips? All his
soul went out to her in a great cry.

"Oh God! you are mine—you are mine! What
do I ask else—or care?"

It was the baser strength of his passion that cried
out in those burning words; their fire thrilled her, their
echo awoke in her; yet with them the force, which had
never before then failed her, revived. Here lay his
danger—this danger, born of her own loveliness, that
would abase him, and allure him, and destroy him;
this danger, which filled her with one instinct alone,
the instinct to tear him at all cost from the snake's
nest which held his foe, to compel him at · all
hazards from herself, through whom his destruction
came. She rose and locked her hands upon his arm,
and pressed him forward out towards the mouth of the
cavern.

"Go—go! This place is death for you."

"What!—and you are here?"

A smile passed over her face; the smile that is the
resignation, the self-irony, of an absolute despair.

"He doubts at last!" she thought. "He can be
saved through that."

And she had strength in her to hope from her soul that such doubt might wrong her deeply enough to spare this man some portion of his pang—might make her in his sight loathsome enough to be thrust out from every memory, cursed yet unregretted.

That smile stung him as scorpions sting; he crushed her in his arms, ere she could escape him, in the ferocity of an intense torture.

"You smile at my misery? Are you, then, the thing that they say—the beautiful, pitiless, glorious, infamous temptress, seducing men to your will that they may perish in your work, binding them by their passions that they may die at your bidding? Ah! my love, my love! only look in my eyes as an hour ago, and I will curse myself that I ever asked you such shame; only let your lips touch mine with their sweetness, and the whole world shall call you traitress, but I shall know you truth?"

The impetuous, wild words poured out unchecked, incoherent; he scarcely knew what he uttered, he only knew that the kiss of this woman would outweigh with him the witness of all mankind; they burned deep down into her heart, they brought the subtlety of temptation to her, insidious, sweet, and rank as honey-hidden poison. Her honour broken with one, her past withheld from the other; a bond ruptured, a silence kept; this only done, and the sweetness of liberty and the liberty of love were hers.

But she thrust it from her: here she had no pity for herself, and here she had pity—exhaustless and filled with an unsparing self-reproach—for this man, who out of the very nobility of his soul, the very guilelessness of his trust, fell thus beneath her feet,

and hung his life upon her. She had been merciless
to others, devoting them to her need, breaking them
through their own weakness, with the unpitying contempt and rigour of intellectual disdain and of sensuous
allurement; here she was merciless to herself; here she
bent, and broke, and cast away all her own life without
pause or compassion. That which she had done to
others she did also to herself.

She unloosed herself from his hold, and looked at
him with the cold, unnatural tranquillity which had had
its terror even for the Greek.

"Who has called me a traitress?"

His eager eyes gazed down with imploring appeal
into her own; the ardent fealty that would have
disbelieved the voice of Heaven against her glowed
through the heavy shadows of pain and dread upon his
face.

"A traitor himself—a liar who shall eat his lie in
the dust. God forgive me that I uttered the word to
you; but you speak to me strangely, you drive me
beside myself;—doubt has not touched me against
you; I would not soil you with so much as suspicion.
Oh! my loved one, your honour was safe with me;—
do not think that one shaft of his told, that one moment of belief gave him triumph. He spoke infamy
against you, it is true, and I swore to him to bring
that infamy to your hearing, but never because it
glanced by me as truth, never save only for this—to
prove him and brand him in falsehood. You know me;
as I love, so I trust, so I honour."

She stayed him with a gesture; she could bear no
more. The swift, eloquent, generous words seemed
thrust like daggers through her heart. The fearless

light of faith upon his face made her blind as with the lustre of the noonday sun. This was the man she must forsake for ever whilst their lives should last— this was the love that she must change into eternal scorn of her as of a wanton, murderous, living lie! Her martyrdom grew greater than her strength.

"Who was this speaker?"

"Victor Vane; your guest, your friend."

"And he said?"

At the name her old superb irony flashed over her face, her old superb wrath gleamed in her glance, her lofty height rose erect as a palm; her eyes met his in all the fulness of their regard.

"He said?" she repeated.

"What your look has answered enough."

"No. What does he bring to my charge?"

"Vileness that my lips will never repeat. Half-truths wrung into whole lies, as only such men can wring them. Chiefly—he bade me ask you two things——"

"They were?"

"Who it is that sought my life in the mountains, and what tie a Greek—Conrad Phaulcon—bears to you?"

A change passed over her face, like that change which steals all the living warmth and hue from features that the greyness of death is approaching. He saw it, and his voice came in broken rapid breaths, imperious and imploring.

"Are they one—this Greek and my murderer?"

She answered him nothing; he saw a hot flush rise upward over her face and bosom—the flush of a bitter degradation.

A moan like a wounded animal's broke from him; he could not bear to live and see shame touch her! He stood above her, while the flicker of the fire glowed duskily upon the dilated wondering misery of his eyes.

"Are they one? Answer me!"

She did not answer, nor did her look meet his.

"That man I showed you sleeping is ,this Greek!"

She held silence still.

"What! You screen him in his crime? What tie has he to you, then?"

Her teeth clenched tight as a vice to keep herself from utterance of the words that rushed to her tongue.

He stared blindly at her; he felt suffocating, drunk, mad; he stood beside this woman, whose every tress of hair he loved, whose mere touch could send the vivid joy like lightning through his veins, and he arraigned her as her judge for having union and collusion with his attempted slaughterer!

"What is he to you? Where is he now?" he panted. "You called him your worst foe. Do women shelter their foes' guilt thus? You would not let me take my justice on his life. What is his life to you?"

She looked at him with the rigid calm returned upon her face, impenetrable as a mask of stone.

"I said that there were things that you could never know. This is of them. I have withheld your justice from you; I have known your assassin, and kept the knowledge untold to you. I have erred against you —greatly. Think of me what you will, what you must."

The reply was spoken with a cruel mechanical

precision: she moved from him and stooped above the pine-logs, seeking their heat. She felt as she had done when once, in a Livonian winter, the night-snows had overtaken and enshrouded her, and the life had begun to turn to ice in her veins.

Something in the very action bespoke a suffering so mute and so intense that it struck to his heart, still so closed to evil and so open to faith, so slow to give condemnation, so quick to render trust and pity. He threw himself beside her, drawing her hands against his breast, searching her eyes with the longing love, the bewildered incredulity, of his own.

"Think of you! What can I think? You are my mistress, my sovereign, my wife; you take my love and yield me yours; you have smiled in my eyes, and lain in my arms, and spoken of a lifetime passed together; and now—now—it is my murderer who is sacred to you and beloved by you—not I!"

As though the fire of the words stung her into sudden life, she turned swiftly, all the light and the fever, and the anguish of passion breaking one moment through the frozen tranquillity of her face.

"Not you? Ah! would it were not, my love, my love, my love!"

In the yearning of the accent a tenderness unutterable broke out and burst all bonds; as he heard the darkness passed from his face—a glow like the morning shone there.

"You love me thus! You cannot have betrayed me——"

She stayed him; she knew that this glory of re-awakening joy must be quenched in an eternal night.

"Wait. I love you. I cannot lie to you *there*.

But that ends, now and always. I say, you have been
sinned against heavily; I must sin also against you—
sin without shame by forsaking you, sin with shame
by life with you. I choose the least. We are divorced
for ever. We must be as are the dead to one another.
Forgive me, if you can; curse me, if you cannot.
Whatever you do—leave me, as though death were in
my touch."

All the ardour, and the yearning, and the warmth
had passed from her voice; it was sad as despair, and
as inflexible.

He listened, watching her with a grave wondering
pain and pity; he had his own construction of the
meaning of her words, and the patience and the belief
in him were infinite.

"Though death came by you, do you think that I
would leave you?"

The great salt tears sprang into her aching eyes.
She could have set the muzzle of the rifle to her forehead, and died there at his feet. She had a more merciless ordeal—to live and make herself loathsome in
his sight.

"No; not for death," she answered him. "But—
if dishonour came by me?"

His frame shook with a sudden shudder, but still
she could not turn away the enduring tenderness that
would not take even her own witness against her.

"You use cruel words," he said, while he stood
above her with the dignity of a judge, with a great
nobility in the pity of his gaze. "Hear me a while.
I have learnt more of your past to-day; I think that
I can imagine what I do not know of it. I think that
you have been involved in evil, but through errors

that had root in virtues. I think that many have betrayed you and attainted you through the very bravery
and generosity of your nature. I think that you have
been bound with criminals because you first held them
to be patriots, and because your bond was sacred to
you even when sworn to worthless men. Do I think
aright?"

She heard in silence; her soul went out in honour
and adoration to this man, who, from the truth and
the virtue of his own heart, judged and divined her
life thus rightly, despite all weight of circumstance, all
darkness of calumny. But she knew that to leave him
to believe this was to bind her to him for evermore.
She knew that he must believe else than this ere he
would be forced from allegiance to her.

"You think nobly, because you think by the light
of your own heart," she said, in her teeth. "But it is
not this that you were warned to think to-day! Your
counsellor was nearer right. Believe him."

"Were you what he said, you would not tell me
that. I judge you thus by the light of your own nature.
You speak to me of divorce—of dishonour. You know
the coward who attempted my life, and will not render
him up to my justice. These are bitter things; yet I
can see day through them. It may be that you have
fallen amongst much guilt, and yet are unstained amidst
corruption. It may be that you shield a crime, because to expose it would be treachery in you. It may
be that you elect to forsake me because you cannot reveal to me that full truth of your past which should be
one of my marriage-rights. This is how I judge you.
If I judge rightly—I said to you that you could not
stretch my tenderness further than I would yield it. I

say so now; trust only my love, it shall never fail you."

"Oh, God! cease, or you will kill me!"

She swayed forward and sank down at his feet, her brow and bosom bruised on the cold jagged floor of the cavern. She had exceeding strength, but she had not strength enough to hear those tender words and give them no response; to behold this limitless forgiveness stretched to her, and leave him to think her too callous, too abased, to return to it even gratitude and repentance; to know that, as he judged her, he struck to the very core of fact, and rendered her but sheer and rightful justice, yet that the acceptance of even this justice at his hands was denied her through an alien crime.

He stood above her, the great dew gathering on his forehead; the evidences against her that her accuser had uncoiled one by one in so close a sequence thronged on his memory; her attitude, her misery, her abasement, had so much of guilt in them, yet had so far too much of suffering to be the cruel, wanton, voluntary guilt of such a woman as her calumniator had declared her to be—to be guilt, sensual, tyrannous, and self-chosen.

He stooped to her, and his voice was so low that it was hardly heard above the beatings of his heart.

"I cannot tell; is it—not justice that you need, but pardon?"

She answered him nothing where she had sunk in that abandonment. The nobler his pardon, the darker was the wrong against him. She could have kissed his feet, and cried out to him for forgiveness, as though her own hand had done that murderous iniquity against him. She could better have borne his curse than she could bear his tenderness.

He touched her; his hand shook like a leaf.

"Is it so? I can bear to know you are human by error; you shall be but dearer to me for the truth with which you redeem it."

She looked at him with a swift sudden movement that raised the full beauty of her face upward in the tawny flame-light; it was colourless, and lined with the marks of the damp stones, and had all its proud glory soiled and dimmed, yet it had the grandeur of an intense sacrifice, of an intense passion, in it.

"Ah, you are just and pitiful as a god! Give no pity, give no justice here. Only leave me—leave me, and never look upon my face again!"

"For what cause?"

"For the cause—that of my people—your murderer came."

He looked at her with a terrible incredulity, that was slowly hardening into the stern chill desolation of doubt that he had put from him so long with so leal an allegiance.

"Of your people! You called the Greek to me your deadliest foe?"

She was silent once more: the testimony of half the nations of the earth would have failed to weigh with him against her; but by her own blows the storm-proof fabric of his faith was swaying to its fall.

He laid his hands upon her shoulders, crushing under them the loose masses of her hair.

"First your foe, then your comrade—hated and sheltered—condemned by you, and screened by you.

What is he to you, this man for whom you forswear yourself thus?"

She answered nothing; the red shadow of the fire gleamed upon her face, but it was not so dark or so hot as the flush of shame that scorched there. His hands held her like iron. The force of jealousy rose in him; the ferocity of bitter suspicion worked in him; against all witness he had disbelieved every accusation brought to stain her, but he could not disbelieve the meaning of that silence, of that humiliation, of that conscience-stricken abasement.

The patience, so long strained, broke at last.

"They say this brute was once dear to you? Is it true, since you cover his crime so fondly?"

She did not reply; her head was bent so that he could not look upon her countenance, but he could see the heaving of her breast with its rapid, laden breathing.

His hands grasped her with unconscious violence; he knew neither what he did or said; he knew only that she could not meet his eyes, that she could not answer his challenge.

"Is it true?—that you once loved him?"

She bowed her head; a faint, chill, deadly smile crossed her lips one moment, she smiled as men, lying broken on the wheel, have laughed.

A cry rang from him down the stillness of the vault; he staggered where he stood, and loosed her from his hold, and stretched his arms out mechanically, as though he had grown blind and sought support. The merciless light of certainty seemed to have stricken his sight as lightning strikes it; that hideous assurance of conviction had come on him, against which the mind is at once and for ever conscious no appeal is possible.

Had she denied it, by the trustful tenderness of his nature, the evil told against her would have passed, leaving no stain, no shadow even, of mistrust of her; but before that affirmation of her gesture, before that condemnation of her silence, it lay no more with him to choose between belief and disbelief. His faith fell, as a tree must fall when its roots are severed.

"There is one man—one man only—that your mistress ever loved."

The words seemed whispered by a thousand voices that rushed down the empty air; he had been betrayed by her that this criminal might be sheltered from his vengeance!

He knew it; in that horrible hush of stillness that fell between them, his heart stood still, his very life seemed to cease; it was out of her own mouth that he condemned her. His throat rattled, his words burst, scarcely with any human sound in them, from his parching lips.

"What! you kneel there and tell me this thing— you who swore to me that no kiss but mine ever touched you? What? you fooled me with love-words that you might lead me off the scent of my vengeance; you turned a living lie to harbour a murderer? Such vileness is not in woman! You a slave of your senses!— a priestess of vice! Oh, God! Say the whole world is false, but not you!"

She held silence still. Her head dropped lower and lower, as though each word of that appeal were a hurled stone that beat her down lower and lower in her abasement.

He forced her upward in his arms with the unwitting violence of suffering, and strained her once

more to his embrace, and covered with kisses her lips,
her brow, her bosom.

"Say it—say it. Say the world lies and you are
true, or—or—I shall end your life and mine!"

Her eyes, heavy with the mists of a great misery,
fathomless and hopeless like the eyes of the Fates in
Greek sculptures, gazed up to his.

"Do you dream *I* would stay your hand? It were
best so—so I should be yours yet."

"Mine! What then?—you love me though you are
my traitress?"

"One may have guilt and yet have love," she muttered, faintly.

He shuddered as he heard her; in the answer a
subtle tempting coiled around him; the perfection of
her earthly beauty might be his, though it were but
the love of the wanton wherewith she loved him; the
taint on her soul could not steal the fragrance from her
lips, the voluptuous light from her eyes, the mortal
glory from her loveliness. The baser passions of his
soul longed for her, though every evil that swells the
sum of human crime had place in her—though through
her should come to him sin, and desolation, and dishonour. Yet—he was not their slave; the greatness
of his nature rose above them, and trampled out their
tempting. He put her from his arms lest his strength
should fail him, thrust her back from him so that her
breath should be no more against his cheek, her heart
throb no more on his own.

"Love that is faithless and shameful? What is that
to me? If you have wronged my vilest foe, the woman
I loved is dead."

Where she stood before him she bowed her head,

as beneath words that had the weight of a righteous law. For this—that he rose higher than his passions' tempting, that he strangled the assailants of his senses, that infidelity to his enemy would have been as dark in his sight as infidelity to himself—she honoured him with a great reverence.

"Yes. She is dead," she answered him, with a strange dreamy repetition. "Where has she ever lived save in your visions? She is dead — go. Do not wait by her grave."

There was a terrible meaning in the hushed, hopeless words; across their calmness a single cry broke— a cry that had in it all the despair of a ruined life, of a breaking heart.

Then silence fell between them. She had no courage to look upon his face; she dared not read all that she knew was written there.

The drooping flames reached a dry bough of pine, and flared afresh with it, and rose up in a writhing column of light. As the flames darted into lustre they shed their hue on the fair head of the Greek stretched out from the deep gloom of the farther vault. He drew back swiftly, as the tell-tale glare searched for him, and fell upon his face.

Yet before he could reach the shelter of the inner den, the one he had wronged saw him, and, with the leap of a staghound, hurled himself upon him, and dragged him from the depths of the vault forward into the full light of the flames. The slight limbs of the Athenian had no force against the vengeance of the man who found in him at once his murderer and her paramour; he was torn out from his lair and tossed upward, as a wrecker's hands may toss a beam of driftwood.

Erceldoune forced him downward into the circle of the burning pines, full in their light and full in her sight. He only knew that this was the man who had sought to assassinate him; that this was the man for whom and to whom she betrayed him. Yet, beyond the memory of his vengeance, beyond the violence of his hatred, beyond the rage of jealousy in his soul, was a terrible pathos of wonder that looked out at her from the reproach of his eyes;—it was for a thing so vile as this she had betrayed him! it was for a life so infamous as this that she had given herself to guilt!

Reeling, swaying, striving, they wrestled breast to breast, strangers from the far ends of the earth, yet bound together by the kinships of wrong and of hate, while she, who had cast herself between them, strove to part them—strove to tear them asunder—strove with desperate strength to end their contest. Erceldoune flung her heavily off him.

"You stayed my hand once—not again. Stand there, and see the felon you harbour die as curs die!"

His face was black and swollen with the lust for blood that she had seen there when he had fought with the Neapolitan Churchman. Wound in one another, they struggled together, seeking each other's lives, with the breath of the flames hot upon them. The Greek's lips were white with fear, but they laughed as he glanced aside at her.

"You love to see men at each others' throats? You

love to see tigers play? So, so, Miladi!—then look
here."

He slipped loose with a swift, supple movement,
and freed his right arm. There was the glisten of
steel in the light; the blade quivered aloft to strike
down straight through heart or lung; before it could
fall, his wrist was caught in a grip that well-nigh
snapped the bone, and wrenching the knife from his
hand, flung it far away into the depths of the cavern,
while the sinewy arms of the man he had wronged
gathered him fresh into their deadly embrace. The
slender southern limbs had no chance, the serpentine
suppleness had no avail, the fox-like skill had no
power, against the mighty frame and the ruthless will
of the avenger who at last had tracked him; a shrill
scream broke from him as the steel was twisted from
his grasp, the numbness of dread overcame him as he
was choked in the arms of his victim, and down into
his looked the unbearable fire of the eyes he had left
for the carrion-birds to tear. A sickly horror, a fascination of terror, held him breathless and unresisting to
the will of his foe; Erceldoune swung him upward, and
held him, as though he were a dog, above his head,
his own height towering in the glow of the flames.

"Oh, God!" he cried, in the blindness of his agony
and of his hate. "Is there no death worse than what
honest men die for this brute?"

She threw herself on him, she seized the loose
folds of his linen dress, she held him so that he had
no power to move unless he trod her down beneath his
feet.

"Spare him!—for my sake, spare him!"

"For your sake! You dare plead by that plea to me?"

"Oh, Heaven, what matter what I plead by! Give me his life—give me his life!"

"The life of a murderer to the prayer of a wanton? A fit gift? Stand back, or I shall kill you with your paramour."

"Wait!—you do not know what you do! I saved your life from him—let that buy his life from you!"

He stood motionless, as though the words paralysed him; all the tempests of his passions suddenly arrested; all the wild justice of revenge, that had made him strong as lions are strong, turned worthless as at last he grasped its power in his hands. The blow that struck him was memory—the memory of that death-hour when through her hands life had been given back to him.

By that hour he had sworn that she should ask what she would of him, and receive it. At last she claimed her debt; claimed by it the remission of her sins—claimed by it mercy to the companion of her guilt.

He stood motionless a moment, the leaden night-like shadows heavy as murder on his face and on his soul—then at her feet he dashed the Greek down, unharmed.

"What you ask by my honour — take by your shame."

And, without another look upon her face, he went out to the air, to the sea, to the day, ere his strength should fail him, and the stain of blood-guiltiness lie on his hands.

CHAPTER XIII.

"I lean toward the Stroke with silent Mouth and a great Heart."

CONRAD PHAULCON slowly gathered himself from the ground, faint, blind, staggering from the force with which he had been thrown, and looked on her where she had fallen senseless—her proud head sunk on the grey wood-ashes, her face white with the whiteness of death. He thought her dead: and a mortal dread fell on him, a mortal chillness froze his heart. In his own cruel, tyrannous way he loved her still, and he thought that he had killed her. Moreover, she had been faithful to him. Listening and watching there, he had found that she had kept her bond to him, and had not betrayed him. The evil against her died out from him; a shame that was almost remorse stole on him. Senseless there, like some fair statue shattered down by a hand that stayed not for sake of beauty or of genius, she smote his conscience, all dulled, and crushed, and burnt out though it was. Throughout their lives he had betrayed, and oppressed, and goaded, and dishonoured her, throughout them she had done him good for evil, and been true to him against his own untruth. This strength and this fealty pierced him harder, because of their utter unlikeness to the cowardice and the greed of his own nature.

With hands that trembled, and tears that stood thick in his eyes, he touched her, and sought to revive her; his temper was the temper of a child, and he had a child's fleet facile emotions, a child's wanton cruelty and worthless repentance. Like a child, he could wring his bird's throat without mercy, and weep useless tears when the victim lay cold and huddled in death.

After a while sense returned to her; her lips parted with slow struggling breaths, her veins grew warm, her eyelids quivered and opened heavily to the glare of the resinous flames. She knew him where he bent above her, and lifted herself with a sudden breathless shuddering force.

"Go, go, go! Never dare to come again in my sight!"

He lingered, scared and awed by the words and the gesture that were like an imprecation upon him, by the blaze of her eyes as they unclosed, wide and wild, to the tawny light.

"Go, go!" she cried afresh. "You could hear what he called me, and yet hold your peace! Go!—there are wrongs gods themselves could not pardon."

He knew it; he turned slowly away, and went from her glance, from her presence.

She rose faintly, and reeling slightly; looking out at the darkness that closed her in, whilst for all the world without the morning sun was shining. She was like one drunk with alcohol; her brain was stunned, yet her force intensified; the power and the vitality in her were strong almost to ferocity—the ferocity of that unbearable suffering which is in itself a madness. Like some lithe-limbed leopardess stung to blood-thirstiness by the shot that has struck it from an unseen hand, she passed swiftly across the depths of shadow, to the place where the boy Berto lay sleeping still in the intense slumber of long fatigue.

She laid her hand upon him. "Wake."

He did awaken, and sprang wonderingly from his bed of dry sea-grasses.

"Illustrissima! What is there?"

"There is need of you."

"I am ready." The fair, pale, boyish face had the calm keenness of the Napoleonic type. "It is——?"

"Treason."

"Ah!"

His eyes caught the meaning, his mouth the smile, that were on hers.

"Treason—against me; if to me, so to all; so to Italy. A traitor never sins *once*. Seek Lousada and Veni; seek your brethren, seek any one of our people. They know how to avenge the unpardonable sin. Bid them bring him here; I will give him his sentence."

The boy smiled; the smile of a St. Just.

"He has lived his life," he said, in the old Roman idiom. "His name, Eccellenza?"

She stooped and breathed it on his ear: the name of Victor Vane.

Without word or pause he bowed low, took his rifle, and went on her errand; a child by years, yet already weighted with the weariness and the wisdom of maturity, by reason of the penalty he paid for having let his childish soul brood over the burdens of the peoples, and dream of liberties under the leprous shadow of a dominant priesthood, whilst other children laughed, and played, and only asked of life that the vine should give fruit, and the sleek herds milk, that their gay feet should ply in the tarantula's measure, and the sweet sun dance in their own bright eyes.

She, left there in solitude, and bound by her word to keep the limits of her den, paced to and fro in the fire-lit darkness in that fierce, futile rebellion with which she had paced the dungeon of the church. Her eyes were burning, her throat was swollen with long thirst, her teeth were locked like a vice. All sense, thought, volition, seemed scorched up and withered in one intolerable misery, one unalterable shame. One thing alone seemed left to her—her vengeance.

She was of the nature which happiness makes sweet, rich, generous, as southern sunlight; which calamity renders fearless, strong, and nobly calm beneath all adverse fate; but which, beneath wrong and treachery, in an instant turns hard, dark, dangerous as the force of iron.

She laughed aloud, in the loneliness.

"He played the traitor!—so! Well, he will learn how we deal with traitors. Fool, fool, fool!"

Then, as that laugh died, the weakness of her bodily frame, the agony of her soul, beat down the false alien strength of bitter passions.

"Oh, my love!" she moaned. "It was for your life, not for mine."

And she sank amidst the grey ashes by the fire that was slowly dying out, with the stupor of exhaustion stealing on her, and her eyes fastened on the gloom beyond, strained, and senseless, and savage with pain, like those of an animal that is chained to a stake for the torture.

To her, there could have been no martyrdom like this martyrdom of undenied dishonour. ·

Without, the boy Berto passed into the glare of day. His errand was perilous; and he knew what Tedeschi rods were like, how Papal steel could thrust; but he had the firm, silent heart that Nature early gives to those whom she will hereafter make leaders amongst men, and, having a purpose to accomplish, he did it unflinchingly, through to the end. He went swiftly and straightly now over the lonely shore, with the eye of a hawk, with the speed of a greyhound, glancing on every side for those he sought, and going warily, lest he should be seen by the soldiers, whom he knew were out, more or less near, seeking for the proscribed who had escaped them. He ran swiftly, mile on mile; reaching a crest of land, he paused at last for breath. On one side lay the sea, now blue and laughing in the full noon-day; and the other, mountain-bounded, the low-lying lands, with their broad sun-lit desolate tracks dotted with the herds of swine and grazing buffaloes, with thickets of wild myrtle and green pools of water. There he saw what made him drop suddenly, and hide like a young hare.

What he saw were the barrels of carbines among some acanthus-covered stones that screened a score or so of soldiers, and further onward the solitary figure of a man in the clothing of the Capri fishers. The soldiers lay close, their heads alone above the fallen blocks of shattered marble; the tall form of the Capriote, dark and towering against the intense light, came onward, fast, blindly, taking heed of nothing, seeing nothing, in his path, passing straight through the horned cattle as though they were an insect cloud, with his head bare to the heat, and his eyes without sense in them; headlong, as if he were deep in drink, yet with a nameless misery on him that had as terrible a majesty.

Fascinated by it, the Roman boy watched him as he reeled through the sunlight, while the browsing herds were scattered by the tornado of his course. The soldiers watched him also, as he came nearer and nearer straight across the plain, pausing for no obstacle, breaking through all vegetation, rushing like the wind over

the width of the country. Then, rapidly as a lasso is
thrown, they sprang upon him as he passed; his arms,
his limbs, his body, were bound and knotted with cords
ere he could cast off 'one of the score of hands that
seized him; fettered in an instant, with the naked
blades flashing round him, he stood like a wild horse
netted by guachos, his muscles panting under the
close-drawn bonds, his eyes wide-opened on his captors,
red and glaring and senseless. There was no escape
possible.

IIe stood a moment, looking vacantly down on his
bound limbs and the savage wolf-eyes of the soldiery.
All consciousness seemed dead in him; he was passive
from the sheer intoxication of suffering, and he was
weak in his body also, for from a wound on his shoulder
blood was oozing through his shirt. Yet, as he felt
the withies on his limbs, he fought against his captors
on the sheer instinct of combat, with his head dropped
like a bull of Aragon when it charges to give to the
torreador the fatal blow of the *cogida*, and with his firm
white teeth, the only weapon left him, clenched hard
and fast at the throat of the soldier nearest him.

For some minutes there was a struggle that made
even the bold veins of the Roman boy run chill—
weakened, hampered, jammed, powerless as the captive
was, he had terror for his assailants, as the bull when
its black hide is steeped scarlet with gore, and its flanks
are transfixed with the lance-heads, carries death for
picador and banderillo still. But brute force conquered;
the hirelings of Francis were scarce better than brigands,
and courage awakened no homage in them. When they
fell away a little from each other, and the dust of the
parched plain that had risen in clouds above the scene

of the conflict sank, they had pulled him down as with a lasso—he was stretched there on the short burnt turf, his eyes distended, his mouth filled with sand, his limbs lashed fast with cords.

To them he was but a Capri boatman, a thing of the people, a scum of the sea, a rebel on whose life a good price was set, an animal to be thrust to the shambles, how roughly mattered little so that out of his heart they should cut that which they sought to know.

They heaved him up, with a kick, by the ropes they had passed round his waist and under his shoulders; they loosened a little the cords binding his ankles, and bade him stand, holding a carbine at his head; then they fastened him by his belt to two of the strongest-built of their band, and, with bayonets fixed in his rear, drove him on in their centre, as the Aragon bull is driven on at the point of the lance from pasture to circus.

So they took their way through the white breath of the sunlight over the brown lonely plains, with their prisoner set in their midst. He had never spoken once.

The child Berto rose slowly from his hiding-place in the low myrtle-bushes; many a time his hand had been on his rifle to send a message of death through these wolves of the mountains who wore the King's livery, and dishonoured the title of soldier; as many times he had paused, knowing that one shot could avail nothing, and that, were it fired, he would only share the captivity of the man whom he sought to release. As his slight, girlish frame rose up out of the leafy screen and against the sunny blue of the sky, his teeth were set tight, his pale features had grown like marble.

"They go to take him to their captain;—they will make him tell where her refuge is. If he will not tell, they have rods, they have the water-torture—drop, drop, drop, ah! till one is mad!" he muttered aloud, in his breathless rage. He knew nothing of this stranger, save that he guessed him by his dress to be the sailor whom he had heard had rescued her from Taverno—in the cavern his sleep had been too profound to awake to any distant sound—but the sight of the conflict and the capture alone sufficed to rouse all the revolutionary and patriotic soul that was in him. He wrung his hands as he watched the soldiers move over the plain, growing dark and distant as some far-off troop of buffalo.

"Ah, the brigands! the assassins! And I could not fire a bullet for him!" he cried in his solitude. "Miladi must know of it. She can say whether he will bear the scourge and be silent. If I had thought he would speak, I would have shot him dead before they could have got him. Almost I wish I had. It had been surer."

For the Roman lad knew the means—passing the strength of humanity to endure—by which men who were mute against royal or priestly will were made to find voice in that fair dominion of Naples.

"She must know," he mused;—waited an instant, then with the speed of a lapwing, once having the swell of the hillocks between him and the soldiery, he retraced his way over the lowlands to whence he came, until out of the laughing brilliance of the noon-sun he came into the darkness of the cave, which now

was only lightened by the low flicker of the expiring
pine-flames.

Her attitude had never changed. There was that
in it, as she sat beside the great heap of silvered ashes
and of burnt-out wood, that struck the boy's heart
with a sudden awe and fear. The abasement, the subjection, of a fearless life has ever in it a certain terror
—the mournful terror of every fallen greatness—for
those who look upon it.

He went softly to her, and spoke low in her ear
before she saw him by her.

"Eccellenza, the soldiery are out."

She gave no sign that she heard him.

"The soldiers have him! Can you trust him,
Illustrissima?"

She still seemed to hear nothing where her gaze
was fixed upon the dying fire. The boy touched her
timidly.

"The King's people have him, Miladi. Will he be
true?"

She started, as though some corpse had been gal-
vanised to life, and turned her face to him.

"True? Will who be true? He whom all are false
to? Yes, true to death—true to death!"

He saw that her mind wandered, that she had not
aright understood him.

"Eccellenza, hear me," he said, softly. "The
soldiers have made that friend of yours their prisoner."

She sprang to her feet, convulsed to passionate
energy, to fresh existence.

"Prisoner? The King's prisoner?—*he!*"

The boy's voice sank to a whisper; he had not

thought it would move her thus; he knew she was well used to send men out to die.

"They took him on the shore there, by the ruins. They caught a brave man like a snared wolf, the cowards! He fought—gods! how he fought; but they threw him like a bull in the lasso. Will he keep silence, think you?"

"He will keep silence till they lay him mute in death. Ah! God reward you that you came to tell me!"

She put the wondering child aside, and swept across the vault to the far-off shadow where the Greek had crouched; she stood before him ere he had seen her move.

"I break my word to you. I go from here."

"Go!"—he echoed dizzily; the violence of his fall had stupified him. "Go! Not where I do not follow."

"Follow, if you will."

"Where, then?"

"To the soldiers of Francis."

She laughed aloud as she spoke; she knew that the cowardice of his nature would no more let him pass out where she went than if gates of adamant opposed him. He was startled and bewildered; he felt tenfold fear of her as she stood there in the shadows before him, with that despair on her face and that laugh on her lips; he had thought her dead or dying; a superstitious hesitation held him afraid and irresolute.

"Wait—wait," he said, stretching his hands out to hold her. "What is it you dream of? What mad thing would you do?"

"Save the life you and I have sent out to destruction."

Before he could arrest her she had passed him, and was far out beyond the watch-fire, and lost in the gloom of the entrance-passage; her hand was on the boy Berto's shoulder, and thrust him down the tortuous passage, swiftly and silently up to the open air. When once more the darkness lay behind her, and on her face was the breath of the morning, she bent to him.

"Which way?"

He pointed to the northward, looking with wistful anxiety in her face.

"Miladi, what is it you will do?"

"My duty—late in the day."

The hound had followed at her side; she stooped and kissed his forehead, then sent him from her back into the shelter of the cavern, reluctant yet obedient.

"Will you not need him?" the boy asked.

"No. Even a dog's life is too noble to perish for mine. See you to him, and cherish him for my sake."

"I! I go with you, Eccellenza."

"No—go rather on the errand I gave you."

"But——"

"Hush! I have said -- none go with me. And—for that you came and told me this thing—may the beauty of life rest with you ever, my child."

She passed her hand softly over his fair curls.

Then as rapidly and silently as a shadow passes she went from him on her fatal way.

Over the heavy, rugged ground the soldiers forced their prisoner, with his arms lashed behind him, and the carbines held at his temples. They were a dozen men under a corporal, scouts sent out by the commandant of the gendarmerie scouring the shore; low scoundrels

who had been thieves ere they donned the King's
uniform, and would be brigands when they doffed it.
So that they dragged him to their captain, and compelled him to tell what they sought from him, they
heeded nothing beyond. His bound feet stumbled over
the rough declivities, his chest was stifled under the
crossed cords till he could barely breathe; with every
jerked step that his guards took over the roughness of
the ground their shot might be lodged in his brain; the
red ants, disturbed in their hills, swarmed up his limbs
and clung there; the open wound of his shoulder was
cut by the tight-drawn ropes; still he said not one
word, but went on in their midst, with his bloodshot
eyes staring out at earth and sky yet seeing nothing,
and with a heavy, sullen, murderous darkness on his
face and on his soul.

Of physical suffering he was insensible; the dead-
ness of despair had numbed in him all corporeal consciousness. There had only survived in him the mere
mechanical brute instincts of defence and of resistance.
Beaten in these he resigned himself, passively, dumbly;
too vast a ruin had fallen on his life for him to heed
what befel his body. So far as thought still was distinct
to him, so far as any ray of it pierced the blackness
of desolation in which every memory save one was lost,
he wished that they would strike him dead upon the
plain they traversed.

They wondered that, cramped and bruised as he
was, and strong to ferocity as they had found him,
he went with them thus mutely and unresistingly; they
did not note the keen, hard, ravenous, longing look,
as of one starving at sight of food, that his eyes ever
and again cast upon the steel tubes of the slanted

carbines which carried death and oblivion so near, and yet denied them, to him.

Beyond this he knew nothing; he was dragged over the low-lying country at a pace as swift as the heat of the day and the unevenness of the uncertain paths would allow; whether he had force to bear it, in the sultry noontide of summer, they never heeded. If he had fallen, they would have pulled him on still, as best they might, with his head striking the stones. He knew nothing; the sunlight was like a blaze of fire over about him; the hard, hot skies seemed to glitter as brass; water, mountain, the darkness of myrtle, the rush of wild birds, the blue gleam of the sea, the brown baked earth beneath his feet, these were all blurred, shapeless shadows to him, while his eyes looked out, straight onward, with the red, dusky, mastiff flame in them that made his guards mutter among themselves that this man was mad, and should be shot like a mad dog.

And they judged right: he was mad, with the Othello madness that believes what it adores dishonoured.

At last their march paused; the silence was broken by the noise of loosened tongues; there were stir, and tumult, and the clash of arms around them; they had joined their comrades,—they had brought their prisoner to their captain to be judged. Under some mighty pillars of yellow travestine, the lonely relics of some forgotten temple, four or five score of black-browed, loose-harnessed soldiers, the worst of a worthless army, were scattered, lying full-length in the shade, taking their noonday meal, or slaking their thirst at a sluggish noxious streamlet stealing by the columns' base amongst the violet-roots. They had been checked a moment in their search by the sea for the fugitives; and lay like hot, panting, ferocious dogs, ready to rise and use their teeth at a moment's tempting.

They swarmed round him like a pack of wolves, but no change came on his face; with a hundred soldiers beside him, lean, savage, ruffianly, for the most part, as any Abruzzian banditti, with the glitter of their steel, the muzzles of their carbines, the yelling of their oaths, the clamour of their triumph about him where he stood powerless in their midst, they could not tell that he even saw them there. His eyes never glanced to them; they looked still, straightly, sightlessly, to the low line where sea touched sky; there was no consciousness in them; but there was that which stilled their riot of exultation with a vague sense of danger in this chained man standing so calmly in their hostile crowd.

They fell back, as their commander, told of the capture, came from the nook of shadow, where, with his subaltern, he had been at rest apart. He was little more than a *guerillero*—a course, rough, careless, Calabrian-born filibuster.

"A fine animal," he muttered, as he glanced over a paper of instructions, comparing the details there with the personal appearance of his prisoner. "So! you are the sacrilegious scoundrel who broke into the monastery of Taverno, and used foul violence against the august person of his sacred grace of Villaflor?"

"I am."

Erceldoune answered mechanically; his tongue clove to his mouth; his voice was hoarse and savage.

"Basta! you are in haste to be hanged!" swore the Calabrian, half disappointed at an avowal which left him no excuse for the ingenuity of threat and torture. "Since you confess yourself guilty, go further, and tell us—what have you done with the bona-roba you stole from her prison?"

The word struck like the stroke of lightning.

Life, sense, shame, grief, rage, rushed over his hearer with a torrent's force; the foam gathered on his lips; he strained for a moment like a fettered lion at his bonds;—then he was still as with the stillness of death.

"Speak—where is she?"

He made no answer.

"Have you no tongue? We will make you find it, and use it Tell me—quick!—where is this woman hidden?"

His vengeance was in his hands; one word, one gesture only, to where the sea-cave lay, and his wrongs would be avenged, without the lifting of his hand.

"Speak out," hissed the soldier, whose rage was rising. "Where is this empress-democrat? Where does she hide? She knew how to use that buffalo strength of yours; but she will fool you, once she be free. We know what Miladi is! Give her to us; and you may save yourself a necklace of hemp, mayhap?"

There was still no answer.

"Has the sorceress put a spell on you?" swore the Calabrian. "Look you—you are safe to go to the gallows. Corpo di Christo!—it will be odds if his Grace do not think a quick twitch of the noose too gentle a punishment for you: Monsignore has a long arm and a heavy hand! You are a fine animal—it were a pity all that sinew should rot in quick lime; we will get your life saved somehow, if you put us this minute on the track of your mistress?"

He might never have spoken for aught by which he could tell that he was heard. The threat that his body would be given to slaughter had little import to the man in whom all life, save the mere breath of existence, had already been slain by worse than a thousand deaths.

"Have you no voice?" yelled the commandant, infuriated that his unwonted offer of mercy met no response. "We will find a way to make you speak, with your will or against it! Once for all—will you show us where this woman is sheltered?"

"No."

The Calabrian gnashed his glittering teeth.

"*Altro!* You defy us, you hound? We will see how long that obstinacy lasts. I have licence to deal with you as I see fit; to string you up by the throat to that column if I judge it right in the need of my service. We will soon make you find voice, you dog of a rebel! Here; take him, and lash him to that pillar; there, in the full sun."

He was already bound, in cords that crossed and recrossed, and left him scarce liberty to draw the air through his lungs; it was an easy matter to fasten him to the shaft of the shattered column that stood in the glare of the noon, unshaded even by a branch or a coil of ivy.

"Strip his shoulders, and let the gnats find him out," laughed the Calabrian, moving away to finish his meal and take a mid-day slumber. "We will see if we do not make him give tongue."

He was obeyed.

They stripped the linen from his chest and shoulders, and left him in the fullest force of the vertical rays; his wound uncovered, and his head bare. At his feet ran the half-dry brook. They went themselves into the shadow, and lay laughing, swearing, mocking, taunting, chanting obscene songs, and holding up to him in the distance the wine-cans they had drained.

The insults passed by him unnoted, the jeers unheard; in the desolation of his life they were known no more than the sting of an insect is felt by one whom the smoke and flame of a burning pile is consuming.

Yet they had chained him to a martyrdom.

The intense heat poured upon his brain; the scorching light quivered about him; his veins swelled till it seemed, with every fresh pulse of the blood, they must burst; the innumerable winged insects, humming through the summer hours, attracted one by another, settled on his naked breast, and thrust their antennæ into the bruised skin, and pierced their stings into the opening of the wound. He could not free his hands to brush one of them away. His throat was dry as leather; his tongue was swollen and black; his thirst was unbearable; and at his feet the shallow water stole, to madden him with the murmur of the cool ripples he could not touch. The moments were as hours; the minutes as years. The earth, the air, the sky, were as one vast furnace that enclosed him; where the jagged and beating nerves had been laid open by the hatchet-stroke, the buzzing gnats alit, and clove, and stung, and feasted. Weaklier men would have had the mercy of insensibility;—with him the vital strength, the indestructible force of life within him, kept every nerve and every sense strung to their keenest under the torture.

Yet when they came to him ever and again and asked him if he would speak at last, his silence remained unbroken. He was faithful to those who had betrayed him.

He could receive release, as he could take vengeance, by the utterance of one word. He could deliver over his assassin to justice, and unloose his traitress to the doom that waited her, by the same sign that should free him from this slow excruciating death. He could cease to suffer, and become the just accuser of those by whom he was destroyed. He could sever his bonds, and divide those whose guilty union was a worse agony to him than it lay in the power of his torturers to deal. His own fate and theirs rested in his choice.

And he bore his martyrdom and kept silence. The supreme hour of his passion had come to him and tempted him, and found him strong. The purity of his honour would not let him take a traitorous shame even against those who dealt him treachery; the great love in him could not forsake her utterly, although itself forsaken and betrayed.

The bond of his word was as religion to him still; and in his sight, though fallen, lost, dishonoured, she still was sacred.

So far as thought could come to him, his thought was still to save her.

And he hung there, bound by the waist, with the blaze of the sun in his blind eyes and on his throbbing brain, and the clouds of the booming circling gossamer wings growing darker and larger as his tormentors swarmed down to fasten upon him.

One of the soldiers, whom he had heavily bruised

in the struggle for his capture, came out of the shade and dipped a wooden cup in the brook, and held it just beyond the reach of his lips.

"Speak, and you shall have drink!"

His throat was baked like burnt clay, his mouth was full of dust, his tongue was cloven to his teeth; he longed for water with the death-thirst of the desert.

The Italian reached and touched his beard with the rim of the cup, so that the coolness of the draught mocked him close.

"Will you speak?"

He faintly moved his head in denial.

The soldier laughed with taunting mirth, and shook the water from the bowl out on to the herbage at his feet: he knew that every wasted drop would be an added pang.

Still he never spoke.

They left him again to the Tantalus torture. He had his freedom in his own choice; in the utterance of one word; and he let them do their worst upon him rather than turn traitor to the woman whom he held his traitress.

They came and grouped about the pillar, and looked up in his face again with riotous laughter and foul-mouthed outrage at him in his defencelessness. The brazen sky burned above in pitiless fire; the smiling cruelty of the salt sea mocked him with its tossing sunlit freshness; the red ants were slowly climbing the base of the column, scenting blood, and swarming upward to fasten on him; through the air the first mosquito winged its way, herald of troops to come.

"Will you answer now?" asked the chief.

"No!"

The Calabrian flung himself round on his men in the rear.

"Take him down, and scourge him till you cut the truth out of his heart!"

They were like a herd of Pyrenean dogs; the sight of prey roused all their ravenous instincts. Men tasting once the power and the pleasure of torture rarely pause till they lose their sport to the king-player, Death.

They unbound him from the column, and fastened him afresh to a low block of stone, stripped to the waist, so that his chest and back should be left undefended for the curling thongs of the lash; his face was set still seawards, so that the fair breadth of the free waters mocked him with its liberty. His head hung heavily downward; throes of pain, like the scorching of fire, throbbed through his wounded flesh; the rushing of pent-up blood filled his lungs, his brain, his ears, his throat to suffocation. There was a pause of some moments; they were weaving together some cords and some leathern bolts into the thing they needed. The chief sauntered near him once more, and looked at him doubtingly: he knew the Capri mariners could be dogged in brainless obstinacy as any Capri mule, but he saw that this man's endurance was far more than the mere mute, contumacious persistence of a sullen ignorance. He struck away, half compassionately, a gnat that was alighting on his prisoner's bare breast.

"You are too fine a brute to be cut in pieces with the lash. Look you, they have tough arms, have my men; they will make their belts lay your lungs open if you keep silent. Do you know how the leather can eat a man's flesh?"

He bent his head in assent; in Russia he had seen a serf die under the scourge.

"You do? Well, that grand frame of yours will not spare you; they will mash it to pulp. Will you not speak—now?"

"I have answered."

"You are a fool and a madman!" swore the Calabrian. "You lose your life for a worthless woman."

A spasm that the bodily torture had never brought there passed over his captive's face. He kept silence still.

The Italian shrugged his shoulders, and strolled away.

There was a moment's longer pause, then two soldiers came to their work; they bore the whips that they had made, with the heavy buckles at the end of the belts serving as the leaden points with which the lash is commonly weighted. The blows would fall from either side, as the strokes of the woodman's hatchet fall on a tree. The rest of the band closed round in a semicircle, their commandant slightly in advance.

Then—then only—as he saw the scourges in their hands, and knew the indignity that approached him, the mute calm of his endurance, the apathy of that desolation of the heart in which all bodily suffering passes as nought, changed and broke. All the fire of his nature, all the bride of his race, all the dignity of his manhood, flashed to sudden life. He never spoke—he was bound, motionless—but he raised his head and looked them full in the eyes with all the haughty wrath of his fearless blood once more aflame. It was but one look; his arm could not avenge him, nor his strength resist the outrage; yet before it they paused and quailed. For the instant they stood irresolute, cowed by the challenge of that unshrinking leonine regard; then, savage at their own sense of shame, they threw themselves forward, the metal-weighted thongs swirled round their heads, gathering full force to curl around him like a serpent's folds; the watching soldiery drew deep noiseless breaths in silence, the hot hushed air of noon had not a sound upon it; he stood erect to his full height, the courage of the soul victorious over the torture of the body. Before the uplifted hands could fall, a single word echoed down through the stillness—"Wait!"

The scourgers paused; the chief swung round to see who dared bid his men's obedience halt. Into their startled crowd came the woman they sought. Against the glitter of the sea and the brown desolation of the plains, they saw Idalia.

From the captive they had bound a long bitter cry rang—a cry that the lash would not have forced from him, though it should have cut his heart in twain.

Breathless and toil-worn, she pressed her way to him and fell at his feet, and strove with both hands to wrench apart the knots that held him. The Calabrian seized her; he knew her but by name, and her face was strange to him.

"Woman!—how dare you? Who are you——?"

"I am Idalia Vassalis. Take me—-bind me—scourge me. But let the guiltless go."

The rough mountaineer looked at her amazed, awed, dazzled, doubting his own senses.

"You are the Countess Vassalis?"

There in her masque-robes, with the gold all soiled and blackened, the scarlet aflame against the sun, exhausted by that mid-day travel through the blaze of noon, yet with so much command in her eyes, with so much majesty in her glance, she moved him to fear as the sight of Cleopatra, captive, would have moved a Latin boor of the cohorts.

"Yes, yes, yes! Are there no men here who can swear to me? I am the rebel you seek. Take me; do what you will with me; deliver me up to your masters—but free that man, who is innocent!"

The Calabrian shaded his eyes with his hand; he felt giddy before her.

"Is it she?" he whispered a comrade.

"It is she," said a Lombard, from the ranks. "I saw her before Verona; my shot killed a horse under her."

She turned her head to the soldier.

"I thank you for your witness. Now—do your duty. Bind me, and free your prisoner."

"Free him! So!—he has as much guilt as you."

"He has no guilt. Unloose him, I say; fasten me there in his stead; use those thongs upon me; it will not be the first time you scourged a woman. Take him down, and bind me there in his place, by every justice in earth and heaven!"

Erceldoune's voice crossed her own, husky and forced with difficulty from his swollen throat.

"Do not heed her. She speaks only to save me——"

The Calabrian laughed coarsely.

"Ah! This fine Capriote dog, is he your love-toy, then, 'llustrissima?"

"He is my victim. May not that better release him?" The coarse outrage had no power to wound her; she had no consciousness except of the man who, for her sake, was bound in the cruel scorching noonday well-nigh to the pangs of a crucifixion. "Is he to suffer for those who have wronged him? He does so when he suffers for me! If I be your enemy, I am tenfold his; will not that quell your rage against him? I have ruined him; that should give him grace in your sight? From first to last he has been wronged by me. Plundered, wounded, left for dead by those who were of my people; used by me, forsaken by me, driven to peril and bondage by me—has he not more to hate me for than you? In the nobility of his heart he shields me still, because he once has pledged me shelter, because his honour still is greater even than his immeasurable wrongs; but he does so only because he is above even his own just vengeance, only because he will not purchase freedom even at cost of lives that are his curse."

She sank down at his feet once more; she strove to rend his bonds asunder;—he seemed to her great as never man was great in that silent martyrdom, endured for those who had betrayed him. He looked down on her, doubting his own senses, doubting that the burning of the sun made him, in delirium, dream the words he heard, the face he saw.

"Free him!" she cried aloud, with that ferocity of unbearable misery which makes the gentlest savage. "What plea have you to hold him? I am here; I surrender to you. Take me to king or priest, as you choose; give me only his liberty for mine!"

Instinctively his heart went out to save her; his consciousness awakened through the feverish mists of pain enough to know that remorse flung her here to perish for him, enough by unconsidered impulse to seek to save her still

"Do not heed her, I say," his lips breathed hoarsely. "She only speaks to spare me——"

"Ho!" laughed the Calabrian, "how you quarrel for the kiss of the lash! Now we have you we will keep you—both."

She turned on him with her old imperious command:

"O God! you will not dare to take his life! He is of England—not of Italy. Such things as he has done against your king and your laws he has done never for himself, only at my instance——"

"A likely tale, to screen your fellow-rebels, Miladi! Tell it to more credulous hearers——"

"You think that *I* speak falsely?"

For the moment the old glorious challenge of her disdainful pride beamed from her face;—they who saw it thought, despite themselves, that if this woman were not above a lie, then never truth was uttered in this world.

"It is no matter how you speak," the Italian made her answer. "You are my prisoners; I shall but give you over to those who will judge you."

"Give *me*, then. Am I not here that you may do your worst with me? But by all justice, all mercy, all pity, leave him free!"

"It is impossible!"

She threw herself before him; she let her fallen hair bathe his feet, she poured out the vivid utterances of an eloquence that none ever heard unmoved, she sued to him as never for herself would she have sued an emperor; for the only time in her life she abased herself to supplication—she to whom the praying of such a prayer was worse than the endurance of any chastisement.

The Calabrian heard her, startled, dazzled, shaken, but he would not yield.

"It is too late," he said, abruptly. "Miladi, why did you not think before what serving you might cost to a brave man? You treated him like a dog: well he must die a dog's death. The blame of·it is not *mine*."

There was a certain pathos in the words; he was brave enough himself to honour the courage he had so mercilessly tried; her head sank as though the rebuke of Deity spoke by the rough soldier's mouth; she crouched with a low moan, like a stricken animal's, at the foot of the column where Erceldoune was bound.

He turned on her his strained and aching eyes.

"Why have you so much mercy on my body?"

There was an infinite reproach in the infinite patience of the wondering words. Why had she who had slain his soul, his spirit, his hope, all in him that made the living of his life of any peace, of any worth, thus have mercy on the mere torture of limb and nerve and sinew? Why did she who had been so pitiless, so wanton in her cruelty, feel compassion and contrition before the coarse, indifferent doom of merely physical pain?

The Calabrian looked at them in silence, then motioned to his men.

"Take them from the sun-glare, and bind them together."

In a sense he felt pity, because he felt the homage

of courage to courage, for this man whom he had seen so loyal at such awful cost; but for her he had no emotion, save dread of her as a sorceress, save wrath against her for one whose fell temptations had been so fatal and so ruthless.

She made no resistance; she never felt the grating of the leathern thongs upon her wrists; she had lost all consciousness of personal suffering; she had come to deliver up her life for his, and the sacrifice was given too late. She had no knowledge left her save this, no heed for whatsoever they might do to her, though she had given herself back to a worse captivity than the prison of the grave. As the leash with which the soldiers coupled them like hounds was pulled tighter, her hand touched his. He shuddered as he had never done when the mosquito had thrust its sting into his unshielded breast.

She felt rather than saw it; it passed through her in tenfold bitterness. This man, who had held himself unworthy to touch but the hem of her garment, who had deemed himself blessed as with the gift of gods if her eyes but dwelt with a smile on his, now shrank from the contact of her hand as from pollution, from iniquity!

"Take me away," she moaned, wearily. "Would you chain him to his murderess?"

They hesitated, and looked towards their chief.

"Leave me, and take him down!" she said, with that vibration in her voice that scared them like startled sheep. "He dies there, and you have not mercy enough even to lift him up one drop of water. If you are men, and not fiends, unloose him!"

They had been as fiends in their sport; the southern

22 *

cruelty that will rend a bird's wings from its body, or
a butterfly's dainty beauty asunder, laughing softly all
the while, had been awakened in them; they were loath
to quit its indulgence.

He looked as though she said aright, and that he
was dying lashed there to the column; his eyes were
blood-red, his mouth open and swollen, his forehead
purple with suffused blood; his heart beat visibly, great
slow laboured throbs, under the cords.

She wrenched herself from their hold, and caught
the wooden cup the soldier had cast down, and filled
it with the water of the stagnant stream, and held it
upward to his lips. He quivered from head to foot,
and shrank from the draught that through the parching heat he had been athirst for with so deadly a longing.

"Do not torture me—more?"

The whisper was almost inarticulate from his dry
stiffened lips: the cup fell from her hold. She knew
his meaning; she remembered the memory which made
the thirst that he endured more bearable than that action from her hand. She turned passionately on the
nearest soldiers.

"Show some human mercy! Bind me there in his
stead, tear me limb from limb as children tear the fireflies; it will be rarer pastime for you to put a woman
to torment! You know what manner of thing is justice?
Then if you do, by every law of justice make me suffer,
and spare him."

Under their drooping lids, his eyes lightened a
moment with a gleam of consciousness: his instinct was .
still for her defence.

"Let me be. So best," he said, faintly. "It will
soon end."

She was worthless—she had so declared herself; she was his traitress and another's paramour; yet the loyalty in him survived still—still, to lay his life down for her had its sweetness for him.

A shrill wailing cry broke from her, like that of some creature perishing in the trough of waves or under billowy flames.

"O Christ! have you no pity? Take him down while there is breath in him, and bind me there in his stead. I will never bid you spare *me* one pang!"

They looked doubtfully at their chief: he signed them to obey her.

"She says justly; it is she who ought to suffer. Loose him, and bring him out of the sun."

They unloosened the knotted cords that swathed his limbs to the column. When they were wholly un-fastened, he swayed forward, his head fell on his breast, his body bent like a reed, there was foam upon his beard, and his eyes were closed.

A great stillness came then upon the soldiery about the place; through them, under their breath, they whispered that their work was done—that he was dead.

She alone thought not as they thought, that his sacrifice for her was crowned by the last sacrifice of all.

"He is not dead," she said, simply.

There was a strange calmness and certainty in the words that thrilled through those who heard them. They looked at her, neither touching nor opposing her; she had terror for them—terror for them as of some great, fallen, half-shameful, and half-glorious thing. Every intense passion carries its reaction of fear upon those who witness it: hers had such on them now. They dimly felt that if they, in their wanton cruelty, had been the actual murderers of this man, she knew herself for more utterly his destroyer than they could be, who had but harmed his mortal form.

"He is not dead," she said, with that vibration of an exquisite joy crossing the icy desolation of despair, which smote the most callous there to some vague sense of answering pain;—as though her voice reached him, he raised himself slightly, where two soldiers held up his sinking frame, his lips gasped for breath, his eyes unclosed to the dazzling gleam of the day, he stood erect, while a loud cry broke from him:

"O God!—I *cannot* die!"

The English words missed the listening southern ears; she alone knew the agony in them of the great imperishable strength that would not let life leave him, that would survive all which strove to slay it—survive to keep sensation, memory, knowledge in him, and to refuse the only mercy he could ever know, the mercy of oblivion and annihilation.

The Calabrian went and laid his hand upon his prisoner's shoulder.

"You are a fine brute. I am sorry you provoked us. See here—this woman is the guiltier: she says so: she is come to suffer in your stead."

He heard, though all his senses still were dim—though earth, and sea, and sky, and the ring of the armed men, and her face in the white furnace-heat of the sunlight were all one misty blaze 'of colour to him. He heard, and his lips moved faintly.

"She shall not suffer—for me."

So far as thought could be clear to him, he thought

that, having sinned so deeply against him, remorse at
the last had struck her, and drawn her here to bear
witness for him. He thought that there yet dwelt in
her too much still of native courage, of inborn nobility,
to let her rest in safety and security, whilst through
her sin, and to give her freedom, he endured the doom
to which she had cast him out; he thought that, so far,
she was true to herself, though false with worse than a
Delilah's treachery to him. To take vengeance upon
her was a poor, vain, wretched quittance that never
glanced by him; a grossness, a baseness that could have
no place with him; his great tortured passion could no
more have slaked itself in such a payment than it could
have wreaked its wrong by the bruising and the marring of that mere loveliness of form which had been
the lure and instrument of his destruction.

The Italian swore a heavy oath.

"Are you mad? Why, of her own testimony she
has been your ruin?"

"Of a woman's compassion she says it—out of her
own mouth you would not condemn her?"

It was the sole denial, the sole evasion of the truth
that ever his voice had spoken. To save himself, he
would not have borrowed the faintest likeness of a lie;
but in the dizzy mists of his reeling senses this one instinct remained with him—to save her even from herself, to screen her even from the justice that would
avenge him.

As she heard, where she stood bound, held back
by the guards who had seized her, her eyes met his;—
guilty or guiltless, faithful or faithless, by that look
he knew that she loved him as no woman will love
twice.

His head sank, his eyelids closed, he shivered in
the scorching day. She loved him, or she had not
come thither; she loved him, or never that language
had burned for him in her glance. But this love—
love of the traitress, of the voluptuous betrayer, of the
temptress of sin, of the "queen of evil, lady of lust,"—
what was this to him?

Some touch of veneration for the courage they had
witnessed, for the self-sacrifice they vaguely understood,
had come upon the brigands round him—brigands in
their coarseness, their training, and their brutality,
though they wore the livery of a monarchy. They had
seen that this man could hold his own in contest with
the strength, and the rage, and the prolonged resistance
of lions; they saw now that he could suffer and submit
with the mute-enduring patient self-surrender and self-
command of those saints of whom the priests had told
them, in their boyhood, dim, pathetic, ancient legends,
half forgot and half remembered. They yielded him
a certain reluctant, wondering respect, and they brought
him, with more gentle usage, where the thickly-woven
olive and acanthus made a shadow from the sun, and
gave him water to slake his burning throat, and drew
the linen folds of his dress over his wounded chest with
what was, for them, almost tenderness. To her they
had no such pity; they knew her a revolutionist, a rebel,
an infidel, as they were told, a woman of evil, murderous, and fearful sorcery, who could revenge with the
"evil eye" all those who incensed her by resisting her
seductions; they hated her with a great sullen hate,
the stronger, because it was the barbarous hatred that
is born of fear. But for their commander they would
have shot her down with a volley from their carbines,

that the fatal regard might gaze on them no more with the glance that they believed could wither them like a sorceress' incantations. They bound her arms behind her with ruthless severity, till her fair skin was lacerated and bruised; then they forced her down on to the yellow grasses that grew lank and long among the fallen temple-stones, and passed the ropes that bound her round a block of travestine. From the moment that she had asked for his deliverance, she had never spoken.

He was so near her that, stretching her hand out had she been free, she could have touched him where they had laid him down. His pain-racked limbs were stiff and motionless; he could not have stirred one step to save his life; his frame was racked with cramp, and the virus from the insects' teeth seemed to eat like vitriol into his flesh; his face was buried in the grasses as his forehead rested on his arm; he could not bear to look upon her; he could not bear to feel her gaze was on him. To the watching eyes of the soldiers about them, to the certainty of captivity, or worse, that waited them, they were both unconscious; all that either knew was that presence of the other, which surpassed any martyrdom to which military and priestly power could ever bring them.

There was silence for some time around; the chief of the scanty troop had sent northward for orders. He was uncertain what to do, and whither to take them. In a thing of so much moment he feared to move rashly or wrongly; the people were inflamed, moreover; the times were rife with unrest and sedition, the mouths of the populace were whispering tales that made the national blood burn hot against the Bourbon; he feared a riot—even it might be a rescue—if he bore this woman, to whom his superstition gave such spells, and to whom the revolutionists gave such homage, in the full noonday captive towards Naples.

Where they had fastened her she sat with her head bowed down, and her eyes, that burned like fire under their swollen aching lids, fastened on him where he lay. He had lost all actual knowledge that she was near, in the exhaustion that had succeeded to the long strain on every nerve and fibre. Delirious teeming fancies swam before his brain even in that lethargy of worn-out powers; in them he had no sense of the reality of her presence beside him; but in visions he believed he beheld her, the priestess of passion and pain, the goddess of darkness and of the spells of the senses, whom no man shall worship and live.

The messenger returned. The answering command was whispered by him to his officer. There was noise and movement and haste and delay around them under the shadow of the aged silvered olive-trees. Neither knew nor heeded it. Fate had wrought its worst on them.

The soldiers brought a long low waggon, taken from a homestead some way in the interior, oxen-drawn, and commonly used to bear the load of millet-sheaves at harvest, or the piles of purple fruit at vintage time. They half-dragged, half-lifted him upon the straw within it, and motioned her to a place beside him. She stooped over him where he lay, half-senseless.

"O Heaven! how you suffer!"

The darkness of his eyes, humid and lustreless, gleamed on her a moment under his half-closed lids; he turned with restless fever on the straw.

"You think *this* pains?"

CHAPTER XIV.
"I would have given my Soul for This."

THE oxen toiled laboriously on their wearisome way; the waggon jolted on its large unpainted wheels; the soldiers marched on either side, and in the van and rear: the tawny leathern covering flapped idly to and fro, whilst about it clung a faint sweet fragrance from grass crops and vine-loads carried through many changing seasons of the earth.

Where they went she had no knowledge; they had bound her eyes; that the noon in time passed and the cooler day followed she could tell by some diminution in the intensity of heat, and by the tender music of birds' throats that every now and then broke out from myrtle thickets and lemon-gardens that they wended their way through as the hours advanced. The measured march of the men, and the heavy tread of the cattle, at intervals paused; then she heard the muttering of voices, and some change in their guards' position round the waggon, as though uneasiness or insecurity was prevalent amongst the scanty troop. Time seemed endless; but she knew that she might easily err in its reckoning, for the oxen moved with great tardiness, and neither man nor beast could press on with any swiftness till the sun had sunk lower. At her feet Erceldoune lay motionless; she could not see or touch him, she could only listen for each sigh of the painful breath he drew through his aching chest. A feverish lethargy held him insensible. They had screened him from the heat with some broken boughs;—the soldiers compassionated him as the prey of the "evil eye." At times, from the weakness that had followed on the ordeal he had endured, his breathing and the pulsations of his heart were so low, that neither could be detected by her eager ear; she could not tell whether life had ceased or not, and her own heart stood still with a fear that no jeopardy of her own life had ever roused in her. And yet—what would existence, if it lingered in him, be to him! Only an existence dragged out at the galley-oar amidst the companionship of felons. Or,—even if his country and his friends gained freedom for him,—only one unending misery through his memory, through his loss of her.

Through the darkness and the stillness round her the sounds of the declining day, that was still bright upon the world, came with strange distinctness. The song of a child's voice on the air; the noise of a water-wheel in a stream; the slow droning notes of monastic bells; the laughter of vinedressers among the budding vines; the mournful chaunt of a requiem as a village funeral passed with the crucifix borne aloft; a thousand murmurs of sweet sunlit idyllic life, came on the stillness with a jarring cruelty through the ceaseless tread of the soldiers' feet, and the slow creaking of the reluctant wheels.

At length they paused and bade her descend. She drew back: "Where he goes, I go!"

She spoke, not with the supplication of a woman who loved to rest near what she loved, but rather with the entreaty of remorse to share the victim's fate, with the demand of a leader to endure whatever fell to the lot of one who too loyally obeyed such leadership. The soldier laughed noisily:

"Oh, yes! you shall have your lover, 'llustrissima. Come!—or it will be worse for him."

She obeyed, obliged to be content with such a promise, lest the threat against him should be borne out. Her eyes were still bound from the light. She heard them lift him down from his bed of straw. She thought they bore him after her, as heavy steps followed in her rear; and a heavy hand thrust her forward down long stone passage-ways. Where they had brought her was a large granary, or group of store-houses, very lonely, and built strongly in early days, when the ungathered grain had to be not seldom defended with a fierce struggle from the raids of foreign bands that fought their quarrels out upon Italian soil. The building was two-storied, and the vast barn-like chambers were of stone, with slender windows barred with rusty iron, and with a faint dreamy odour in them from sheaves of millet stored there, and from a quantity of the boughs of the sweet myrtle, which had been cut away to lay clear the stems of olives to the air.

They undid the cord that bound her hands, and left her as they closed the door, and drew the bolts without.

She tore down the bandage that covered her eyes, and saw that they had played her false. In the darkened room she stood alone.

For many hours afterwards time was a blank to her.

Whether sleep succeeded to the exhaustion, the endurance, and the sleepless toil of the past days and nights, or whether she again lost consciousness, and lay as in a trance, she never knew. The irresistible reaction that follows on over-wrought excitation came on her. The worn-out limbs and the strained nerves succumbed to it, and it stole upward at length to the brain, and deadened it to all sentient life, to all remembrance, to all thought.

When she awakened, she was lying, thrown forward on the heap of dying myrtle. All was intensely still; through the slit of the casement the midnight stars were shining, and the hooting of an owl came wailingly on the stillness.

Her first memory was of him. Her first action was to arise and look out on the night. A beautiful country lay in the pallor of the young moon's rays; she knew the landscape well; it was but few leagues from Naples. Below, under some great trees of olive and of lemon, two sentinels were pacing with their carbines slanted; except for their measured tread there was no sound. The place was lonely and deserted; the out-building among maze-fields and olive-slopes of a farm belonging to the Crown. She looked; then went back to the couch of withering myrtle, and sought to make her thoughts grow clear; and the manifold hazards and remembrances of her past become of use in her extremity. But the task was beyond her strength. She was fasting—she was devoured with thirst; she was conquered by physical fatigue; she could see, hear, remember, nothing but the face of the man who had been willing to perish for her sake,—the gallant beauty bound to the stone-shaft, mutilated, bruised, agonised,—the voice which yet gave her no reproach more bitter than that one rebuke, "Why have you so much mercy on my body?" She loved him with the voluptuous warmth of southern passion; but she loved him also with that power of self-negation which would have made her accept any doom for herself, could she thereby have released him to

freedom and to peace.   Her pride of nature, her imperial ambitions, her habit of dominion, and her desire
of homage, had given her long a superb egotism, even
whilst she had been ever willing to lose all she owned
for the furtherance of lofty aims.   But now all heed of
herself was killed in her; on her own fate she never
cast a thought of pity.   She had played a great game,
won many casts in it, and lost the last.   That was but
the see-saw of life.   But he—for his loyalty he perished;
for his nobility he suffered as felons suffer; by the very
greatness of his faith he was betrayed; by the very
purity of his sacrifice he was lost for ever!

Time crept darkly on.   The odour of the myrtles
was like the mournful fragrance from flowers strewn
upon a coffin.   From below, the monotonous sound of
the slow regular steps sounded faintly; in the gloom
bats flew to and fro, and an owl, who had her nest among
the rafters, flitted in and out through the bars of the
unglazed casement, seeking and bringing food for her
callow brood.   The silence was unbroken; the darkness
filled with a stealing, sickening sense of unseen life, as
rat and lizard darted over the stones, and the downy
wings of the night-birds brushed the air; she felt as
though she should lose reason itself in that horrible
stillness, that fettered misery, that impotent inaction.

Amidst all, there came on her a strange dreamy
wonder how the life of the world was passing.   For
twelve days she had been as dead as though she had
lain in her tomb.   When they had seized her at Antina,
the time had been pregnant of great things; whether
they had been brought forth or strangled in their birth
she could not tell.   All that had been done amongst
men was a blank to her.

Then all such memories drifted far from her again. One remembrance alone remained—that of the man who suffered his martyrdom for her rather than render up to justice one by whom he believed himself betrayed more foully than the sleeping Sisera slain under the sanctity of the roof-tree. She knew it might well be that never again would they look upon each other's face, that they might drag their lives on asunder, chained apart at the labour of felons, with eternal silence betwixt them, and knowing not even when each other's lives should cease.

It is a horrible knowledge—that one living, yet will be for ever as the dead.

Fear had never touched her; yet now a supernatural terror seemed to glide into her veins. The black shades of the stealing lizards, and the cold touch of the bat's wing as it passed, grew unbearable; the darkness seemed drawing in on her closer and closer; the eyes of the night-birds glowed like flame through the gloom; she uttered a bitter cry, and threw herself against the bars, and shook them with all the force of despair. "Let me see him once, that he may know!" she cried out to the peace of the night. "Oh God! that he may know!"

The cry, though not the words, was heard.

The door was unbolted, and opened. The light of a lamp fell on the floor. The Calabrian entered.

"So! what is it, Miladi?"

He came, careless and ready for a braggart's insolence. She turned her eyes on him, and the look smote him speechless.

"You played me false," she said to him. "Where is he?"

He stammered, then was silent. She dazzled and affrighted him, as her sudden apparition had done in the blaze of the noonday. He thought coarse and evil things against her; he had heard them said, and deemed them true; but in her presence, even to think them seemed a sacrilege.

"Where is he?" she repeated. "Answer me."

"He is near you." He spoke at random; with the flicker of the lamp on the scarlet of her dress, and the gleam of her loose-hanging hair, her beauty looked to him unearthly.

"In this building?"

"Yes. You are both—kept here because—until—" He stopped confusedly, and bent above the wick of the lamp, as though it needed trimming.

"Until what?"

"Until the kings pleasure," he replied, sullenly.

She came closer to him.

"You are a soldier?" she asked.

"Yes."

"Well then, brave men are commonly pitiful. Let me see him for one hour to-night."

He would have laughed out a coarse jest; but as he met her look he dared not.

"Impossible!" he answered, curtly. "No prisoners must commune with each other."

"I know—I know!" she interrupted him. "But gold keys unlock all barriers? I am rich. Name your price. You shall have it if you can give me one hour with him."

"Impossible!" he muttered once more.

"No: possible—if you will do it. What can it harm you? You have both under lock and ward. All

I ask is a little speech with him. See—I told you I had wronged him deeply. Can you not think I want his pardon?"

The humility of the words coming from lips so proud, and bending a spirit so indomitable, touched the soldier, who, under a rough rind, had a certain latent kindliness.

"Nay; I would do it for you if I could out of charity," he made answer. "But it is not in my power, I tell you."

"It is in your power, if it be in your will. An hour—a half-hour—but a few moments—and you shall have a thousand—five thousand ducats!"

He looked at her stupefied; he was avaric ous, like most Italians.

"How can you get them? They will have confiscated all you have?"

"In Italy—yes. But that was little. My wealth lies elsewhere. I will write you an order on Paris, that will give you the sum down in gold."

"You speak truth?"

"Did you ever hear that I spoke any other thing?"

He laughed. "Basta, never. They all say that you lash king and priest with your tongue! Well; I will see what I can do."

He left her; barring her in. She waited in an anguish of dread. She had spoken calmly and briefly to him; but alone, the great veins stood out on her forehead, and her limbs shook with the passion of hope and fear. She would have laid her head down on a scaffold with the breaking of dawn if to-night she could thereby have purchased the power to say but a single word to the man who believed her his traitress.

Before long the Calabrian returned; he had nothing of the soft grace common to his countrymen; but he had a rough good faith, which, blent with his liking of gold, served her better. He held her an inkhorn and a slip of paper.

"It was a miracle to get these; I sent to the osteria for them. Write, and you shall see this stricken lion of yours; sure you have wounded him someway worse than ever we did."

She laid the paper on the stone window-sill, and wrote an order for the payment, in Paris, of ten thousand francs in her name to his. He read it with the hesitation of a bad scholar by the feeble oil light; then a laugh spread itself over all his features.

"So! I have a brother, a singer, in Paris who will serve for this work. It were as much as my life, Miladi, were worth for your name and mine to be seen together. Come! you shall go to your comrade; but, of a surety, rich lips like yours might add one another payment?"

The indignant blood flushed her face; but she restrained the haughty impulse that moved her.

"Brave men do not insult captives who cannot resent," she said, briefly. "I have fulfilled my bond. Fulfil yours."

He hung his head ashamed, and motioned her to pass out before him. There was a short broad stone passage, with a door at the further end—the great barn-door of another stone chamber. He drew the bars aside, and pushed it open, setting his lamp down within the entrance. "You shall be alone an hour," he said, as he closed the door afresh, and the bolts rolled back into their places.

The oil-fed wick shed but a narrow circle of light
beneath it; it did nothing to illumine the impenetrable
darkness that lay beyond in the central and distant
parts of the room; there was no more sound here than
in her own prison-place, the same flitting of grey
downy wings, the same gliding murmur of hidden
night-awakened insect life. She thought that again
the Italian had betrayed her; that she was still in
solitude.

But though her eyes could not pierce that dense
wall of unlightened shadow that fronted her, such light
as came from the lamp—for here the moon did not
shine—was cast full about her, and on the dusky scarlet
cloud of her draperies. And on the silence a cry
rang that startled all the night-birds in their restless
flight, circling beneath the rafters. Unseen himself, he
saw her, and deemed it a vision of the bitter dreams
that swam, as shadows seem to swim on waters, through
his aching brain.

He rose slowly from the straw in which he lay,
reeling to and fro in his weakness, and came out from
the gloom, and faced her—silent.

She looked at him a moment, then fell at his feet
as she had fallen when he had been bound beneath his
scourgers.

He did not move, nor touch her; his eyes were
fastened senselessly upon her; he shivered as though
hot iron seared him. "Can you not leave me in peace
to suffer?" he muttered. "Off—off—off! What *I*
loved is dead! Ay—you tempt me—you bring me her
beauty—you would give me her kisses, her passion,
her sweetness, her shame. I will not—I will not!
What I loved is dead. *I* am faithful."

All through the hours of the night, dreams of her had mocked, and pursued, and tortured, and assailed him; he was drunk as with the fumes of wine with the burning of the love that still lived; his mind, weakened and delirious, had only been conscious of phantoms that seemed to throng on him, tempting him in a thousand shapes, binding him down the slave of his senses, forcing on him joys torn out from the hell of guilt. "What matter what you be—what matter what death come by you, so you are mine?" The old, old subtlety that has tempted all men from the first hour that they fell by woman, had besieged him through all the lonely watches of the night. Now he knew not her living presence from the visions of his temptress.

In horror she knelt before him.

"Hush! hush! Ah! for Heaven's sake, believe my love at least, though it has cursed you!"

He thrust her from him, with the senseless blaze still in his eyes.

"Love! Ay, shared with a score. Love that is poison and infamy; love in my arms to-night, in another's to-morrow! Oh, I know, I know,—it is sweet, and cruel, and rich, and men fall by it and perish through it. But to *me* it were worse than nought. Can you not tell how I loved her?"

The words which had been at first raving and violent sank at last into an infinite weariness and pathos. Tears rained down her face as she heard them; never had she honoured him as she honoured him now, when he refused subjection to a vile passion, and held her dead to him because he held her base with the baseness of deliberate and self-chosen vice.

"I can tell!" she murmured. "You love as she merits not, nor any woman. Yet, love further still, and, if you can, forgive!"

He started as the voice thrilled through him, and roused his consciousness of some actual life near him.

"Forgive? forgive?" he answered her. "Do you not know that what men have to pray for, before women like you, is to have the power to *hate?* Forgive? That were sweet as the touch of your kisses! It is to shun, to abhor, to resist you, that strength is needed!"

He was not wholly conscious of her presence; the sense that whilst she had betrayed she yet had borne him a cruel, worthless, sensual passion had been forced on him even whilst he had found her sheltering his foe, had been borne out by her own words, even by her outbreak of remorse, as she had pleaded for his life on the seashore; that sense remained with him, and against the weakness in him that made such a love even as this look priceless, strove that nobler instinct which had governed him when he had said to her, "love that is faithless and guilty,—what is that to me?"

He had thought that, for her sake, he should shrink from no crime, that for the guerdon of her beauty there would be no guilt before which he would pause; but even now, in the semi-insanity brought on him by the torment through which he had passed, he was truer to himself than this, and the caress of a wanton could never have replaced to him the loss of the "one loyalty, one faith" of his life. He would have defended her and cleaved to her in her extremity; and endured in her stead for sake of the imperishable fidelity he had sworn to her; but it would have been only when the last thing was done and the last sacrifice rendered, to have put her from him for evermore, and never to have looked upon her face again.

She lay at his feet, and heard him thus abjure her power; thus entreat for force to be blind and dead to the allurement of what he deemed the voluptuous visions of his cheated passion; and she honoured him as never she had honoured any living man; honoured the slave, who, because his slavery was shame, broke from it, and became her king by virtue of the very majesty of that rebellion. Snakes had crawled and beasts had crouched in human likeness many a time before her; this man alone stood before her undebased, having rent the withies of base desire, having cleaved to the liberty of an unstained honour.

And her heart went out to him in supplication, remembering alone the wretchedness that through her had fallen on him.

"My God, yes! I have brought you only evil. But hear me once before we part for ever. Hear me but once,—you perish by me, but I have no guilt to *you*."

He breathed loud and hard; his eyes stared on her in the dusky light; he took but one sense from her words—that the infidelity of her life had been against others; that though she had lied to him and beguiled him and forsaken him, against his rival she had done deeper sin than against himself.

"You love me?" he muttered, as he strove to thrust her back. "Be silent, then—Go, go, go! I have no strength,—if once I pardon, never shall I resist you!"

Pardon! Its softened mercy took the shape of deadliest temptation. It looked sweet as life to forgive;—to forgive, and steep all wrong, all pain, all hate in one divine oblivion; to forgive, and heed not the pollution of the soul, so only the grace and graciousness of mortal form were his; to forgive, and call sin grace, shame honour, and treachery truth, if so alone the heaven he had lost were his.

She rose up, and faced him, silently awhile; the great slow tears swam before her sight; her tongue was stricken of its fluency; she knew that for her, through her, by her, this man was condemned to a living death; yet that it was not his lost life but her lost purity which was his despair now.

Then she went to him ere he could repulse her, and laid her hands upon his breast, and looked full upward to his eyes: and her voice was low, and had a strange sweetness in it.

"When to-night is over we shall never meet again. The truth may be told now. I have never betrayed you."

A marvellous change passed over his face; the suffering and the darkness, and the haggard desolation on it, were suddenly crossed as with a golden flash of light. He answered her nothing; but his gaze strained down into hers as though it read her soul.

Her hands still leant upon his breast, her eyes still were lifted up to his, her voice had still that sweetness which was so calm as with the calmness of those from whom all hope has passed, and yet had a yearning piteous passion in it that no words could give.

"We may speak now as the dying do—you and I—we die to-night. To-morrow the living world will have no place for us save a prison and a grave. You perish through me; I have killed you! Your murderess —yes; but never your traitress.”

He trembled through all his limbs under her touch and her words; the breath of her lips seemed to toss his life to and fro as the winds play with reeds. His brain reeled. They had said that her voice could steal reason itself from those whom it tempted; they had said that her lie brought a thousand times subtler charm of conviction than the truth of other women ever bare in it; at dawn she had abased herself in guilt before him, now, at midnight, she swore to him that no treachery to him was on her.

“Not mine!” he echoed. “When my foe is your paramour, my assassin your care! Silence! silence! They say that you tempt men till they lose all likeness of themselves—all power to see you as you are; but you died to *me* for ever when you owned yourself dishonoured!”

“Wait! At dawn you gave me your pity!”

“Pity—pity—pity! God! you know what a man's passion is! Can it yield that cold, merciful, sinless thing when it consumes itself in hell-fire? Pity!— what pity had you?”

It was the sole reproach he had cast at her.

“Ah! hear me, only hear me! To *you* I had no sin!——”

He gave but one meaning to her answer; a bitter moan broke from him; for an instant his arms touched her to draw her once more to his embrace, then they fell as though nerveless and useless.

“Then—you had sin to another. I have not the strength I thought; I cannot pardon to the uttermost.

I would not forsake you; I would not harm you. Vengeance! What would that give back to *me?* But the woman *I* loved is dead, I say; do not bring me in mockery of her,—a courtezan."

The words were incoherent and faint; but they had an exceeding pathos; the longing, aching melancholy of a life henceforth without one hope. Her very heart seemed to break as she heard them, as they strove after justice and tenderness to her, even amidst the havoc of his shattered faith, his unutterable desolation.

"Listen;" she answered him, passionately. "I bring you a woman who sinned, if ambition were sin; if too little mercy were sin; if imperious pride and cruel victory were sin; if evil fellowship and enforced sufferance of alien crime were sin; but of all other I am innocent."

His hands fell heavily on her shoulders, in the dim light that flickered on the paleness of her face, his own was wholly in darkness; but through the gloom his eyes burned down upon hers with the glow of wildly-wakening hope straining through the belief—by her own lips—of her guilt.

"Innocent! When you are his mistress!"

"I am not his—nor any man's."

"Ah, God! Take care how you betray me afresh. I am mad, I think, to-night!"

"I do not betray you. I have never betrayed. I left you to believe me dishonoured, lest worse should come unto you."

"What! when you harboured him, forsook me for him, of your own confession loved him!"

"I spared him for my truth's sake, I forsook you

for your life's sake. I loved him in childhood—yes.
Then only."

"In childhood! What are you to him?"

"Wait—wait! It sickens me to tell! Out of the
greatness of your own heart you judged my life—
you judged it rightly——"

"What are you to him?"

"To my eternal shame—his daughter!"

Her head was sunk down on the stone floor of the
prison-chamber as the words left her, slowly, unwillingly, as though her existence itself were torn and
dragged out with them; to the woman who had the
pride of an imperial blood, with all the superb insolence of beauty, genius, and power, without their peer,
it was humiliation, as deep as to lay bare a felon's
brand, to own her kinship with crime and with cowardice, to yield up the secret disgrace of her mighty
race.

He,—dead to all else—heard but the answer that
gave her back to him; doubted not, questioned not,
paused not for proof or for dread, but with a great
cry—the cry of a heart that was breaking with rapture—stretched out his lacerated arms, and drew her
up to his embrace, and crushed her close against his
bruised and aching breast.

"God forgive me that ever I believed even your
own voice against you! God forgive me that I wronged
you!"

His words rung clear and loud, and sweet as
clarion's ring in his unutterable joy. Then his head
sank, his wounded limbs failed him, ecstasy vanquished
his strength as never wretchedness had done; for the
first time in all his years of manhood he bowed him-

self down and wept as women weep, with the agony
of passion, with the abandonment of childhood.

*   *   *   *   *   *   *

Not until long after were other words uttered between them. The first that were spoken were hers,
while the pulse of her heart beat on his, and the low
flame of the lamp sunk out slowly.

"What use! what use that you know the truth!"
she moaned. "You have been martyred for me.
Through me you will perish!"

He smiled, as men smile in some sweet fancy of
dreaming sleep.

"Though I may die with the dawn, I can thank
God *now* I have lived."

"Lived to be cursed by me!"

"Lived to be loved by you;—it is enough."

"Loved by a love that destroys you! Can you
ever forgive?"

"Forgive? What is left to forgive, since you are
mine?"

"Yours—for your ruin, your torture, your slaughter! These are the love-gifts I bring you!"

"Think not of them! Lift your lips to mine, and
they are forgotten!"

His thoughts held no other thing, his consciousness
grasped no other reality, than this one living priceless
surety of *her*, that came home to his heart, beyond
doubt, beyond suspicion, with all the divine force of a
resistless truth. Memories of evil and of crime floated,
shapeless, amidst the sudden glory that seemed to fill
the gloom of his midnight prison with the glow of a
southern dawn: he let them pass,—he could not hold
them. She unloosed herself from his arms, and knelt

once more beside him, so that, in the dim shadowy
rays of the lamp he could only see the paleness of her
upturned brow. She longed to be sheltered even from
his sight, in that hour. She had no fear but that the
greatness of his nature would reach to mercy and to
pardon. She knew that justice to the uttermost, and
an infinite tenderness, would ever be hers at his hands.
But none the less she knew that through her he would
perish; and none the less were the shame that she must
reveal against her race, the taint of cowardly crime
that must rest on her by implication, the degradation
of her name that she must lay bare before him, bitter
beyond all bitterness to the pride that was born at once
of royalty and freedom, to the courage that would
have faced a thousand deaths rather than have bent
down to one act of baseness.

"Forgotten!" she echoed, where she bowed herself
at his feet. "You are wronged so deeply, that no love
but yours could ever outlive such wrong. Listen! I
have spoken but truth to you. I have striven to save
you with all the might that was in me. I have never
been false to you by deed, or word, or thought. But
—all the same—your life is lost through me; and in
me you see the daughter of your vilest foe, of the
man who shot you down with a brigand's murder and
a coward's secrecy. Yes! I!—I!—I!—who believed
no · empress never had wider reign, who have treated
men as dogs beneath my feet, who have told you the
legends that gave me heroes' and sovereigns' blood in
my veins; I have greater shame upon me than the
poorest serf that ever crawled to take bread at my
gates. I am the associate and the accomplice of an
assassin. I am the daughter of Conrad Phaulcon."

He heard; and the words carried their way to his mind, that had been delirious with the weight, and now was giddy with the release, of pain. He heard; and the violence of the hatred he had borne this man shook him afresh, as tempests shake strong trees. He breathed slowly and heavily. With the rich liberty of his arisen joy came a deadly and heartsick oppression; with the sweet daylight of his renewed faith came the poison-mists of a dead crime.

"My God!—how you must have suffered!"

The suffering that such a tie as this had cost her was his first thought, before all other.

"You think of me, and for me still—still!"

"When I shall have ceased to think of you, I shall have ceased to live."

Burning tears fell from her eyes upon his hands. She would not let him raise her nearer him, but knelt there, where the faint and gold-hued light of the dying lamp strayed softly to her, and fell upon her head like a halo of martyrdom in the pictures of old masters. He stooped to her.

"Tell me all."

"All my shame!"

"Not yours; you had no share in it; or you would not kneel there to-night."

"Yes, mine; for the shame of one man is the shame of his race, and the evil that is shielded is shared."·

She felt him shudder for one moment from her.

"Stay! You were never leagued with that infamy?"

"Against your life? No. I suspected—I feared— but they dreaded me, and hid it from me. Once I brought it against him, and he swore by the memory of my mother that he was innocent. This one oath he had used to hold sacred. By it he duped me—that once."

A hate, unforgiving and deadly, ran through the thrill of the words. In the sight of her fearless eyes the one unpardonable guilt was the dastardly guilt of a lie.

"Tell you all?" she pursued, while her voice rose swifter, and gathered the fluent eloquence which was natural to her as its warmth to the sun. "In years I could not! Tell the torture of that companionship I have endured so long? Ah! you must paint it to yourself; no words of mine could give it. Look! I am brave, I was born linked with a coward; I am proud, I have been bound to a man who never knew what it was to wince under the lash of dishonour; I am ambitious, and I have been leashed with an adventurer whom the whole continent brands as a knave; I have loved truth and the people's rights—it is all that has redeemed me—and I have been fastened hand and foot to the baseness of intrigue, the venality of mock patriotism, the criminal craft of secret societies. Look! That man could hear what you called me and deemed me a few hours ago; and he could hold his peace, and laugh, and never breathe one word, or strike one blow, to defend my honour, to redeem my name. That will tell you what his life has been."

A bitter curse moved his lips as he heard.

"Why did you stay me when my hand was on his throat?"

"Could his guilt annul his tie to me? By that one bond he has claimed his immunity, and enforced my forbearance, through all the evil of his years."

"Yet,—why not have told me?"

"Because I was bound to silence by my oath. Look! I told you how my early life was spent, but I could not tell you the influence Conrad Phaulcon had on it. My mother died whilst I was in infancy. She was the love of his youth, and she had passed away from him ere she had worn that love out. There are green places which never wither in the hearts that are searest: such was her memory to him. But her race he hated with a reckless hatred; he had looked to share their dominion when he wedded her; but there was feud between him and Julian. And Julian read him aright, and held him in distrust, and none of their wealth came to him, and he hated their greatness with a bitter envy. I have heard him curse my face because it was like the Byzantine line; yet, on the whole, he loved, and was gentle to me. And I—I thought him a god, a hero, a patriot. He was a communist, an agitator, an adventurer; but I knew none of those names. I thought mankind was divided into the oppressors and the oppressed, into the haters and the lovers of liberty, and I revered him as a Gracchus, a Drusus, an Aristogiton, stoned by the nation's ingratitude! Once he was proscribed, and I knew where he lay hid, though I was but a few summers old, and they took and starved me to make me speak. Because the food would not tempt me, they tried blows; and when I still kept silent, they wondered, and at last let me go, because one of their patriarchs reproved them, saying I was more faithful to man than they were to God."

"And he knew that you—his young child—suffered that for him?"

"Surely he knew it, later, in Athens."

"And it failed to make you sacred in his sight?"

"Nay, it only showed him that I was perhaps of the steel that would furnish him forth a choice weapon! I was proud to suffer for him; I adored him; and chiefly of all because I believed him sworn to the people's good, and a martyr for the sake of freedom. Whilst I was still so young those things were still so close at my heart! And he loved me in answer then, though I saw him seldom, and might have lived on charity but for Julian Vassalis;—then and until the time came when, there being no male of the great Byzantine race left, I succeeded to the whole of its splendour, and by the will of the dead chief, bore its name. From that moment the hate his foiled ambition and his cheated avarice bore against the Vassalis line, blent against me with the old tenderness that he bore me, and from that moment he saw in me only—his prey."

She felt his hands clench; she heard his breath catch on passionate words of imprecation.

"Ah, peace, peace!" she murmured to him. "Aid me rather to forgive—if I can. My own wrongs I might, but yours——"

"Nay, mine are but of the hour, yours are lifelong. Tell me all—all."

"I could not if I spoke for years! A brave nature bound to a coward, a proud one leashed with dishonour —that is an agony that lies beyond words. When he saw me thus, so young, given this wealth and this power he had so vainly desired, a desire of vengeance entered him against me; and also, with the craft of his school, he saw in me a fitting instrument for his many schemes! Well he knew his sway over me; Julian

dead, there remained none to counteract it. A revolutionist ere I could reason, and ambitious with an ambition far out-leaping all the goals of the modern world,
a child still in my ignorance of actual things and my
belief in the omnipotence of truth, yet already mistress
of what seemed to me the magnificence and the dominion of a Cleopatra, I came to his snare as a bird to
the fowler's. I would have gone to martyrdom to have
liberated the nations; I would have sold my soul to
have reached the sovereignty of a Semiramis. By these
twain—my strength and my weakness—he ruled me.
And through them, in all that glorious faith of my
youth, he bound me by oath to himself and his cause.
That oath I have never broken."

There was silence for many moments. Then she
spoke again, while the dying lamp sunk lower and
lower, and the halo ceased to fall upon her brow.

"Many besides me, unseen of men, wear those
secret fetters of political vows, sworn in the rashness
of their youth and faith to what they believed the cause
of freedom—to what too late they know an inexorable
and extortionate tyranny that through all their after-
lives will never spare. While I thought myself an empress they were fastened round me, and made me a
slave. Ah! I cannot travel back over that waste of
years! It is enough that I swore fealty to his cause
and obedience to his order—that I swore, moreover,
adhesion with him in all things, and secrecy upon the
tie he bore me. This last thing I promised because he
willed it—it was easy to maintain. His marriage had
long been concealed from fear of the Vassalis' wrath;
and when the world knew me, I bore another title than
his. Too late I learned what this fatal exaction cost

me. Had I been known as his daughter, the evil notoriety he had gained would have sufficed to blemish my own repute. As it was, I might as well have come forth from a lazar-house or a felon's cell. None knew his tie to me, except, of late years, the traitor who taught you to see in him my lover, my accomplice. True, my riches, my youth, my ancient name, my brilliancy and extravagance of life—other gifts that men saw in me—all brought me celebrity, notoriety, triumphs, such as they were. But from the first to the last—companioned by him—they were darkened by slander and falsehood. And he—ah! you may well ask if a man's heart ever beat, if a man's blood ever glowed in him!—knew it, knew it long ere ever I dreamt it, and let the shadow of his own evil fame lie upon me, because, through it, his schemes were best served; because by it, he could best secure what no other should ever share with him—the wealth that I held and he coveted. He feared that I might one day break from him, that I might one day give the love I give you. So he desired men to think me worthless as they would, and his presence beside me sufficed to fulfil his desire! No, no! do not pour on me those noble words, I am not worthy of them. Though sinned against, I am not sinless. When too late I saw what my fatal promise had wrought for me, I was in love with the dangers, the victories, the sway, the excitation I had plunged into; I had drunk so deeply and so freshly of the draught of Power, I could not have laid down the cup though I had known there was death in it. And under scorn and hate, and all the unutterable misery that came to me when I saw myself betrayed by him, my very nature changed. I grew hardened,

24*

reckless, pitiless. My loyalty to liberty, to truth, to
the peoples, never altered; but that was all the better
thing left in me. I remained faithful, even to a traitor.
But the world and I were for ever at war. I cared not
how I struck, so that I only struck home. Evil had
been spoken against me falsely, and I lived in such
fashion that they should know one woman at least
breathed whose neck could not be bent, nor whose
spirit bowed by calumny. Men came about me, mad
for the smile of my lips, but not true enough in themselves, as you were true, to pierce to the truth in me,
and I gave them a bitter chastisement for their blindness: I slew them with their own steel. But—Oh
God! what avail to tell you this? I can tell you how
that which was spoken against me has, in part, been
truth deserved, and, in part, the malignant coinage of
envy. I can tell you that at dawn to-day I had no
choice but to leave myself a traitress in your sight, or
see you slaughtered by him as the issue of my love. I
can tell you this—but what avail? You perish through
me, for me, by me! What use that you should hold
me faithful to you? I am none the less your murderess because I would give my life for yours, my love,
my love, my love!"

Her voice, that had been sustained and eloquent
with the vital strength of remembered wrongs, failed
her over the last words. The memory of the martyrdom which he had borne for her; the memory of the
destruction of all his future, which through her befell
him; the memory of the only existence that could ever
now be his dragged out beneath the galley-chains, and
companioned by the worst of criminals, alone remained
with her. Guilty or guiltless, faithless or faithful,

having cleaved to him or having forsaken him,—what mattered it? Wherein could it serve him? He was lost through her.

But this thought never came to him. His eyes looked down on her through the heavy shadow with a light in them that had the sweetness of release, the glory of victory, through all the infinite pain and hopelessness of their fated love.

"What avail?" he answered her. "Do you know me yet so little? Do you not know that I could lie down and die content, since I have heard that you are sinless?"

"I know, I know! You would have died for me when you thought me vile with the vice that I cherished, branded with the kisses of shame. And yet—is there no doubt with you now?"

"Doubt? Did ever I harbour it save at your own bidding?"

"Yet—what have you but my word, the word which that Iscariot told you was only a dulcet lie, soft and false on every ear?"

She felt the tremor of his passion run through all his limbs.

"Were I free but for one hour——"

"Be at peace. I have given him to vengeance. Have you not heard how traitors end even in these days, even in European capitals? So will be is end, for his sin against us."

Her voice had in it that strong immutable merciless vengeance that came to her with her eastern blood; that smote rarely, but when it smote, never wavered and never failed. Then once more she shrank from his hand as though unworthy of its touch.

"Vengeance!" she moaned, "what use is it to us? You are lost through me—lost for ever! You pity, honour, love me still! I could better bear your curse!"

In the darkness that was about them, she rather felt than saw the infinite tenderness of his eyes as they gazed down on her:

"Hush! Would you wrong me still? Can you not think one hour that lays your heart bare to me thus, and brings me thus the surety of your innocence, is worth to me a lifetime of common joy and soulless pleasure? Let its cost be what it will—it is well bought."

She knew he held it so; and for this, that he loved her with this exceeding holiness of love; for this, that the restoration of her nobility and honour in his sight was priceless to him, as no paradise purchased by her crime could ever have been; for this, the woe that she had wrought him, eat like iron into her soul.

"Well bought!" she echoed. "It will be bought by a living agony of endless years! Manhood, pride, peace, joy, all killed in you; your very name lost, your very fate forgotten, till your hair is white with sorrow and your eyes are blind with age! Ah, my beloved, what matter what I be! It is I who have condemned you to this! It is I who have been your ruin!"

His arms drew her upward, close against the heart that only beat for her; his hot lips quivered on her own; in the night-silence and the darkness that was on them his voice thrilled through her "sweet as remembered kisses after death."

"Do you think they shall ever part us now? Death shall unite us, if Life would divorce us."

The hours passed, and they were left in solitude. As they had forgot all other life save their own, so by it they seemed forgotten. Through the heavy masonry of the iron-bound walls, no echo of the world without came to them; on the hush and the gloom of the chamber there was no sound, save only the soft gliding of a night-bird's restless wing. Whatever fate rose for them with the dawn, this night at least was theirs: there is no love like that which lives victorious even beneath the shadow of death; there is no joy like that which finds its paradise even amidst the cruelty of pain, the fierce long struggle of despair.

Never is the voluptuous glory of the sun so deep, so rich, as when its last excess of light burns above the purple edge of the tempest-cloud that soars upward to cover and devour it.

The hours passed, and the rays of the morning slowly stole inward through the narrow casement, bedded high above in the granite-blocks, whilst with the coming of the day the birds of the night returned from their outward flight, and nestled in their dark haunts with their eyes hid beneath their wings. As the first light touched her brow,—and the dawn came not there till it was full-risen for the earth without,—she smiled in his eyes, and loosened from her bosom the slender steel blade, scarce broader than a needle's width, that had rested there so long.

"Take it. You have said—they shall not part us now."

His hand closed on it while his smile answered
hers.

"I will find strength enough for that;—it shall
give us eternal liberty, eternal union."

Once before he had pledged this promise to her.
And as she had known then, so she knew now, that he
would find strength to deliver her from dishonour and
himself from captivity; strength to be true to her,
even to this last thing of all.

Having reached the supreme ecstasy and the supreme
anguish of life, death was to them, as to the races of
the young world, the god of deep benignant eyes, whose
touch was release, and whose kingdom was freedom,
on whose face was light, and in whose hands was balm.

As the words left his lips, on the quiet of the air a
single shot rang.

The first sunbeam had slanted through the slender
chink above; the stillness was intense; far below the
measured step of the sentinel fell muffled on the turf,
and the liquid stealing music of water, that fell down
through thick acanthus foliage without, alone was dimly heard. At that moment, as the brightness of the
day reached high enough to enter the vaulted chamber
of the upper story of the granary, the stillness was thus
broken. There was a stiffled cry; then silence reigned
again; and on that silence there was heard no more the
monotonous tread to and fro of the soldier on guard.

He started to his feet, his hand on the Venetian
steel he had just grasped.

"The man is shot!"

His voice was low and rapid, his eyes turned on
hers with the same thought that came to both alike.
There were those in that world they had lost who

would have done all that courage and true friendship could in his service had they known of his extremity; there were those also by the score who would have let their lives be mowed down like the millet sheaves around them in her cause, had they had power to reach her from the grip of priest and king.

Hope had been dead in them.

In the lowest depths of woe the oblivion of passion had made them senseless to all else—senseless even to the fate that must await them with the awakening of the dawn. But no thought of deliverance had ever come to them. It had seemed meet that their lives should end, once having reached the deepest joy that life could hold;—joy taken from the very jaws of the grave;—joy burning through the frozen chillness of despair.

Yet now, when hope, vague as remembered dreams, once touched them, they felt drunk with it as with the fumes of wine.

They listened, as none ever listen save those on whose straining ear the first sound that falls will bring the message of death or life.

For a moment that hushed stillness lasted, unbroken now by even the treading of the soldier's feet. Then there broke forth the loud rejoicing bay of a hound loosed on to his quarry: shot answered shot, steel clashed on steel: the din of tumult filled the soft peace of the early day; the old-remembered rallying words that had so often floated to her ear above the din of conflict, vibrated on it now—"Italia!" "Idalia!" —the two names blent in one.

As she heard, she rose erect; her whole frame seemed

to strain upward to the sun that glanced through the high bars of their prison-room; there was fire in her eyes, light on her lips, the glow of liberty on all her face and form. She was the living symbol of Italy unchained.

"Do you hear? Do you hear?" she cried to him. "*She* is free!"

Before her own freedom—even before his—the liberation of the nation, so long enslaved, came to her heart first; then, while the great tears coursed down her cheeks, she clung to him, trembling with a terror that had never touched her—the terror less for him, as for the land for which she had so long endured and suffered, this hope only dawned again to die out in endless night.

"Ah, God! give them strength—courage—victory!" she prayed, as she lifted her face to the sun. "My love—my love! listen for me, listen! I cannot hear. Hope kills me—hope for you!"

They stood there, barred in, in the shadows which the ray of wandering sunlight on high alone parted, whilst beneath them unseen raged the struggle on which their lives hung. Confused, broken, indistinct, the echoes of the contest came strangely through the hushed prison-chamber. The bitter riot of war tossed to and fro the fate of their coming years; the balance of chance swung, holding their destiny, and they could not tell to which side the scale was swaying; the measure of blood would be the purchase-coin of their ransom, or the price of their bondage, and they could not know whether foe or friend now claimed it. They stood, locked in, in solitude, with but a hand's-breadth of the morning sky through the grating above their heads the only thing visible of all the living world without, and heard the tumult striving far beneath upon whose issue all their future hung.

The time was very brief; a little bird upon an ivy-coil outside the window-bars, had lifted its voice in daylight-song as the first shots were fired, and still was singing softly and joyously, untired; but to them the moments seemed as years. Then, loud and rejoicing on the summer air, wild vivas broke the bitter noise of conflict, and crossed the moans of fallen men; the dropping shots grew fewer and fewer. Upon the stone stairway the rapid upward rush of feet came near; the bolts were drawn back, the door was flung aside, with his flanks white with foam, and his mighty jaws crimson with gore, the great dog sprang on her with a single bound; behind him, upon the threshold, stood Conrad Phaulcon.

His eyes met theirs one instant; then headlong at her feet he fell, a deep slow stream of blood staining the grey stone of the floor.

Thus at last he met his foe. Thus at last his foe looked on him after the weary search of baffled vengeance, long and hot as tiger's thirst.

As he fell his hands caught the hem of her dress.

. "Idalia! Idalia——"

The word died as his head smote the granite, and the broken sword which he had pressed into his side to lend him strength for a moment, pierced further, driven in by the weight of the fall.

Erceldoune staggered forward and raised him.

"He is dying!" he said, as he looked at her.

There came upon him a strange awe as he saw the death that at dawn he had so nearly dealt, smite thus, as another day broke on the world, the man from whom he had fled, as David from the sight of Saul, lest murder should be upon his head if longer he lingered where his enemy lay.

She never spoke, but sank on her knees beside her father where he had fallen, held up in the arms that a score of hours before had flung him upward like some worthless driftwood to be cast into the flames. Her eyes were fastened on his flushed and haggard face, that still had so much left of the old bright classic beauty.

"You have saved us! You——!"

She doubted her own senses; she thought she dreamt as madly as though she were dreaming that the heavens opened and the angels and archangels of mediæval story descended with the sword of Michael, with the spear of Ithuriel, to their rescue.

He drew his breath with a great sigh, and his voice came in broken whispers.

"You said right—there are things gods would not pardon,—your wrongs are of them. You stung me at last!"

She did not answer; she gazed at him with blind tearless eyes that saw his face, but only saw it as in the mists of dreams.

He pressed the sword that had broken off in his loins closer and harder to staunch the blood, while his voice rose ringing and resonant.

"Our day has come! They have Palermo; Naples must follow. The king has enough to do to think of his capital. They fear the news should get to the populace. We have done a bold stroke to-day; they have been hunting us down like wolves, but we have

turned and torn them. The sentinel killed, the rest
was easy. Ah! look you,—there is vengeance for you
too. That white-faced Northerner betrayed you to
Giulio Villaflor. Well, the boy Berto caught him in
his own toils. They hold him safe; they will kill
him like a cur at your word. Ah, Christ! how the
steel pierces! I would not die if I could help it.
Not just now—not till I have seen that traitor's face.
It is hard—hard—hard. He has cut and galled me
so often; it is hard to die just when I could pay
him all!"

The ferocious words gave way as his breath caught
them; he moved restlessly, driving the blade in still,
so that by this means he might yet gain a moment's
force. As his wandering glazing eyes glanced upward
he saw whose arms supported him; and the old relentless hate glowed in them—dark and deathless.

"So! you have your vengeance, and I am baulked
of mine. Lay me down, signore. I would sooner
die a minute earlier than gain the minute by your
help."

The old savage tiger lust was in the words. Erceldoune never heeded them, he rested the Greek's head
on his own breast, and held him upward with gentleness and in silence.

Idalia hung over him.

"Tell him—tell him! If you would atone for your
sin—if you would redeem your infamy—if you have
ever known remorse—bear me witness what you are
to me!"

The evil faded off his face; a softer look came back
there.

"Late—late—late!" he sighed: yet he lifted his head and made the sign of the cross with that latent superstition which lingered in him even whilst he made reckless jest of Deity, and denied with flippant laughter man's dreaming hope of God.

"By her mother's memory I swear,—Idalia Vassalis is my daughter. To her most bitter calamity. Those who have spoken evil against her have lied. I have been a coward, a traitor, a shame, and a darkness for ever on her path; but—she has ever been loyal to me. She never feared, and she was never faithless; I loved her for that; but,—for that too,—I hated her."

As the words, more vivid in the southern tongue he used, left his lips firmly and distinctly, her eyes filled slowly with tears, and across the stricken form of the wounded man, met those which had seen her aright through all the mists of calumny, which had looked down through the shadows of doubt, and read, despite them, the veiled truth of her life. The faith in him had been sore tried; but at length, after many days, his reward came.

Neither spoke. That one look uttered all between them.

Conrad Phaulcon pressed his hand closer yet upon the jagged steel that for a few brief moments still could thus hold life in him. Something of his old laugh hovered on his lips.

"Look! I make a fair ending. Pity there is no priest to crow above me. Death-bed repentance!— there is no coin like it; you sell the game you have lost already, and you buy such a fine aroma for nothing—"

She shivered at the awful mirth as she stooped to him, and passed her hand over his forehead.

"Silence! Live rather to repent! He will forgive; and I—you have tried my mercy long, you need not fear it now."

"No," he muttered, more huskily, more faintly. "If you had been willing to take your vengeance you could—long ago—you knew what would have sent me to the galleys. But you were true to your word. Strange, strange enough! You were so bold, so careless, so proud, so reckless; but one could hold you in a bridle of iron, if once you had given your word!"

His sight, that was beginning to fail him, sought her face with a wondering, baffled glance; through her whole life this loyalty to her pledged honour had bewildered him, even whilst by it he had found so merciless a power to bind and to drive one whom fear could never have swayed, nor force have moved. As she heard she lost remembrance of the deadly wrongs done against her by the man who should have been her foremost guard, her surest friend; all the long years through which he had persecuted and poisoned her freedom and her fame fell from her; lying, in his last hour, at her feet, having thus at last, however late, however slightly redeemed the cruelty of his past against her, he brought to her but one memory;—that of a long perished time, when on her childish ear his voice had come like music, breathing the poetry and the heroism of the world's dead youth.

"Be more just to us both!" she murmured, while the salt drops fell from her eyes upon his brow. "What I remembered always was what you at last remember too,—the love you bore my mother, the love she gave to you. Let it bring peace at last between us."

He shuddered as she spoke.

"God! if priests' and women's tales be true, and she lives in another life! I would go to hell, if a hell there were, sooner than see her face,—sooner than hear her ask of you at *my* hands."

"Hush! Have I not said *I* forgive?"

The soft and solemn cadence of the mournful words seemed to fall upon his ear with a deep calm he dared not, or cared not to break; he lay silent some moments, breathing heavily, while his drooped lids hung as though in sleep; then with a sudden upleaping of the vivid life within him, he raised himself once more, while the careless melody of his sweet laugh echoed with its old chime through the air.

"I have been a coward all my life. Well—I will die like a hero. They will make me a martyr when I am gone! Why not? Let my epitaph lie as it will, it cannot lie like a priest's or a king's! So this is the end of it all; the drama is not worth the playing. They have taken Palermo, I tell you;—Well! they revile us, but after all, we have truth in us; the people will see that one day. The capital is all in confusion. They could only leave you a half-dozen guards. Lousada and Veni, and a few others, thought we could do something if we struck well,—they have got a brigantine too,—if you fly at once, you will be safe."

The incoherent fragments of speech were panted rapidly out; scarce pausing for breath, he looked once more upward at Erceldoune; with the old unquenched hatred still burning dark in his glance.

"You will have the Vassalis' fief!   Ah! that cuts harder than the sabre.   I would give twenty lives now to keep you asunder from her.   But—she stung my memory; conscience, fools call it; I could not free her without freeing you, or I would have done.   You hate me?"

"I pity you—beyond all words."

"Because I lie here like a shot cur?"

"No.   Because you wronged her."

There was a meaning in the grave and weary answer that checked the fretting and galled passions of the dying man.

"Yes, I wronged her.   It was for Julian's wealth that I hated her.   Sir—you swore to deal me my mortal stroke.   Keep your oath.   Pluck that broken steel out of my loins; I shall not live a minute.   You will not?   Why, you break your vow!   Christ!—how the pain burns!   Look here, then!"

With a sudden movement he drew the blade out from the wound in which it was bedded; the pent-up blood, let loose, poured from it: he smiled.   It seemed as though in that hour the courage of his Achæan fathers flowed into the veins that were fast changing to ice beneath the throes of dissolution.

"My life has disgraced you: my death will not," he said, as his heavy eyes were lifted to hers.   "Can you forgive all?"

"God is my witness,—all."

"Ah, you were ever generous!   Idalia——"

And with her name thus latest upon his utterance, as it had been the latest utterance of so many, his head fell back upon her bosom, and through his

parted lips the lingering breath came in one long deep-
drawn sigh.

When that sigh ceased to quiver in the silence, he
lay dead in the morning light.

The low dark entrance had filled in that moment
with armed men; their weapons dropped blood, their
faces were hot with the heat of war and of victory,
their passions were at white heat with the madness of
joy; they were of that nature which long before showed
its southern grandeur in the midnight charge of the
Aurelian trench, and made the five hundred of the
Legion pierce their way through the dense and hostile
host at Mazzarene. At their head was the young boy
Berto; all his slender limbs quivering with the glory of
triumph, and his fair face, with the yellow hair flung
back, transfigured like the face of some angel of
vengeance. He came eagerly through the gloom of the
porchway, followed by the Italians, who obeyed him
as though he were a god; he had received the baptism
of blood when his mother had been shot down by the
Papal troops; he was the son of a great patriot who
had fallen at the gates of Rome; and whilst yet in the
first years of his infancy he had stood at the knee of
the Liberator, and laughed to see the balls pour down
upon the Savarelli roof around them, while the hands
of Ugo Bassi had been laid in benediction upon the
golden curls of the young child of liberty. His word
was the law, his sword was the sceptre, of the men
who came with him now.

Breathless, covered with dust, bruised, wounded,
but with a marvellous luminance beaming through the
calm unchanged repose of his colourless face, he came
to her in the flush of his triumph.

"Eccellenza, we bring you the best gifts of life!
—we bring you liberty. We bring you vengeance."

Then as he saw the dead man lying there his
proud and glad voice dropped, he made a soft backward movement of his hand, signing his followers to
pause upon the threshold, he bent his delicate head in
reverence.

"He has won higher guerdon than we," he said
gravely; "he has died for you."

For he had no knowledge that this one hour of
remorse had been the single narrow thread of gold un-
ravelled from the long, twisted, tangled, poisoned web
of a lifetime of wrong.

CHAPTER XV.
"Lost in the Night, and the Light of the Sea."

AROUND the high-leaping flames of a fresh pile of
pine-boughs, that flashed their lustre on the hanging
crystals and the hollow depths of the cavern by the
sea, the Italians who had freed her were gathered when
the night had fallen.

They stood in a half-circle about the great pyramid
of fire, whose heavy aromatic scent rolled out down
the vaulted space; the light and shadow played upon
their bronzed faces, on the metal of the rifles, on those
muzzles they leaned their hands, and in the darkness
of their eyes that were lustrous with longing rage, and
impatient joy. Joy for the sweetness of the surpassing
hope that the past day had brought, Palermo won
Naples would follow, their sail once loosened to the touch,
they would be with the Thousand of Marsala, with
the deliverers of Sicily. Rage against a prisoner set in

their midst, a prisoner who had been false to Italy,
and false to the woman whom they loved, as soldier
and servant, noble and minstrel alike, loved Mary
Stuart. The quiet was unbroken even by a loud-drawn
breath; the sound of the flame consuming the lithe limbs
of the wood was the only thing that stirred it. They
waited for her judgment, and they had known that
judgment inexorable as those given from the stone
justice seat in the early ages of her own city of the
Violet Crown. With his arms bound behind him, whilst
they stood around him, ready to spring at a word upon
him and sheathe their steel in his body with the fierce
swift justice of the south, they held captive the man
who had sold her to Giulio Villaflor.

To this end had his high ambitions come!

He had known that, soon or late, his sin of treachery
would surely find him out; would reach him though he
were housed within kings' palaces; would strike him
down even amidst those gods of gold and silver for
which he had bartered his brethren. Yet the vengeance
he had looked for had been the concrete vengeance,
for his outraged oath, of his forsaken order; of that
body politic to which he had sworn the secret vows of
his implicit obedience; and even this vengeance, in the
oversight of that intelligence which deems itself safe
enough and sure enough to play with all, and remain
true to none, he had held lightly. Rulers who wore
the purple of power had been scarcely less false to
such oaths than he, and he had thought that for him
as for them the blow might be temporised with, warded
off, bought off, until he like them, should have risen
too high for even that unerring and invisible hand to
reach. But now, by the men whom he had scorned

with all the scorn of his astute abilities, as the mere
raw material that may be turned to the statesman's
successes, the fools of patriotic visions and rude honesties,
of childish faith, and of barbarian warfare; by these he
had been baffled, checked, vanquished, meshed in the
intricate web of his own treacheries; by these he had
been conquered and dragged down, to stand in his dishonour before the one glance which had power to make
that dishonour worse to him than a thousand pangs of
death. To this end had his life come!

An end more bitter to him it could never have
reached, if his limbs had swung in the hot air of
Naples from the hangman's chains. The hooting lips
and ravenous eyes of the million of upturned faces of
a railing populace would have been powerless to bring
home to him his shame, as one regard bent on him,
brought it now.

For, beyond the undulating wave of flame, and
with that gulf of fire and of shadow parting them, the
gaze of Idalia rested on him.

At her side Erceldoune stood. His head was bent,
his eyes were on the ground, and his arms were folded
on his breast; he knew that if he looked up or unloosed his hand, he should break the word that he had
passed to leave their vengeance with her, he should
forestall the death-stroke that the soldiers of the Re-
volution waited there to strike.

She faced them in the hush of the silence; so intense that through the cavern the far-off chiming of
the waters on the shore could be faintly heard. The
warm glow of the pine-flames, like the red sun that
burns on the Nile, fell about her in a splendour of hot
tawny gold. Her eyes were dark and dreaming, as

with the memories and secrets of innumerable ages,
like the unfathomable lustre of the eyes that poets
give to Cleopatra; her mouth was grave and weary as
with the languor of past and deadly pain; her brow
was in shadow, as though the shade of the thorn-crown
of those who suffer for the people still was there, yet
on her face there was a light beyond that which the
burning sea-pines shed; it was the light of the dawn of
freedom.

She never spoke; but her gaze rested on the man
who had betrayed her into captivity—who had spoken
falsely against her honour, who had given her beauty
to the scourge, her freedom to the chains of her enemies;
and he who was no coward, but bold and sure, and of·
self-control passing those of most men, closed his own
eyes involuntarily, as though the lightning smote them,
and cowered downward like a shrinking dog.

For what that long, deep, silent gaze had quoted
against him was wrong far heavier than that against
her own life; wrong against all manhood, as in him
stained; against all human nature, as by him shared;
against all bonds that bind man to man, as by his
treachery dissevered; against all liberty sought for by
the nations, as, by his false adoption of its fair name,
prostituted.

It was this which that one unvarying gaze spoke
to him; and there was soul enough left in him to
make him know its deepest meaning, and taste its
deepest agony.

"A traitor!"

Her lips had never spoken the word; but its shame
ate into his heart as it ate into the heart of Iscariot. In
that one moment the austere, the divine, the supreme

majesty that lies in Truth was revealed to him, and blinded him as the blaze of the heavens blinded Saul of Tarsus. In that one moment he knew what he had denied all his years through—that men who, for it, render their lives desolate and barren, and, for it, die unloved and forsaken of the world, may know in life and in death a beauty that never comes to the multitudes who grasp at gold, at power, at the sweetness of lascivious ease, and at the wide fools’ paradise of lies.

The Italians who stood around him, leaning on their loaded rifles, while ever and again upon him turned the waiting savage brilliance of their glances, gave an impatient movement that shook the clangour from their arms out in a shrill echo.

“His sentence, Eccellenza!”

They were thirsty to deal him a traitor’s due; to lead him out yonder on to the starlit sand, and, with one volley fired on the still night air, give him the death that all deserters meet, and see this justice done ere their boat should be thrust through the foam, and their oars should cleave the waters apart, and their vessel should be reached, that would bear them southward to where the Sicilies lay.

She made them no reply. Still with her eyes fixed on him she stood with the light that was like the afterglow of Egypt full upon her. To him she ceased to be the woman he had loved and coveted; she seemed to him transfigured; with that mystery of thought, with that infinitude of reproach, with that passionless scorn, and with that passionless pity on her face, she looked to him like the avenging shape of the honour he had sold, of the land he had betrayed, of the freedom he had surrendered, of the cause he had forsaken. The rebuke of her regard was not hers, but the rebuke of the peoples, weary and abandoned by the leader who bartered them for gold; the scorn of her gaze was not hers, but the scorn of the martyrs of liberty, who through all ages perish willingly, if with their bodies they can purchase one ray of higher light for the world which knows them not until too late.

By her he saw how vile he had become.

By her he saw how high he might have reached.

She had her vengeance.

The impatient fire of the same demand ran afresh through the revolutionists around him:

"His sentence, Eccellenza?"

He never heard. He had passed through all the bitterness of death; it was her look that killed him.

The cry rose louder: "His sentence!"

Then at last she answered them:

"Loose him, and let him go."

A sullen furious yell of dissent that not even their loyalty to her could still, rolled through the vault.

"A traitor dies! A traitor dies!"

By his crime they claimed their justice.

A heavy sigh parted her lips; then the full sweet melody of her voice came on the clamour like music that moves men to tears.

"A traitor he is! And for that you would deal him death? Nay, think me not gentler than you. I meant to deliver him up to your hands. I bade him be brought to my judgment, that your vengeance might strike him, and lay him dead at my feet. I am no holier than you. There was an hour in which I longed

for his life with that thirst you know now; there was
an hour in which I would have taken it, and not
spared, though his mother had prayed to me. Ah,
friends! such hours come to all. But now, the darkness has passed. I see clearer. Death is not ours to
deal. And were it ours, should we give him the nameless mystic mercy which all men live to crave—give
it as the chastisement of crime? Death! It is rest to
the aged, it is oblivion to the atheist, it is immortality
to the poet! It is a vast, dim, exhaustless pity to all
the world. And would you summon it as your hardest
cruelty to sin?"

They were silent; she stirred their souls—she had
not bound their passions.

"A traitor merits death," they muttered.

"Merits it! Not so. The martyr, the liberator, the
seeker of truth, may deserve its peace; how has the
traitor won them? You deem yourselves just; your justice errs. If you would give him justice, make him
live. Live to know fear lest every wind among the
leaves may whisper of his secret; live to feel the look
of a young child's eyes a shame to him; live to envy
every peasant whose bread has not been bought with
tainted coin; live to hear ever in his path the stealing
step of haunting retribution; live to see his brethren
pass by him as a thing accurst; live to listen in his
age to white-haired men, who once had been his comrades, tell to the youth about them the unforgotten
story of his shame. Make him live thus if you would
have justice."

They answered nothing; a shudder ran through
them as they heard.

"And—if you have as I—a deliverance that

forbids you even so much harshness, still let him live, and bury his transgression in your hearts. Say to him as I say;—'your sin was great, go forth and sin no more.'"

Then, as the words left her lips, she moved to him from out the fire-glow, and stooped, and severed the bonds that bound him, and left him free; and none dared touch that which she had made sacred, but stood mute, and afraid, as those who stand in the presence of a soul that is greater than their own. And the man who had sinned against her, fell at her feet.

"Oh, God! If I had known you as I know you now!"

"You never had betrayed me. No!—Live, then, to be true to greater things than I."

While the night was still young, a ship glided southward through the wide white radiance of the moon. The waters stretched, one calm and gleaming sheet of violet hues; from the fast-retreating shore a fair wind came, bearing the fragrance of a thousand hills and plains, of golden fruits and flowers of snow, and passion-blossoms of purple, and the scarlet heart of ripe pomegranates; through the silence sounded the cool fresh ripple of the waves as the vessel left her track upon the phosphor-silver, and above, from a million stars, a purer day seemed to dawn on all the aromatic perfumes of the air, and all the dim un-measured freedom of the seas. And she, who went to freedom, looked, and looked, and looked, as though never could her sight rest long enough upon the limit-less radiance, nor her lips drink enough in of the sweet fresh delicious treasure that the waters gave and the winds brought;—the treasure of her liberty.

"You come to my kingdom!" she said softly, while her dreaming eyes met her lover's.

And he who had cleaved to her with that surpassing love which calumny but strengthens, and fire but purifies, which fear cannot enter and death cannot appal, drew her beauty closer to his breast:

"My kingdom is here!"

And the ship swept on through the stillness of the hushed hours, through the glory of the light, to glide out through the eternal sea-gates of the old Roman world, and pass into the cloudless warmth of Eastern skies, where already through the voluptuous night the star of morning rose.

THE END.